# CONTEMPORARY VERSE

KATHARINE LEE BATES AND SIGURD

# CONTEMPORARY VERSE

NEW EDITION EDITED WITH
A PROLOGUE AND NOTES

BY
**A. MARION MERRILL**
AND
**GRACE E. W. SPRAGUE**

Granger Index Reprint Series

**BOOKS FOR LIBRARIES PRESS**
Freeport, New York

Library of Congress Cataloging in Publication Dat

Merrill, A        Marion, ed.
    Contemporary verse.

    (Granger index reprint series)
    1.  American poetry--19th century.2.  America
poetry--20th century.  3.  English poetry--19th
century.  4.  English poetry--20th century.
I.  Sprague, Grace Eliot Winthrop, joint ed.
II.  Title.
PS612.M4  1972        821'.008        72-8281
ISBN 0-8369-6392-X

DEDICATED
TO
THE BOYS AND GIRLS OF AMERICA

# POETRY

I am the reality of things that seem;
The great transmuter, melting loss to gain,
Languor to love, and fining joy from pain.
I am the waking, who am called the dream;
I am the sun, all light reflects my gleam;
I am the altar-fire within the fane;
I am the force of the refreshing rain;
I am the sea to which flows every stream.
I am the utmost height there is to climb;
I am the truth, mirrored in fancy's glass;
I am stability, all else will pass;
I am eternity, encircling time;
Kill me, none may; conquer me, nothing can —
I am God's soul, fused in the soul of man.

ELLA CROSBY HEATH

THE biographical sketches seek to present somewhat of the personality of the authors and the atmosphere in which they wrote. Though poetry is "an open page", yet without guidance many points escape the young reader. Such guidance the "Notes and Questions" aim to give, but in no case to rob him of the joy of discovery.

The editors have long labored in the field of poetry, gleaning widely, in the companionship of their pupils, and with much enjoyment. To facilitate their own work by having at hand a convenient collection of poems for ready use, and perhaps to offer some aid to other workers in the same field, especially for schools which have not access to any considerable library, this volume has been prepared.

The editors offer it now, with cordial good wishes, to their fellow workers, the Teachers of English Poetry, and to that best reading public, the Boys and Girls of America.

A. M. M.

G. E. W. S.

# ACKNOWLEDGMENTS

To both poets and publishers who hold copyrights on the material used in "Contemporary Verse" indebtedness is cordially acknowledged by the editors:

To Barse and Hopkins for poems by Robert W. Service. To The Bobbs-Merrill Company for poems by James Whitcomb Riley. To The Century Company for the poem by William Rose Benét. To Dodd, Mead & Company, Inc., for poems by Angela Morgan. To George H. Doran Company for poems by Joyce Kilmer and Charles Hanson Towne. To E. P. Dutton & Company for poems by Katharine Lee Bates and Winifred M. Letts. To Doubleday, Page & Company for poems by Richard Le Gallienne, and for poems: "O Captain", "The Ox-Tamer", "I Hear America Singing", "When I Heard the Learn'd Astronomer", and "Years of the Modern" from "Complete Leaves of Grass" by Walt Whitman. To Harcourt, Brace & Company, Inc., for poems by Thomas Augustine Daly and Carl Sandburg. To Henry Holt & Company for poems by Robert Frost, Walter de la Mare, Carl Sandburg, and Margaret Widdemer. To King Features Syndicate, Inc., for poem by Angela Morgan. To Lothrop, Lee, and Shepard Company for poems by Sam Walter Foss. To The Macmillan Company for poems by Wilfred Wilson Gibson, Vachel Lindsay, John Masefield, Edwin Arlington Robinson, and William Butler Yeats. To David McKay Company for poems by Winifred M. Letts. To Charles Scribner's Sons for poems by Edwin Arlington Robinson and Henry van Dyke. To Small, Maynard & Company for poems by Bliss Carman. To Frederick A. Stokes Company for poems by Alfred Noyes. To Yale University Press for poems by William Rose Benét. To *The Bookman* for the poem "Purple Grackles" by Amy Lowell. To *The Gleam* for "A Bargain" by Abbie Farwell Brown. To *Good Housekeeping* for "The Watcher" by Margaret Widdemer. To *The Literary Digest* for "The Outlaw" by Robert W. Service; "Rebecca and Abigail" by Katharine Lee Bates; and "The White Ships and the Red" by Joyce Kilmer. To *The Youth's Companion* for "The Vigil" by Abbie Farwell Brown.

The editors extend sincere thanks and appreciation for sympathetic interest and many valuable suggestions to Professor Katharine Lee Bates, Miss Abbie Farwell Brown, and Mrs. Sam Walter Foss; to Mr. Wilfred Wilson Gibson for manuscript poems; and to Miss Amy Lowell, Professor Lionel Marks, Miss Angela Morgan, Miss Margaret Widdemer, and Miss Edna C. Woodbury, Librarian, Somerville High School.

# CONTENTS

# ILLUSTRATIONS

# PROLOGUE

THIS collection of verse has been prepared for the use of classes beginning the study of Poetry.

In junior high schools, and in the freshman class of the general high school, a milestone seems to be passed; dawning maturity makes possible a broader horizon. The pupil may well and happily discover that poetry is no mere harmony of sweet sounds, as he thought, if he liked poetry, and no intricate saying of things in an order unusual and hard to understand if he "doesn't care much for that rhyming stuff." Now poetry may stand revealed to him as the mirror of human life and of nature; its material the sky above and earth around, the songs of birds, the rippling waters, the rustling leaves. Its happenings are the experiences of human beings. Poetry is "a true thing", true to life in all time, for nature and the human heart change not.

This volume aims to emphasize a second point: Poetry belongs not alone to the past but to the living present. From the ranks of Industry, of Journalism, of War, alike as from the ranks of literary workers, arise to-day strong hearts to express in poetic terms the experiences they have lived, and to these poems the glowing heart of youth gives quick response.

No attempt is made to teach structural poetry as such; that may well be left for later years. Attention is called to the musical quality of poetry and to the simpler arrangements of rhythm and metre, some understanding of which is an aid both to reading and appreciation.

# INTRODUCTION TO THE STUDY OF POETRY

POETRY is beautiful thought beautifully expressed in rhythmic language. Its chief characteristics are: rhythm, rhyme, pauses, melodious language, frequent use of figures of speech, and an abundance of pictures.

RHYTHM. The underlying principle of all art is *contrast*. Rhythm is but another name for contrast and is the fundamental law of the universe. Consider the rise and fall of the waves, the ebb and flow of the tides, the rising and setting of the sun, the beat of the heart, breathing, the blowing of the wind, the ripple of the brook, and the song of the birds. The three great allied arts, dancing, music, and poetry, are based on rhythm, and so, too, in a less apparent way, are painting and sculpture.

By *rhythm* in poetry we mean the regular succession of stressed (or long) syllables and unstressed (or short) syllables.

*Example:*     I *think* that *I* shall *never see*
A *poem lovely as a tree.*

*Note:* All diction has stressed and unstressed syllables, the difference between poetry and prose being that in poetry the succession of stressed and unstressed syllables is *regular*, — while that in prose is *irregular*. The more regular the succession becomes, the more poetic becomes the prose.

*Example:*

The Lord is my shepherd, I shall not want,

He maketh me to lie down in green pastures, etc.

The novel, "Lorna Doone", by Blackmore, is a remarkable example of the sustained use of rhythmic prose throughout.

## FIRST RESULT OF RHYTHM

This regular succession of stressed and unstressed syllables causes a division of syllables into Metrical Feet.

A Metrical Foot is a group of syllables containing one stressed and one or more unstressed syllables.   *Or:*

A Metrical Foot is a group of two or more syllables, one of which must be stressed.

Principal Types of Metrical Feet, divided:

I.  According to Number of Syllables
    *a.*  Dissyllabic
        1.  Iambus  la *lá* or ∪∠ as in defy
        2.  Trochee *lá* la or ∠∪ as in tender
    *b.*  Trisyllabic
        1.  Anapæst la la *lá* or ∪∪∠ as in cavalier
        2.  Dactyl *lá* la la or ∠∪∪ as in silently

II.  According to Place of Stressed Syllables
    *a.*  Unstressed followed by stressed, *i.e.,* rising or ascending rhythm
        1.  Iambus
        2.  Anapæst
    *b.*  Stressed followed by unstressed, *i.e.,* falling or descending rhythm
        1.  Trochee
        2.  Dactyl

An Iambus is a metrical foot containing an unstressed syllable followed by a stressed syllable.   (Adjective, iambic)

*Example:* The *mou*ntain *nymph*, sweet *Li*berty

(la *lá* | la *lá* | la *lá* | la *lá*)

A Trochee is a metrical foot containing a stressed syllable followed by an unstressed.   (Adjective, trochaic)

*Example:* *Once* up*on* a *mid*night *dreary*

(*lá* la | *lá* la | *lá* la | *lá* la)

An Anapæst is a metrical foot containing two unstressed syllables followed by a stressed.   (Adjective, anapæstic)

*Example:*  The As*syr*ian came *down* like a *wolf* on the *fold*.

(la la *lá* | la la *lá* | la la *lá* | la la *lá*)

A Dactyl is a metrical foot containing a stressed syllable followed by two unstressed.   (Adjective, dactylic)

*Example:*  *Just* for a *hand*ful of *sil*ver he *left* us.

(*lá* la la | *lá* la la | *lá* la la | *lá* la la)


## SECOND RESULT OF RHYTHM

VERSE.  A number of metrical feet so grouped as to form a larger metrical unit is called a Verse or Line of Poetry. These verses are named according to the number of metrical feet composing them.

Monometer (monom′eter) — one foot

*Example:* A-way !

Dimeter (dim′eter) — two feet

*Example:* None but | the brave

Trimeter (trim′eter) — three feet

*Example:* He made | and lov | eth all.

Tetrameter (tetram′eter) — four feet

*Example:* Or sweet | est Shake | speare Fan | cy's child

Pentameter (pentam′eter) — five feet

*Example:* The cur | few tolls | the knell | of part | ing day.

Hexameter (hexam′eter) — six feet

*Example:* As one | for knight | ly giusts | and fierce encoun | ters fit

The full name of a verse of poetry consists of two parts; an adjective giving the prevailing foot, and a noun telling the number of feet in the line.

*Example:* Iambic tetrameter, meaning four metrical feet all of which are iambic.  A trochee is frequently substituted for an iambus if the pronunciation of a word forbids the use of the iambus, but since the two are metrically equivalent, the rhythm is not affected.

## RHYME

RHYME is the recurrence of similar sounds (the same vowel and succeeding consonant sounds) in accented syllables at the end of lines of poetry.  Sometimes, though infrequently, we find rhyme in the middle of the lines.  This is called Internal Rhyme.

*Note.*  Rhyme, unlike rhythm, is an ornament rather than an essential of poetry; in fact, much of the noblest poetry in the English language is written in blank verse; for example, Milton's "Paradise Lost" and all of the Shakespearean dramas.

Blank Verse is poetry that does not rhyme.

RHYME is the means by which poetic lines are bound together into stanzas, the larger unit of poetry.

Functions of Rhyme:
1. Giving of pleasure by the similarity of sounds.
2. Emphasizing the end of a verse.
3. Uniting verses into stanzas.

## THE STANZA

A Stanza is a group of poetic verses usually containing a single idea.  Roughly speaking, it corresponds to a paragraph in prose.

Kinds of Stanzas:

Couplet, shortest possible stanza — two rhyming lines.

Triplet, three rhyming lines.

Quatrain, four lines with varying rhyme-schemes — the most common form in English poetry.

Stanzas of five, six, seven, and eight lines are found with varying rhyme-schemes.

Refrain Stanzas — stanzas where a refrain takes the place of a rhyme.

## PAUSES

Two kinds of Pauses:

1. Those that fill in the time of a missing syllable and correspond to rests in music.

*Example:* Souls of poets dead and gone.

2. Those that have to steal their time from adjacent periods or syllables and correspond to phrase pauses in music. A pause within a line is called a Cæsura, from the Latin word *caedere*, meaning to cut off.

*Example:* Then fell thick rain, plume droopt, and mantle clung.

## POETRY IS SONG

Poetry is song, or, in other words, it is addressed to the ear and therefore should always be read aloud to be appreciated. There are various aids to musical sound, the knowledge of which will help you to understand in part at least the magic of the poet.

## AIDS TO MUSICAL SOUND IN POETRY

1. Alliteration, which is the repetition of initial *consonants*.

*Example:* The lisp of leaves and ripple of rain.

2. Assonance, which is the linking together of words repeating the same *vowel* sounds.

*Example:* It is an isle under Ionian skies.

3. Onomatopœia, which is the effect produced by words or groups of words whose sound suggests their meaning.
*Example:* Clang battle axe, and clash brand.

4. Skillful use of conspicuous consonant sounds.

   *a.* Liquid sounds produced by frequent use of "l", "r", "m", and "n."

   *b.* Explosive sounds like "p", "b", and "d."

   *c.* Hissing sounds like "s" and "z."

## SYMBOLIC VALUE OF VOWEL SOUNDS

Vowels are quite as important as consonants, if not more so, in the magic hands of a poet, and a knowledge of the table given below will make plain the fact that words are not haphazard things but the result of thousands of years of human experience.

The following vowels "are especially fitted to express uncontrollable joy and delight, gayety, triviality, rapid movement, brightness, delicacy, and physical littleness."

| | | | |
|---|---|---|---|
| i | as in little | ai | as in fair |
| e | " " met | a | " " mate |
| a | " " mat | i | " " I |
| e | " " mete | | |

The following vowels "are especially fitted to express horror, solemnity, awe, deep grief, slowness of motion, darkness, and extreme or oppressive greatness of size."

| | | | |
|---|---|---|---|
| a | as in father | ow | as in cow |
| oi | " " boil | o | " " gold |
| u | " " but | oo | " " gloom |
| oo | " " wood | aw | " " awe |

From an essay on "The Symbolic Value of English Sounds", by Prof. Tolman.

## KINDS OF POETRY

*A.*  Narrative Poetry is that form of poetry which relates events.  There are four kinds of narrative poetry, namely, the Epic, the Metrical Romance, the Metrical Tale, and the Ballad.

1. The Epic has a noble subject, serious treatment, a heio, events largely under superhuman control, and a consistent plot. *Example:* "The Iliad", "Paradise Lost."

2. The Metrical Romance is less serious than the epic, its metre is lighter and the control of events is mainly human. *Example:* "The Lady of the Lake."

3. The Metrical Tale is a narrative poem, somewhat simpler than the metrical romance, more complex than the ballad. *Example:* "Enoch Arden."

4. The Ballad is the shortest and most simple of narrative poems and deals with a single event, the treatment of which is most direct. *Example:* "Robin Hood."

*B.*  Lyric Poetry expresses the poet's emotions or feelings and is generally so written that it may be set to music.  The most important kinds of lyric poetry are Songs, Odes, and Elegies, though there are a vast number which refuse to be classified except under the general term of lyrics.

1. Songs are lyrics written expressly to be sung.
   *a.* Secular, *Example:* "Annie Laurie", "America."
   *b.* Religious, *Example:* "Lead, Kindly Light."

2. Odes express exalted emotion and are more complex than songs. *Example:* "To a Skylark", by Shelley.

3. Elegies are formal and elaborated expressions of serious emotions. *Example:* "Elegy in a Country Churchyard."

4. Sonnets.

A Sonnet is a lyric consisting of fourteen lines of ten syllables each, and is divided into two parts, the first eight lines or the octave, and the last six or the sestet. These two parts usually express successive phases of the same thought, the octave setting it forth in some specific form and the sestet as a general truth.

*C.* Dramatic Poetry is that form of poetry in which a story is told by means of dialogue and action. *Example:* "The Merchant of Venice."

# SUGGESTIONS FOR THE USE OF THE BOOK

THE earliest English poet made his appeal to the imagination of his audience through the ear alone, as he sang his rude but often inspiring songs to the accompaniment of the lyre or harp. In the childhood of individuals, as in the childhood of the race, poetry appeals first through the ear, and the nonsense rhyme with its jingle is easily and eagerly memorized. Too often, as the student advances, the opposite extreme is realized — his attention is focused on silent reading.

But poetry was never meant to be appreciated merely through the eye alone, since the primary purpose of the study of poetry is enjoyment. The reader should, to this end, have the aid of the double appeal that every poem makes, namely, to ear and eye.

Reading aloud furnishes a ready opportunity for studying *the musical quality* of poetry, the force and power of the thought brought out by the beat of the rhythm, the stress and cadence on important words and on the rhyme. Pupils greatly enjoy such study and speedily develop considerable skill and much satisfaction in the ability to recognize their favorite authors by their style and to judge how much the musical structure of a poem aids in bringing about the effect produced.

Careful study of the musical quality of verse and much reading aloud are suggested for the best enjoyment of this little book of present-day poetry.  To enable the pupil to understand how some of the music of a poem is produced, frequent reference should be made to "Aids to Musical Sound in Poetry", in the Introduction to this book.

The following questions may serve to guide the pupil in the study of the personality of a poet.

## LANGUAGE AND METHOD

What sort of words does the poet use — simple and natural, those of everyday life, or words unusual and difficult to understand?  Are the sentences in general in natural grammatical order, or complicated and therefore difficult to follow?  Does he use literal language or figurative?  If figurative, does any one figure of speech prevail?  Does he use subtly suggestive or photographic words?  Are there many color, sound, odor, or action words?  Does the poet simply photograph people and nature or does he philosophize about them?  Are his pictures given in detail or merely flashed?

## MELODY OF THE POEMS

Does the poet use diction, rhythm, and rhyme in keeping with the subject and feeling of the poem?  Has he favorite ways of using rhyme?  What devices does he use to add music to his lines?

## PERSONALITY OF THE POET

Is he a keen observer of life about him?  Is he most interested in people, animals, or nature?  If in people, what method does he use in describing them?  Is he more fond of the city or the country?  What impresses him most about either?  Is he most interested in the present, the past, or the future?  Is he optimistic or pessimistic, thoughtful, religious, sympathetic?  Has he imagination?  Can you tell from his poems whether he is American or British?

# CONTEMPORARY VERSE

# WALT WHITMAN

Walt Whitman is the first truly American poet because, unlike Long-fellow, Holmes, and Bryant, who wrote chiefly about Europe and its traditions, or gave themselves up to poetic translations of the classics, he chose themes purely American. You should know him also because he had a tremendous influence on future generations, not only in America but also in Europe, since he was the first of the Imagists, poets whose creed is to use the language of everyday life in their poems. He is the singer of democracy and the laudator of the average man, and his appeal is to the brotherhood of man and the great destiny of America, which he was among the first to express. He also uplifts into poetry the whole of modern life and man, thus revealing "the glory of the commonplace." By so doing he became the forerunner of the host of modern poets who voice the same gospel.

Whitman was born of Dutch and English parentage in West Hills, Long Island, New York State. His formal education was slight, as he left school at the age of twelve. His self-education is included in his experience from printing office to the editor's chair of the *Brooklyn Eagle*. His editorials, dealing with education, capital punishment, and intemperance, showed deep sympathy for the working classes and championed civic improvements of all kinds. In 1855 he published "Leaves of Grass", the first collection of poems written in "free verse." As it first appeared it contained but ninety-four pages. The third edition was published in 1860, but almost immediately the publisher failed and the book passed out of public notice in America; however, Whitman was winning enthusiastic recognition in England from such men as Carlyle and Ruskin, and slowly and reluctantly his own countrymen accepted him. Before he died he saw a seventh edition published, containing nearly four hundred pages.

During the Civil War he was summoned to care for his brother, who had been wounded, and thereupon he became the brother nurse of hundreds of wounded Northern soldiers, caring for them tenderly, reading to them, writing their letters, and sending the last sad news home to the stricken families of those who passed on. As the result of

1

the exertion, exposure, and high nervous strain, he became at the end of the war a shattered and almost aged man.  His valiant services were rewarded by a subordinate clerkship under the government and in 1874 he retired, partially paralyzed and prematurely aged. He then went to live at Camden, New Jersey, where he would have suffered from absolute poverty had not his English admirers provided help.  Later some wealthy American families saw that his simple wants were satisfied.  He died in 1892.  Recently a movement has been started to purchase the ramshackle house at 328 Mickle Street in Camden, where he passed his last years, and to restore it as a permanent memorial.

## O CAPTAIN! MY CAPTAIN!

O Captain! my Captain! our fearful trip is done,
The ship has weather'd every rack, the prize we sought is won,
The port is near, the bells I hear, the people all exulting,
While follow eyes the steady keel, the vessel grim and daring;
But O heart! heart! heart!
O the bleeding drops of red,
Where on the deck my Captain lies,
Fallen cold and dead.

O Captain! my Captain! rise up and hear the bells;
Rise up — for you the flag is flung — for you the bugle trills,
For you bouquets and ribbon'd wreaths — for you the shores a-crowding,
For you they call, the swaying mass, their eager faces turning;
Here Captain! dear father!
This arm beneath your head!
It is some dream that on the deck
You've fallen cold and dead.

My Captain does not answer, his lips are pale and still,
My father does not feel my arm, he has no pulse nor will,
The ship is anchor'd safe and sound, its voyage closed and
    done,
From fearful trip the victor ship comes in with object won;
  Exult O shores, and ring O bells!
    But I with mournful tread,
      Walk the deck my Captain lies,
        Fallen cold and dead.

NOTES AND QUESTIONS ON "O CAPTAIN! MY CAPTAIN!"

This beautiful lyric setting forth Whitman's love and admiration
for President Lincoln is in the form of an extended metaphor. To
whom is Lincoln compared throughout?

*Stanza 1.* What is meant by "our fearful trip" and what is the
ship referred to in line 2? Note how vivid is the description of the
victorious ship entering the port.

*Stanza 2.* What makes the appeal to Lincoln to "rise up and hear
the bells" so sad? Is "trills" a good word to describe the bugle-
notes?

*Stanza 3.* What is gained by expressing this stanza in the third
person instead of the second? What by calling Lincoln "My father"
instead of "My Captain"? Look up other poems on Lincoln in this
book and see what one you like best.

*In General.* Unlike most of Whitman's poems this one rhymes;
trace the rhyme-scheme of all the stanzas; is it the same for all of
them? What is gained by the unrhymed lines? What by the variation of length of the lines? What idea is repeated in the last two
lines of each stanza?

## THE OX-TAMER

In a far-away northern country in the placid pastoral region,
Lives my farmer friend, the theme of my recitative, a famous
    tamer of oxen,
There they bring him the three-year-olds and the four-year-
    olds to break them.

He will take the wildest steer in the world and break him
    and tame him,
He will go fearless without any whip where the young
    bullock chafes up and down the yard,
The bullock's head tosses restless high in the air with raging
    eyes,
Yet see you! how soon his rage subsides — how soon this
    tamer tames him;
See you! on the farm hereabout a hundred oxen young and
    old, and he is the man who has tamed them,
They all know him, all are affectionate to him;
See you! some are such beautiful animals, so lofty looking;
Some are buff-color'd, some mottled, one has a white line
    running along his back, some are brindled,
Some have wide flaring horns (a good sign) — see you!
    the bright hides,
See, the two with stars on their foreheads — see, the round
    bodies and broad backs,
How straight and square they stand on their legs — what
    fine sagacious eyes!
How they watch their tamer — they wish him near them —
    how they turn to look after him!
What yearning expression! how uneasy they are when he
    moves away from them;
Now I marvel what it can be he appears to them, (books,
    politics, poems, depart — all else departs,)
I confess I envy only his fascination — my silent, illiterate
    friend,
Whom a hundred oxen love there in his life on farms,
In the northern country far, in the placid pastoral region.

### NOTES AND QUESTIONS ON "THE OX-TAMER"

Why is the northern country described as a "placid pastoral
region"? Why does the Ox-Tamer carry no whip? Pick out the

fine words used to describe the untamed bullocks. Contrast this picture with that of the tamed steers further on. Note the effect of speaking of his friend as "illiterate" in contrast to books, politics, and poems, which make up all of Whitman's life but of which the Ox-Tamer is utterly ignorant. Why did the poet make the last line vary slightly from the first?

This poem is in Whitman's usual style of freely flowing rhythms, long lines and abrupt expressions. Note how skillfully he uses breaks and pauses to prevent the long lines from becoming tiresome. Find lines that are made beautiful and forceful by alliteration.

WALT WHITMAN'S HOME AT CAMDEN
(The two-story house on the right)

## I HEAR AMERICA SINGING

I hear America singing, the varied carols I hear,
Those of mechanics, each one singing his as it should be
    blithe and strong,
The carpenter singing his as he measures his plank or beam,

The mason singing his as he makes ready for work, or leaves
    off work,
The boatman singing what belongs to him in his boat, the
    deckhand singing on the steamboat deck,
The shoemaker singing as he sits on his bench, the hatter
    singing as he stands,
The wood-cutter's song, the ploughboy's on his way in the
    morning, or at noon intermission or at sundown,
The delicious singing of the mother, or of the young wife
    at work, or of the girl sewing or washing,
Each singing what belongs to him or her and to none else,
The day what belongs to the day — at night the party of
    young fellows, robust, friendly,
Singing with open mouths their strong melodious songs.

NOTES AND QUESTIONS ON "I HEAR AMERICA SINGING"

What relation do all the other lines bear to the first line?   What
makes each song differ from all the rest?   Notice that only two of the
songs are described by the use of adjectives; can you see any reason
for this?   Try to write some similar lines describing new songs to be
heard to-day.   Is Whitman a true American poet?   Can you see now
why he is spoken of as the "first of our poets to reveal the glory of the
commonplace"?

## WHEN I HEARD THE LEARN'D ASTRONOMER

When I heard the learn'd astronomer,
When the proofs, the figures, were ranged in columns be-
    fore me,
When I was shown the charts and diagrams, to add, divide,
    and measure them,
When I sitting heard the astronomer where he lectured
    with much applause in the lecture-room,

How soon unaccountable I became tired and sick,
Till rising and gliding out I wander'd off by myself,
In the mystical moist night-air, and from time to time,
Look'd up in perfect silence at the stars.

NOTES AND QUESTIONS ON "WHEN I HEARD THE LEARN'D ASTRONOMER"

Why did the poet become "tired and sick" while listening to the learned gentleman? If you have never seen any charts and diagrams of the heavens, get a book on astronomy and compare the uninteresting pictures with the beauty of the starlit sky. What fine descriptive words are there in the last two lines? Why was the poet looking at the heavens "in perfect silence" happier than when in the lecture-room looking at the diagrams?

## YEARS OF THE MODERN

Years of the modern! years of the unperform'd!
Your horizon rises, I see it parting away for more august
    dramas,
I see not America only, not only Liberty's nation but other
    nations preparing,
I see tremendous entrances and exits, new combinations,
    the solidarity of races,
The earth, restive, confronts a new era, perhaps a general
    divine war,
No one knows what will happen next, such portents fill the
    days and nights;
Years prophetical! the space ahead as I walk, as I vainly
    try to pierce it, is full of phantoms,
Unborn deeds, things soon to be, project their shapes around
    me,
This incredible rush and heat, this strange ecstatic fever
    of dreams, O years!
Your dreams, O years, how they penetrate through me!
    (I know not whether I sleep or wake.)

The perform'd America and Europe grow dim, retiring in
    shadow behind me,
The unperform'd, more gigantic than ever, advance, ad-
    vance upon me.

NOTES AND QUESTIONS ON "YEARS OF THE MODERN"

Note that Whitman uses "Years of the Modern" in the sense of
"Years of the Future." If he had lived until to-day, how much of
his prophecy would he have seen come true? Can you think of "more
august dramas" in which America has taken part since Whitman's
time? Name some "tremendous entrances" made by nations of
Europe since the World War; some exits; some "new combinations."
Might lines 5 and 6 be written of to-day? "Project" in line 8 is
a verb; how then should it be pronounced? "The perform'd America
and Europe" means America and Europe of the past. One of the
chief services which a poet does for his people is to interpret them and
their lives for them and for others; does America owe Whitman anything?

# EMILY DICKINSON

Emily Dickinson, "a poet of Nature's own making", was born in Amherst, Massachusetts, in 1830, the daughter of the Hon. Edward Dickinson, a prominent lawyer and for some years treasurer of Amherst College. As a child she was fun-loving and gay of heart, though shy and delicate. She attended a private school in Amherst and later entered Mt. Holyoke Seminary, — a brilliant student, with an unusual fund of general information. As years passed she devoted herself more and more to her two great interests, books and Nature, forsaking society. It is said that if she saw a visitor entering the gate she would at once disappear, retiring to her room or to some secluded nook of the garden. The only exception to her seclusion was the annual reception given by her father to his college associates and friends. Then Emily came forth, took her place as genial hostess, and neither by dress, manner, nor appearance suggested any lack of familiarity with social events.

Her poems, all of them short, and many of the best lyrical, show the mood of the moment. They were often intended for some friend and

EMILY DICKINSON

9

were frequently enclosed in letters quaint and original as the writer. Few bore any title. Wonderful power of imagination and vivid descriptive ability are shown in her poems. Flashes of humor and originality are often present, and unusual spirituality of nature is constantly evidenced.

Miss Dickinson's death occurred May 15, 1886, in the house where her entire life had been spent.

## A BOOK

There is no frigate like a book
  To take us lands away,
Nor any coursers like a page
  Of prancing poetry.

This traverse may the poorest take
  Without oppress of toll;
How frugal is the chariot
  That bears a human soul!

NOTES AND QUESTIONS ON "A BOOK"

This bit of imagination graphically tells the effect of a book upon the mind. We are transported to distant lands with incredible speed and these journeys are alike free to the poorest as to the richest.

Explain frigate, coursers, prancing poetry, traverse, oppress, frugal.

## ASPIRATION

We never know how high we are
Till we are called to rise;
And then, if we are true to plan,
Our statures touch the skies.

The heroism we recite
Would be a daily thing,
Did not ourselves the cubits warp
For fear to be a king.

NOTES AND QUESTIONS ON "ASPIRATION"

The thought, so often spoken, that we never know how well we can do, or how much we can accomplish until we try, is well put in this poem, as well as the sad suggestion that our own lack of confidence prevents our upward progress.

Explain: "true to plan", "our statures touch the skies", "ourselves the cubits warp."

What other poem by Emily Dickinson has the same rhyme-scheme?

## IF I CAN STOP ONE HEART FROM BREAKING

If I can stop one heart from breaking,
I shall not live in vain;
If I can ease one life the aching,
Or cool one pain,
Or help one fainting robin
Unto his nest again,
I shall not live in vain.

NOTES AND QUESTIONS ON "IF I CAN STOP ONE HEART FROM BREAKING"

What kind of sentence is used here, and why is it a good one to use?

Note the unusual rhyme-scheme and the varying length of the lines.

Put the thought of the poem in a shorter sentence.

Memorize the poem.

## IN A LIBRARY

A precious, mouldering pleasure 'tis
To meet an antique book,
In just the dress his century wore;
A privilege, I think,

His venerable hand to take,
And warming in our own,

A passage back, or two, to make
To times when he was young.

His quaint opinions to inspect,
His knowledge to unfold
On what concerns our mutual mind,
The literature of old;

What interested scholars most,
What competitions ran
When Plato was a certainty,
And Sophocles a man;

When Sappho was a living girl,
And Beatrice wore
The gown that Dante deified.
Facts, centuries before,

He traverses familiar,
As one should come to town
And tell you all your dreams were true:
He lived where dreams were sown.

His presence is enchantment,
You beg him not to go;
Old volumes shake their vellum heads
And tantalize, just so.

### NOTES AND QUESTIONS ON "IN A LIBRARY"

What rhetorical figure does the poem as a whole represent? How
do you understand the words, "A precious, mouldering pleasure" in
the first line? Have you ever seen a book printed on vellum?
Explain: "When Plato was a certainty,
       And Sophocles a man."
Who were Sappho, Beatrice, Dante?

# HELEN HUNT JACKSON

The group of later writers usually includes Helen Hunt Jackson among those of the West. She was born in New England, and her poetry bears the stamp of New England thought and feeling. The daughter of Professor Fiske of Amherst College, she early began writing poems under the initials "H. H." Removing to Colorado Springs she became greatly interested in the Indian question, and her indignation at the government's unjust treatment of the "real Americans" is strongly evident in her two best-known prose works: "A Century of Dishonor" and "Ramona." The latter, a story of Southern California, is regarded as her best work.

## OCTOBER'S BRIGHT BLUE WEATHER

O suns and skies and clouds of June,
　　And flowers of June together,
Ye cannot rival for one hour
　　October's bright blue weather,

When loud the bumble-bee makes haste,
　　Belated, thriftless vagrant,
And Golden-Rod is dying fast,
　　And lanes with grapes are fragrant;

When Gentians roll their fringes tight
　　To save them for the morning,
And chestnuts fall from satin burrs
　　Without a sound of warning;

When on the ground red apples lie
　　In piles like jewels shining,

13

And redder still on old stone walls
  Are leaves of woodbine twining;

When all the lovely wayside things
  Their white-winged seeds are sowing,
And in the fields, still green and fair,
  Late aftermaths are growing;

When springs run low, and on the brooks,
  In idle golden freighting,
Bright leaves sink noiseless in the hush
  Of woods, for winter waiting;

When comrades seek sweet country haunts,
  By twos and twos together,
And count like misers, hour by hour,
  October's bright blue weather.

O suns and skies and flowers of June,
  Count all your boasts together,
Love loveth best of all the year
  October's bright blue weather.

### NOTES AND QUESTIONS ON "OCTOBER'S BRIGHT BLUE WEATHER"

The poem begins and ends with a stanza asserting the superior attractiveness of October over June. Give reasons why you do or do not agree.

Note the appeal to the external senses: the sound of the bumble-bee, the fragrance of the grapes, the glowing color of the apples and of the woodbine.

Explain: vagrant, gentians, satin burrs, aftermath, miser. What is referred to by the words "bright blue weather"?

Compare the last couplet of the third stanza with William Cullen Bryant's "The Death of the Flowers."

And the sound of dropping nuts is heard
Though all the leaves are still.

Which is the more cheerful poem? Do you see why Bryant wrote so sadly?

Is June or October regarded as the more joyous month by people in general? Why?

What special information is to be gained from this poem?

Notice the frequent use of alliteration in the poem. How many examples do you find? What other figures of rhetoric appear?

## SPINNING

Like a blind spinner in the sun,
    I tread my days;
I know that all the threads will run
    Appointed ways;
I know each day will bring its task,
And, being blind, no more I ask.

I do not know the use or name
    Of that I spin;
I only know that some one came,
    And laid within
My hand the thread, and said, "Since you
Are blind, but one thing you can do."

Sometimes the threads so rough and fast
    And tangled fly,
I know wild storms are sweeping past,
    And fear that I
Shall fall; but dare not try to find
A safer place, since I am blind.

I know not why, but I am sure
    That tint and place,
In some great fabric to endure
    Past time and race
My threads will have; so from the first,
Though blind, I never felt accurst.

I think, perhaps, this trust has sprung
   From one short word
Said over me when I was young, —
   So young, I heard
It, knowing not that God's name signed
My brow, and sealed me his, though blind.

But whether this be seal or sign
   Within, without,
It matters not.   The bond divine
   I never doubt.
I know he set me here, and still,
And glad, and blind, I wait His will;

But listen, listen, day by day,
   To hear their tread
Who bear the finished web away,
   And cut the thread,
And bring God's message in the sun,
"Thou poor blind spinner, work is done."

### NOTES AND QUESTIONS ON "SPINNING"

Human life is portrayed in the picture of the blind spinner in whose hand a thread has been placed with the command, "Since you are blind, but one thing you can do."

Through storms which terrify lest she should fall, and ignorant always of the purpose and outcome, yet persevering and patient she is faithful to the spinning until at last the finished work brings release and reward.

Why is the spinner pictured as blind?

To what is the allusion in the fifth stanza?

What is the finished work?

Note the regularity of the rhythm, which makes it easy to divide the long lines into four feet and the short ones into two.   Trace this throughout the poem and, in reading it aloud, note the effect of the short lines and of the rhyme-scheme.

# THE DAY–STAR IN THE EAST

Each morning, in the eastern sky, I see
The star that morning dares to call its own.
Night's myriads it has outwatched and outshone;
Full radiant dawn pales not its majesty;
Peer of the sun, his herald fit and free.
Sudden from earth, dark, heavy mists are blown;
The city's grimy smoke, to pillars grown,
Climbs up the sky, and hides the star from me.
Strange, that a film of smoke can blot a star!
On comes, with blinding glare, the breathless day:
The star is gone.   The moon doth surer lay
Than midnight gloom, athwart its light, a bar.
But steadfast as God's angels planets are.
To-morrow's dawn will show its changeless ray.

The centuries are God's days; within his hand,
Held in the hollow, as a balance swings,
Less than its dust, are all our temporal things.
Long are his nights, when darkness steeps the land;
Thousands of years fill one slow dawn's demand;
The human calendar its measure brings,
Feeble and vain, to lift the soul that clings
To hope for light, and seeks to understand.
The centuries are God's days; the greatest least
In his esteem.   We have no glass to sweep
His universe.   A hand's-breadth distant dies,
To our poor ears, the strain whose echoes keep
All heaven glad.   We do but grope and creep.
There always is a day-star in the skies!

NOTES AND QUESTIONS ON "THE DAY-STAR IN THE EAST"

The beautiful picture of the morning star, "Peer of the sun",
"Co-herald of the dawn", is made the synonym of faith and hope in

human life. Through storm and darkness which surround the earth the morning star makes its sure appearance, even as "Sunrise never failed us yet."

Note in stanza 2 the various similes by which the vast duration of time is emphasized.

Explain the last line.

This poem is written in the metre of Shakespeare's plays and Milton's great epic, "Paradise Lost"; why are the long lines of five metrical feet appropriate to the theme of the poem? What kind of vowel sounds prevail? Consult "The Symbolic Value of Vowel Sounds" (in the Introduction) to see why these are used.

EDWIN MARKHAM
(From the bust by William Ordway Partridge)

# EDWIN MARKHAM

No American poet is better known or loved than Edwin Markham.
His full name is Charles Edwin Markham and he was born in Oregon
City, Oregon, in 1852, of pioneer parents.  After the death of his
father, and before Edwin was five years old, his mother removed to
a wild valley in the Suisun Hills, Central California, where he grew

up on a cattle ranch, herding sheep and riding his broncho over the hills after the cattle. He attended school three months of the year and worked the rest of the time to earn enough to pay his way, reading industriously all the books he could lay his hands on. Later he studied at Christian College, Santa Rosa, and became a teacher and finally a superintendent of schools.

Markham is a disciple of Whitman in that he believes in the brotherhood of man and hates the social injustice that makes some men slaves of labor and others their masters because of their wealth and power. In 1899 he voiced his indignation in the powerful poem "The Man with the Hoe." The world was beginning to think of man's relation to man and this poem caught and crystallized in magic words the unexpressed thoughts of thousands. Its success was instantaneous and universal, and it has burned itself into our American literature as few utterances of man have ever done. In 1901 he came to New York where he became a contributor to periodicals dealing with the brotherhood of man. In an article written for the *Cosmopolitan Magazine* some years ago, entitled "What Life Means to Me", he says, "The survival of the fittest must give way to the fitting of all to survive. The Golden Rule must displace the rule of gold. Man was made for the adventure of love. All true morality for man must be based on unselfish service." Mr. Markham is now living in a suburb of New York City.

## THE MAN WITH THE HOE

God made man in His own image, in the image of God made He
    him. — *Genesis.*

Bowed by the weight of centuries, he leans
Upon his hoe and gazes on the ground,
The emptiness of ages in his face
And on his back the burden of the world.
Who made him dead to rapture and despair,
A thing that grieves not and that never hopes,
Stolid and stunned, a brother to the ox?
Who loosened and let down this brutal jaw?
Whose was the hand that slanted back this brow?
Whose breath blew out the light within this brain?

Is this the Thing the Lord God made and gave
To have dominion over sea and land;
To trace the stars and search the heavens for power;
To feel the passion of Eternity?
Is this the dream He dreamed who shaped the suns
And marked their ways upon the ancient deep?

THE MAN WITH THE HOE

Down all the caverns of Hell to their last gulf
There is no shape more terrible than this —
More tongued with censure of the world's blind greed —
More filled with signs and portents for the soul —
More pack't with danger to the universe.

What gulfs between him and the seraphim!
Slave of the wheel of labor, what to him

Are Plato and the swing of Pleiades?
What the long reaches of the peaks of song,
The rift of dawn, the reddening of the rose?
Through this dread shape the suffering ages look;
Time's tragedy is in that aching stoop;
Through this dread shape humanity betrayed,
Plundered, profaned, and disinherited,
Cries protest to the Judges of the World,
A protest that is also prophecy.

O masters, lords and rulers in all lands,
Is this the handiwork you give to God,
This monstrous thing distorted and soul-quenched?
How will you ever straighten up this shape;
Touch it again with immortality;
Give back the upward looking and the light;
Rebuild in it the music and the dream;
Make right the immemorial infamies,
Perfidious wrongs, immedicable woes?

O masters, lords and rulers in all lands,
How will the Future reckon with this man?
How answer his brute question in that hour
When whirlwinds of rebellion shake the world?
How will it be with kingdoms and with kings —
With those who shaped him to the thing he is —
When this dumb Terror shall rise to judge the world,
After the silence of the centuries?

(Written after seeing Millet's world-famous picture of a brutalized toiler. Copyright, 1899, by Edwin Markham. Used by permission. From the volume, "The Man with the Hoe and Other Poems.")

### NOTES AND QUESTIONS ON "THE MAN WITH THE HOE"

Markham found his inspiration for this world-famous poem in Millet's well-known painting of the same name. Published in 1899, it was hailed as "the battle cry of the next thousand years", and its

effect in making one half of the world realize how the other half lives
was so tremendous that it is said to have "made the whole world kin."
The toiling peasant of the poem represents the worker in any industry,
such as the miner, the iron-smelter, the mill-hand, or the girl or child
toiling long hours in the sweat-shops or the glass-works.

Compare Markham's description of the French peasant with Millet's
picture. Do the expressions "emptiness of ages", "stolid and
stunned", "a brother to the ox" describe the man? Is the jaw
"loosened and let down"?   "brutal"?   Is the brow "slanted back"?

"World's blind greed" contains two figures of speech; metonymy in
"world" substituted for the people of the world, and personification
in "blind greed." What other fine figures of speech add force and
beauty to the poem?

Plato, the great Greek philosopher and pupil of Socrates.

Pleiades, a group of seven small stars in the constellation of Taurus,
often called the Seven Sisters.

Why are the long dignified lines suited to the theme of the poem?
What lines seem to you particularly beautiful because of their sound?
See if by referring to "Aids to Musical Sound in Poetry" in the
Introduction you can tell what makes them so.

Other works which have contributed to social changes: Harriet
Beecher Stowe's "Uncle Tom's Cabin"; Dickens's "Little Dorrit."


# *ANCHORED TO THE INFINITE

The builder who first bridged Niagara's gorge,
Before he swung his cable, shore to shore,
Sent out across the gulf his venturing kite
Bearing a slender cord for unseen hands
To grasp upon the further cliff and draw
A greater cord, and then a greater yet;
Till at the last across the chasm swung
The cable — then the mighty bridge in air!

So we may send our little timid thought
Across the void, out to God's reaching hands —

* Copyrighted by Edwin Markham and used with his permission.

Send out our love and faith to thread the deep —
Thought after thought until the little cord
Has greatened to a chain no chance can break,
And — we are anchored to the Infinite!

#### NOTES AND QUESTIONS ON "ANCHORED TO THE INFINITE"

Since this poem has fourteen lines and is divided into two parts, the first of which contains eight lines and the second six, what is it called? If you do not know, consult "Kinds of Poetry" in the Introduction to this book. Note that the first part of the poem is definite and refers to a concrete incident, while the second is general and teaches a great spiritual truth. This is frequently so in this kind of poetry. What is the climax of the first part? of the second? Observe that it is expressed in the same way in both parts. State the thought of the poem in one sentence.

Do you suppose Mr. Markham was thinking of these lines from Tennyson's "Passing of Arthur" when he wrote "Anchored to the Infinite"?

> "For so the whole round earth is every way
> Bound by gold chains about the feet of God."

## * VICTORY IN DEFEAT

Defeat may serve as well as victory
To shake the soul and let the glory out.
When the great oak is straining in the wind,
The boughs drink in new beauty, and the trunk
Sends down a deeper root on the windward side.
Only the soul that knows the mighty grief
Can know the mighty rapture. Sorrows come
To stretch out spaces in the heart for joy.

#### NOTES AND QUESTIONS ON "VICTORY IN DEFEAT"

Suppose the football or baseball team always wins, what may be the effect on the players? Express the thought of the first two lines

*\* Copyrighted by Edwin Markham and used with his permission.*

in your own words. What is gained by the metaphor of the oak?
Is Markham right about its growth? In how many ways does this
poem say the same thing?

## * OUTWITTED

He drew a circle that shut me out —
Heretic, rebel, a thing to flout.
But Love and I had the wit to win:
We drew a circle that took him in!

### NOTES AND QUESTIONS ON "OUTWITTED"

This is a fine example of the fact that the poet sometimes uses great
economy of words, expressing much in little. How does the very
brevity make the idea clear? The poem is also a fine example of
contrast. Will Love always conquer Hate?

## * HOW OSWALD DINED WITH GOD

Over Northumbria's lone, gray lands,
    Over the frozen marl,
Went flying the fogs from the fens and sands,
    And the wind with a wolfish snarl.

Frosty and stiff by the gray York wall
    Stood the rusty grass and the yarrow:
Gone wings and song to the southland, all —
    Robin and starling and sparrow.

Weary with weaving the battle-woof,
    Came the king and his thanes to the Hall:
Feast-fires reddened the beams of the roof,
    Torch flames waved from the wall.

* Copyrighted by Edwin Markham and used with his permission.

Bright was the gold that the table bore,
　　Where platters and beakers shone:
Whining hounds on the sanded floor
　　Looked hungrily up for a bone.

Laughing, the king took his seat at the board,
　　With his gold-haired queen at his right:
War-men sitting around them roared
　　Like a crash of the shields in fight.

Loud rose laughter and lusty cheer,
　　And gleemen sang loud in their throats,
Telling of swords and the whistling spear,
　　Till their red beards shook with the notes.

Varlets were bringing the smoking boar,
　　Ladies were pouring the ale,
When the watchman called from the great hall door:
　　"O King, on the wind is a wail.

"Feebly the host of the hungry poor
　　Lift hands at the gate with a cry:
Grizzled and gaunt they come over the moor,
　　Blasted by earth and sky."

"Ho!" cried the king to the thanes, "make speed —
　　Carry this food to the gates —
Off with the boar and the cask of mead —
　　Leave but a loaf on the plates."

Still came a cry from the hollow night:
　　"King, this is one day's feast;
But days are coming with famine-blight;
　　Wolf winds howl from the east!"

Hot from the king's heart leaped a deed,
   High as his iron crown:
(Noble souls have a deathless need
   To stoop to the lowest down.)

"Thanes, I swear by Godde's Bride
   This is a curséd thing —
Hunger for the folk outside,
   Gold inside for the king!"

Whirling his war-ax over his head,
   He cleft each plate into four.
"Gather them up, O thanes," he said,
   "For the workfolk at the door.

"Give them this for the morrow's meat,
   Then shall we feast in accord:
Our half a loaf will then be sweet —
   Sweet as the bread of the Lord!"

Oswald, "the most Christian King of the Northumbrians", was born about 604 A.D., shortly after the time of King Arthur. The moral power that reached its height in King Alfred had its first dawn in the character of Oswald. — (*Note by Edwin Markham.*)

### NOTES AND QUESTIONS ON "HOW OSWALD DINED WITH GOD"

Oswald was a powerful king ruling over Northumbria, one of the three kingdoms settled by the Angles in Britain in the sixth century, but his fame rests chiefly on the legends of his piety, for he was among the first of the early rulers to combine Christian mercy with kingly power.

*Stanza 1.* What impression of the country is given by this stanza? How does the metaphor in the last line help? What examples of alliteration do you find? The conspicuous vowels used are those that give the effect of gloom. See "The Symbolic Value of Vowel Sounds" in the Introduction. In "wolfish snarl" we have a fine example of onomatopœia.

*Stanza 2.* This stanza increases the impression given by stanza 1. Apply what is said in the notes on stanza 1 to see how the effect is produced. York is about two hundred miles north of London and was the capital of Roman Britain.

*Stanza 3.* In the great halls of the early castles the beams showed plainly and torches furnished the only light. Why are these said to "wave"?

*Stanza 4.* Notice the difference between the unfinished rafters, the crude lighting of the hall and the sanded floor, and the splendor of the gold platters.

*Stanza 5.* The sounds described make the picture very vivid; could a painter have reproduced that? What fine example of onomatopœia do you find?

*Stanza 6.* "Gleemen", men who sang "glees", light, musical compositions for three or more voices. Study the words used in this stanza to see how the consonants and vowels add to the music of the sound.

*Stanza 7.* A whole animal was often served in those crude days when men ate ravenously.

*Stanza 8.* At that time the poor were largely dependent on the bounty of the rich. Is that a good policy?

*Stanza 9.* "Cask of mead", a small wooden barrel of a mixture of honey and water.

*Stanza 10.* Between the time of stanza 9 and this stanza the food and drink have been carried out to the poor. Tell in your own words why they are not satisfied.

*Stanza 11.* What is the effect of the simile in line 1? "Noble souls are obliged to help even the humblest" is the meaning of the sentence in the parenthesis.

*Stanza 12.* What shows that Oswald was far in advance of his times?

*Stanza 13.* What new quality does this stanza add to the portrait of Oswald?

*Stanza 14.* Express the thought of this stanza in your own words. What is the meaning of the title of the poem?

*In General.* To what class of poetry does this poem belong? Find others in this book belonging to the same class and see if the rhyme and rhythm are the usual ones.

# *THE DEDICATION POEM

Read by Edwin Markham at the dedication of the Lincoln Memorial at Washington, D. C., May 30, 1922.   Before reading, he said:
"No oration, no poem, can rise to the high level of this historic hour.   Nevertheless, I venture to inscribe this revised version of my Lincoln poem to this stupendous Lincoln Memorial, to this far-shining monument of remembrance, erected in immortal marble to the honor of our deathless martyr — the consecrated statesman, the ideal American, the ever-beloved friend of humanity."

## LINCOLN, THE MAN OF THE PEOPLE

When the Norn Mother saw the Whirlwind Hour
Greatening and darkening as it hurried on,
She left the Heaven of Heroes and came down
To make a man to meet the mortal need.
She took the tried clay of the common road —
Clay warm yet with the genial heat of Earth,
Dasht through it all a strain of prophecy;
Tempered the heap with thrill of human tears;
Then mixt a laughter with the serious stuff.
Into the shape she breathed a flame to light
That tender, tragic, ever-changing face;
And laid on him a sense of the Mystic Powers,
Moving — all husht — behind the mortal veil.
Here was a man to hold against the world,
A man to match the mountains and the sea.

The color of the ground was in him, the red earth;
The smack and tang of elemental things;
The rectitude and patience of the cliff;
The good-will of the rain that loves all leaves;
The friendly welcome of the wayside well;
The courage of the bird that dares the sea;

The gladness of the wind that shakes the corn;
The pity of the snow that hides all scars;
The secrecy of streams that make their way
Under the mountain to the rifted rock;
The tolerance and equity of light
That gives as freely to the shrinking flower
As to the great oak flaring to the wind —
To the grave's low hill as to the Matterhorn
That shoulders out the sky.   Sprung from the West,
He drank the valorous youth of a new world.
The strength of virgin forests braced his mind,
The hush of spacious prairies stilled his soul.
His words were oaks in acorns; and his thoughts
Were roots that firmly gript the granite truth.

Up from log cabin to the Capitol,
One fire was on his spirit, one resolve —
To send the keen ax to the root of wrong,
Clearing a free way for the feet of God,
The eyes of conscience testing every stroke,
To make his deed the measure of a man.
He built the rail-pile as he built the State,
Pouring his splendid strength through every blow:
The grip that swung the ax in Illinois
Was on the pen that set a people free.

So came the Captain with the mighty heart;
And when the judgment thunders split the house,
Wrenching the rafters from their ancient rest,
He held the ridgepole up, and spikt again
The rafters of the Home.   He held his place —
Held the long purpose like a growing tree —
Held on through blame and faltered not at praise.

And when he fell in whirlwind, he went down
As when a lordly cedar, green with boughs,
Goes down with a great shout upon the hills,
And leaves a lonesome place against the sky.

THE STATUE OF ABRAHAM LINCOLN IN THE LINCOLN
MEMORIAL

NOTES AND QUESTIONS ON "LINCOLN THE MAN OF THE PEOPLE"

This poem is considered by many the best of the many poems
written about Abraham Lincoln.  It is a wonderful study in symbolism, the qualities of natural objects being used as the symbols of

Lincoln's spiritual qualities; thus the poem is a series of metaphors. Pick out those which seem to you to describe him best.

*Stanza 1.* "Norn Mother." According to old Norse mythology, she was one of the Fates, whose decrees were irrevocable. "Whirlwind Hour", the period of the Civil War. Notice how the long vowels in the first two lines of this stanza give a sense of awe and coming danger, and in the last two lines a feeling of dignity and might. See "Aids to Musical Sound in Poetry", in the Introduction.

*Stanza 2.* Why are "smack and tang" in line 2 the best words that could be used? Note the contrast between "grave's low hill" and the Matterhorn, which is a peak of the Alps rising nearly fifteen thousand feet. What sounds make "The hush of spacious prairies", etc., such a large and quiet line? Why is "granite truth" better than granite-like truth?

*Stanza 3.* What is the wrong referred to in line 3? What figure of speech is in the last line?

*Stanza 4.* Why is "Home" in line 5 a better word than "nation"? A tree is frequently used to symbolize a strong man; why is the simile "as a lordly cedar green with boughs" an appropriate one to use of Lincoln? Why have so many people liked the last few lines of this poem?

# HENRY VAN DYKE

Henry van Dyke was a man of many gifts, none of which he allowed to rust unused.   He was eminently successful as clergyman, professor, diplomat, poet, essayist, and writer of fiction.

Dr. van Dyke was born in Germantown, now a part of Philadelphia, in 1852.  As a child he loved to roam the woods and fields, often in the companionship of his father. He gathered from the songs of birds, the babbling brooks, and the whispering winds a store of material which has reappeared in his writings.

Dr. van Dyke was graduated from Princeton College in 1873 and from Princeton Theological School in 1877.  After a year abroad he became pastor of a church in Newport, Rhode Island, and later of a church in New York City.

Copyright, Pirie MacDonald, N.Y.

HENRY VAN DYKE

His vacations spent in camping and fishing bore fruit in his writings, "Little Rivers" and "Fisherman's Luck."  Several of his religious works were written at this period — the best known is "The Other Wise Man."

33

In 1900 Dr. van Dyke became Murray Professor of English in Princeton University, and in 1913 was appointed United States minister to the Netherlands. A complete edition of his works appeared in 1920. He died April 10, 1933. In all that he wrote was present a spirit of optimism, joy, and hope.

## AMERICA FOR ME (1910)

'Tis fine to see the Old World, and travel up and down
Among the famous palaces and cities of renown,
To admire crumbly castles and the statues of the kings —
But now I think I've had enough of antiquated things.

So it's home again, and home again, America for me!
My heart is turning home again, and there I long to be,
In the land of youth and freedom beyond the ocean bars,
Where the air is full of sunlight and the flag is full of
    stars.

Oh, London is a man's town, there's power in the air;
And Paris is a woman's town, with flowers in her hair;
And it's sweet to dream in Venice, and it's great to study
    Rome,
But when it comes to living, there is no place like home.

I know that Europe's wonderful, yet something seems to
    lack:
The Past is too much with her, and the people looking
    back.
But the glory of the Present is to make the Future free —
We love our land for what she is and what she is to be.

Oh, it's home again, and home again, America for me!
I want a ship that's westward bound to plough the rolling
    sea,

To the blessed Land of Room Enough beyond the ocean
    bars,
Where the air is full of sunlight and the flag is full of stars.

NOTES AND QUESTIONS ON "AMERICA FOR ME"

An American who has travelled extensively in the Old World and
noted in detail the special points of pride in the various cities and
countries realizes that the worth-while country is the one which looks
not to the Past but emphasizes the Present and what it can build for
the Future.

That land is America; as Dr. van Dyke calls it, "the blessed Land
of Room Enough", whose flag is full of stars.

Explain the allusion to the stars of the flag.

Explain the allusion to London, Paris, Venice, Rome. In what
respect has America been said to have no history?

What is it that Europe "seems to lack"?

As you read this poem aloud, note its swing. What do the pauses
have to do with this?

Which poems by Dr. van Dyke do you like better, those written in
blank verse or this one which rhymes?

## LONGFELLOW

In a great land, a new land, a land full of labour and riches
    and confusion,
Where there were many running to and fro, and shouting,
    and striving together,
In the midst of the hurry and the troubled noise, I heard
    the voice of one singing.

"What are you doing there, O man, singing quietly amid
    all this tumult?
This is the time for new inventions, mighty shoutings, and
    blowings of the trumpet."
But he answered, "I am only shepherding my sheep with
    music."

So he went along his chosen way, keeping his little flock
around him;
And he paused to listen, now and then, beside the antique
fountains,
Where the faces of forgotten gods were refreshed with
musically falling waters;

Or he sat for a while at the blacksmith's door, and heard the
cling-clang of the anvils;
Or he rested beneath old steeples full of bells, that showered
their chimes upon him;
Or he walked along the border of the sea, drinking in the
long roar of the billows;

Or he sunned himself in the pine-scented shipyard, amid the
tattoo of the mallets;
Or he leaned on the rail of the bridge, letting his thoughts
flow with the whispering river;
He hearkened also to ancient tales, and made them young
again with his singing.

Then a flaming arrow of death fell on his flock, and pierced
the heart of his dearest!
Silent the music now, as the shepherd entered the mystical
temple of sorrow:
Long he tarried in darkness there: but when he came out
he was singing.

And I saw the faces of men and women and children silently
turning toward him;
The youth setting out on the journey of life, and the old
man waiting beside the last mile-stone;
The toiler sweating beneath his load; and the happy
mother rocking her cradle;

The lonely sailor on far-off seas; and the gray-minded
scholar in his book-room;
The mill-hand bound to a clacking machine; and the
hunter in the forest;
And the solitary soul hiding friendless in the wilderness of
the city;

Many human faces, full of care and longing, were drawn
irresistibly toward him,
By the charm of something known to every heart, yet very
strange and lovely,
And at the sound of his singing wonderfully all their faces
were lightened.

"Why do you listen, O you people, to this old and world-
worn music?
This is not for you, in the splendour of a new age, in the
democratic triumph!
Listen to the clashing cymbals, the big drums, the brazen
trumpets of your poets."

But the people made no answer, following in their hearts
the simpler music:
For it seemed to them, noise-weary, nothing could be better
worth the hearing
Than the melodies which brought sweet order into life's
confusion.

So the shepherd sang his way along, until he came into a
mountain:
And I know not surely whether the mountain was called
Parnassus,
But he climbed it out of sight, and still I heard the voice
of one singing.

NOTES AND QUESTIONS ON "LONGFELLOW"

In this poem Van Dyke shows very plainly that the poet Longfellow made no attempt to write of the problems of his day, but wrote simply to the heart of mankind, to cheer, comfort and to bring peace. You will readily recognize the allusion to Longfellow's poems "The Village Blacksmith", "The Bridge", "The Belfry of Bruges", "The Building of the Ship" and "Resignation."

Explain why the people preferred the simpler music "to the clashing cymbals, the big drums, the brazen triumphs of your poets."

What was Parnassus?

What fine instances of onomatopœia add beauty to the poem?

What is the chief difference between the subjects treated by Longfellow and those of the poets who are writing to-day? Which are more truly American?

## THE ANCESTRAL DWELLINGS

Dear to my heart are the ancestral dwellings of America,
Dearer than if they were haunted by ghosts of royal splendour;
They are simple enough to be great in their friendly dignity,—
Homes that were built by the brave beginners of a nation.
I love the old white farmhouses nestled in New England valleys,
Ample and long and low, with elm-trees feathering over them:
Borders of box in the yard, and lilacs, and old-fashioned roses,
A fan-light above the door, and little square panes in the windows,
The wood-shed piled with maple and birch and hickory ready for winter,
The gambrel-roof with its garret crowded with household relics, —
All the tokens of prudent thrift and the spirit of self-reliance.

AN ANCESTRAL DWELLING

I love the weather-beaten, shingled houses that front the
  ocean;
They seem to grow out of the rocks, there is something
  indomitable about them:
Their backs are bowed, and their sides are covered with
  lichens;
Soft in their colour as grey pearls, they are full of a patient
  courage.
Facing the briny wind on a lonely shore they stand un-
  daunted,
While the thin blue pennant of smoke from the square-
  built chimney
Tells of a haven for man with room for a hearth and a
  cradle.

I love the stately southern mansions with their tall white
  columns,
They look through avenues of trees, over fields where the
  cotton is growing;
I can see the flutter of white frocks along their shady
  porches,
Music and laughter float from the windows, the yards are
  full of hounds and horses.
Long since the riders have ridden away, yet the houses
  have not forgotten,
They are proud of their name and place, and their doors
  are always open,
For the thing they remember best is the pride of their
  ancient hospitality.

In the towns I love the discreet and tranquil Quaker dwellings,
With their demure brick faces and immaculate marble
  doorsteps;

And the gabled houses of the Dutch, with their high stoops
and iron railings,
(I can see their little brass knobs shining in the morning
sunlight);
And the solid self-contained houses of the descendants of
the Puritans,
Frowning on the street with their narrow doors and dormer-
windows;
And the triple-galleried, many-pillared mansions of Charles-
ton,
Standing open sideways in their gardens of roses and
magnolias.

Yes, they are all dear to my heart, and in my eyes they are
beautiful;
For under their roofs were nourished the thoughts that have
made the nation:
The glory and strength of America come from her ancestral
dwellings.


NOTES AND QUESTIONS ON "THE ANCESTRAL DWELLINGS"

In this poem the author emphasizes the thought that America's
success and greatness have sprung from the spirit which developed
in the homes of the early settlers of the country. You will notice how
ingeniously he credits this spirit to the whole country by describing
successively the types of architecture in the various sections of the
country: the New England farm house beneath the elms, with the
gambrel roof and garden of old-fashioned flowers, the gray weather-
beaten houses along the shore, the more pretentious southern mansions
with tall, white columns and avenues of trees, and the Quaker dwellings of Pennsylvania, of brick with marble steps. "Under their roofs
were nourished the thoughts that have made the nation."

Do you think the homes of to-day will do the same for their children?
What great helper has the home in teaching patriotism to-day?

Explain "borders of box", "gambrel roof." Look up Holmes's "Gambrel Roofed House." Why is "blue pennant" a more vivid description than simply "thin blue smoke"? Define "stoops", "dormer-windows", "magnolias", "ancestral." Try to bring to class some pictures of old doorways.

Compare the diction of this poem with that of Walt Whitman's. In what respects are they alike?

# JAMES WHITCOMB RILEY

James Whitcomb Riley, one of the most widely read of the poets
of the latter half of the nineteenth century, was born in Greenfield,

JAMES WHITCOMB RILEY

Indiana, the son of a lawyer who wished him to follow in his own
footsteps. The adventurous spirit of the lad forbade, and at eighteen

he ran away from home and the study of law, to join an itinerant
band of actors.   Riley's versatile gifts enabled him to help with equal
readiness to paint a flaming poster, play any one of several musical
instruments, including the snare drum, or to rewrite old songs, filling
them with local hits.   A little of this life sufficed for young Riley;
already he had sent some of his verses to various papers, which published them under the initials "E. A. P."   Obtaining a position on
the staff of the *Indianapolis Journal* he contributed a series of dialect
poems, assumed to be written by "Benj. F. Johnson of Boone, the
Hoosier poet."   These were somewhat in the style of Lowell's "Big-
low Papers", and were later collected in a volume entitled "The Ole
Swimmin' Hole."

Many honors were heaped upon Mr. Riley: Yale College conferred
upon him the degree of A.M., the University of Pennsylvania made
him Doctor of Letters, and the American Academy of Letters gave
him its gold medal in the Department of Poetry.   But the best
token of appreciation, as he himself would have regarded it, was that
on the occasion of his funeral thirty-five thousand people passed
through the rotunda of the State capitol to look upon his face in death,
and still his native State observes his birthday as "Riley Day."


## THE FIRST BLUEBIRD

The very first bluebird of Spring,
As old Benj. Johnson heard him sing.

Jest rain and snow! and rain again!
And dribble! drip! and blow!
Then snow! and thaw! and slush! and then —
Some more rain and snow!

This morning I was 'most afeard
To wake up — when, I jing!
I seen the sun shine out and heerd
The first bluebird of Spring! —

Mother she'd raised the winder some ; —
And in acrost the orchard come,
　　Soft as a angel's wing,
A breezy, treesy, beesy hum,
　　Too sweet fer anything!

The winter's shroud was rent a-part —
　　The sun bust forth in glee, —
And when that bluebird sung, my heart
　　Hopped out o' bed with me!

### NOTES AND QUESTIONS ON "THE FIRST BLUEBIRD"

A fine example of the author's power to picture by words the scene in his mind — the tardy coming of spring, the frequent lapses of winter — then suddenly abundant sunshine and the first bluebird's song.　Give the meaning of the line, " A breezy, treesy, beesy hum." What is the figure of the last line?

Note the delicate beauty of the poem in spite of the crudity of the dialect.　What lines are especially musical?　What makes them so? Has onomatopœia anything to do with the general effect of the poem?

## MISTER HOP–TOAD

Howdy, Mister Hop-Toad!　Glad to see you out!
Bin a month o' Sund'ys sence I seen you hereabout.
Kind o' bin a-layin' in, from the frost and snow?
Good to see you out ag'in, it's bin so long ago!
Plows like slicin' cheese, and sod's loppin' over even;
Loam's like gingerbread, and clod's softer'n deceivin' —
Mister Hop-Toad, honest-true — Springtime — don't you
　　love it?
You old rusty rascal you, at the bottom of it!

Oh, oh, oh!
I grabs up my old hoe;
But I sees you,
And s' I, "Ooh-ooh!
Howdy, Mister Hop-Toad! How-dee-do!"


Make yours'f more cumfo'bler — square round at your
    ease —
Don't set saggin' slanchwise, with your nose below your
    knees.
Swell that fat old throat o' yourn and lemme see you swaller;
Straighten up and h'ist your head! — You don't owe a
    dollar! —
Hain't no mor'gage on your land — ner no taxes, nuther;
You don't haf to work no roads — even ef you'd ruther!
'F I was you, and fixed like you, I railly wouldn't keer
To swop fer life and hop right in the presidential cheer!
Oh, oh, oh!
I hauls back my old hoe;
But I sees you,
And s' I, "Ooh-ooh!
Howdy, Mister Hop-Toad! How-dee-do!"


Long about next Aprile, hoppin' down the furry,
Won't you mind I ast you what 'peared to be the hurry? —
Won't you mind I hooked my hoe and hauled you back and
    smiled? —
W'y, bless you, Mister Hop-Toad, I love you like a child!
S'pose I'd want to 'flict you any more'n what you air? —
S'pose I think you got no rights 'cept the warts you wear?
Hulk, sulk, and blink away, you old bloat-eyed rowdy! —
Hain't you got a word to say? — Won't you tell me
    "Howdy"?

Oh, oh, oh!
I swish round my old hoe;
But I sees you,
And s' I, "Ooh-ooh!
Howdy, Mister Hop-Toad! How-dee-do!"

From "Home Folks" by James Whitcomb Riley. Copyright, 1900, by The Bobbs-Merrill Company.

### NOTES AND QUESTIONS ON "MISTER HOP-TOAD"

The poem illustrates Riley's love of nature and his friendliness of heart which enables him to greet the homely toad as an old comrade when he returns with the springtime to his old haunts. Note the humor of the second stanza where he bids the toad brace up and rejoice in his independent condition, with no mortgage, debts, or taxes — more fortunate than the President. Note also the hearty comradeship with which in the last stanza he bids the toad "mind" or remember him when next Spring comes.

Define loam, clad. Why is the toad spoken of as "rusty"? What is the meaning of "mor'gage", "furry", "warts"? What is the spirit of the refrain?

Compare the poem with Burns's "To a Mouse."


## THE OLD MAN AND JIM

Old man never had much to say —
   'Ceptin' to Jim, —
And Jim was the wildest boy he had —
   And the old man jes' wrapped up in him!
Never heerd him speak but once
Er twice in my life, — and first time was
When the army broke out, and Jim he went,
The old man backin' him, fer three months;
And all 'at I heerd the old man say
Was, jes' as we turned to start away, —
   "Well, good-by, Jim:
    Take keer of yourse'f!"

'Peared-like, he was more satisfied
　　Jes' lookin' at Jim
And likin' him all to hisse'f-like, see? —
　　'Cause he was jes' wrapped up in him!
And over and over I mind the day
The old man come and stood round in the way
While we was drillin', a-watchin' Jim —
And down at the deepo a-heerin' him say,
　　"Well, good-by, Jim:
　　　　Take keer of yourse'f!"


Never was nothin' about the farm
　　Disting'ished Jim;
Neighbors all ust to wonder why
　　The old man 'peared wrapped up in him:
But when Cap. Biggler he writ back
'At Jim was the bravest boy we had
In the whole dern rigiment, white or black,
And his fightin' good as his farmin' bad —
'At he had led, with a bullet clean
Bored through his thigh, and carried the flag
Through the bloodiest battle you ever seen, —
The old man wound up a letter to him
'At Cap. read to us, 'at said: "Tell Jim
　　Good-by,
　　　　And take keer of hisse'f!"


Jim come home jes' long enough
　　To take the whim
'At he'd like to go back in the calvery —
　　And the old man jes' wrapped up in him!
Jim 'lowed 'at he'd had sich luck afore,
Guessed he'd tackle her three years more.

And the old man give him a colt he'd raised,
And follered him over to Camp Ben Wade,
And laid around fer a week er so,
Watchin' Jim on dress-parade —
Tel finally he rid away,
And last he heerd was the old man say, —
  "Well, good-by, Jim:
    Take keer of yourse'f!"


Tuk the papers, the old man did,
  A-watchin' fer Jim —
Fully believin' he'd make his mark
  Some way — jes' wrapped up in him! —
And many a time the word 'u'd come
'At stirred him up like the tap of a drum —
At Petersburg, fer instunce, where
Jim rid right into their cannons there,
And tuk 'em, and p'inted 'em t'other way,
And socked it home to the boys in gray
As they scooted fer timber, and on and on —
Jim a lieutenant, and one arm gone,
And the old man's words in his mind all day, —
  "Well, good-by, Jim:
    Take keer of yourse'f!"


Think of a private, now, perhaps,
  . We'll say like Jim,
'At's clumb clean up to the shoulder-straps —
  And the old man jes' wrapped up in him!
Think of him — with the war plum' through,
And the glorious old Red-White-and-Blue
A-laughin' the news down over Jim,
And the old man, bendin' over him —

The surgeon turnin' away with tears
'At hadn't leaked fer years and years,
As the hand of the dyin' boy clung to
His father's, the old voice in his ears, —
    "Well, good-by, Jim:
      Take keer of yourse'f!"

From "Poems Here at Home" by James Whitcomb Riley. Copyright, 1893, by The Bobbs-Merrill Company.

### NOTES AND QUESTIONS ON "THE OLD MAN AND JIM"

A graphic word-picture of intense fatherly love which yet lacked words fitly to express itself. "Jim", as the neighbors thought, a dull ordinary fellow, and as a farmer hardly better than a failure, enlisted when the Civil War broke out and fulfilled all his father's belief and confidence.

He passed rapidly from private to officer's rank — still the father's pride and love were dumb. The war ended, and Jim in the last battle was mortally wounded. His father stood by him in anguish so evident that even the surgeon, hardened to pain and grief, shed tears. Still the father's parting words were, "Good-by, Jim. Take keer o' yourse'f."

Do you think dialect improves the poem? Why was it used?
What effective use of repetition do you find?

# SAM WALTER FOSS

No truer picture of Mr. Foss, the man, the poet, could be given than is found in one of his own poems, for indeed he " lived in his house by the side of the road and was a friend to man."

SAM WALTER FOSS

Mr. Foss was of New Hampshire birth and ancestry. Born in Auburn, in 1858, he lived to the age of fifty-three years. The strength of the hills and the beauty and fragrance of the forests, brooks, and meadows are present in his poetry.  Graduating from Brown University in 1882, he at once began contributing to various newspapers and speedily became known as a writer of humorous poems.  He edited successively the *Lynn Union*, the *Yankee Blade*, and was an editorial writer for the *Boston Globe*.  Later he gave up editorial work and devoted his time to writing, lecturing, and reading from his own poems.

Mr. Foss became librarian of the public library of Somerville, Massachusetts, his home city, in 1894.  Here his broad view of the possibilities of the library, and his warm-hearted friendliness to all, brought the library and the public near each other to a degree seldom equalled.

Mr. Foss's published poems number five volumes: "Back Country Poems", "Whiffs from Wild Meadows", "Dreams in Homespun", "Songs of War and Peace", and "Songs of the Average Man." Though humor is a conspicuous element of much of his poetry there is present, behind the humor and within the dialect, truth which reaches the heart of the reader and which furnishes the reason why his poems are increasingly beloved.

## THE HOUSE BY THE SIDE OF THE ROAD

" He was a friend to man, and lived in a house by the side of the road." — *Homer*.

There are hermit souls that live withdrawn
   In the peace of their self-content;
There are souls, like stars, that dwell apart,
   In a fellowless firmament;
There are pioneer souls that blaze their paths
   Where highways never ran; —
But let me live by the side of the road
   And be a friend to man.

Let me live in a house by the side of the road,
   Where the race of men go by —
The men who are good and the men who are bad,
   As good and as bad as I.

I would not sit in the scorner's seat,
   Or hurl the cynic's ban; —
Let me live in a house by the side of the road
   And be a friend to man.

I see from my house by the side of the road,
   By the side of the highway of life,
The men who press with the ardor of hope,
   The men who are faint with the strife.
But I turn not away from their smiles nor their tears —
   Both parts of an infinite plan; —
Let me live in a house by the side of the road
   And be a friend to man.

I know there are brook-gladdened meadows ahead
   And mountains of wearisome height;

That the road passes on through the long afternoon
  And stretches away to the night.
But still I rejoice when the travellers rejoice,
  And weep with the strangers that moan,
Nor live in my house by the side of the road
  Like a man who dwells alone.

Let me live in my house by the side of the road
  Where the race of men go by —
They are good, they are bad, they are weak, they are strong,
  Wise, foolish — so am I.
Then why should I sit in the scorner's seat
  Or hurl the cynic's ban? —
Let me live in my house by the side of the road
  And be a friend to man.

NOTES AND QUESTIONS ON "THE HOUSE BY THE SIDE OF THE ROAD"

This poem expresses vividly the spirit of fellowship which was the author's prominent characteristic.

Note in stanza 1 the excellent choice of words to describe each class of individuals. Consider carefully the meaning of "hermit souls", "souls like stars" and "pioneer souls." Wherein do they have fellowship? Why is "but" a better transition word than "and" would have been?

In stanza 2, how is it shown that the race of men who "go by" are an average group? Define "scorner", "cynic", "ban."

What in stanza 3 suggests that hope and discouragement are part of the common lot of mankind?

What in the 4th stanza suggests that fellowship imparts cheer?

How in the last stanza do you find humility and helpfulness the real lesson of the poem?

# THE CALF-PATH

## I

One day through the primeval wood
A calf walked home as good calves should;

A CALF-PATH
Old Province Street, Boston

But made a trail all bent askew,
A crooked trail as all calves do.

Since then three hundred years have fled,
And I infer that calf is dead.

## II

But still he left behind his trail,
And thereby hangs my moral tale.

The trail was taken up next day
By a lone dog that passed that way;

And then a wise bell-wether sheep
Pursued the trail o'er vale and steep,

And drew the flock behind him, too,
As good bell-wethers always do.

And from that day, o'er hill and glade,
Through those old woods a path was made.

## III

And many men wound in and out,
And dodged and turned and bent about,

And uttered words of righteous wrath
Because 'twas such a crooked path;

But still they followed — do not laugh —
The first migrations of that calf,

And through this winding wood-way stalked
Because he wobbled when he walked.

## IV

This forest path became a lane,
That bent and turned and turned again;

This crooked lane became a road,
Where many a poor horse with his load

Toiled on beneath the burning sun,
And travelled some three miles in one.

And thus a century and a half
They trod the footsteps of that calf.


V

The years passed on in swiftness fleet,
The road became a village street;

And this, before men were aware,
A city's crowded thoroughfare.

And soon the central street was this
Of a renowned metropolis;

And men two centuries and a half
Trod in the footsteps of that calf.


VI

Each day a hundred thousand rout
Followed this zigzag calf about

And o'er his crooked journey went
The traffic of a continent.

A hundred thousand men were led
By one calf near three centuries dead.

They followed still his crooked way,
And lost one hundred years a day;

For thus such reverence is lent
To well-established precedent.

## VII

A moral lesson this might teach
Were I ordained and called to preach;

For men are prone to go it blind
Along the calf-paths of the mind,

And work away from sun to sun
To do what other men have done.

They follow in the beaten track,
And out and in, and forth and back,

And still their devious course pursue,
To keep the path that others do.

They keep the path a sacred groove,
Along which all their lives they move;

But how the wise old wood-gods laugh,
Who saw the first primeval calf.

Ah, many things this tale might teach —
But I am not ordained to preach.

### NOTES AND QUESTIONS ON THE "CALF-PATH"

Note how the first two words suggest a story to follow. Define "primeval." Do you remember another American author who used the word in the beginning of a poem?

In parts 2, 3, what quality caused the increased following of the calf's trail? Define "migration", "metropolis." Draw a line to illustrate "wobbled." How does it differ from "zigzag"?

Why do people continue to follow the "calf-path"? Why does the author say he refrains from mentioning all the lessons the poem might teach? What do you think it does teach?

What is gained by having the stanzas arranged in groups?

# KATHARINE LEE BATES

As author of "America the Beautiful", Katharine Lee Bates is known to all the world. Born at Falmouth, Massachusetts, twenty miles from the nearest railroad, she grew up in close contact with nature and began to write verses as a child. While she was a sophomore at Wellesley one of her poems was published in the *Atlantic Monthly*. The Class of '80 at Wellesley is proud to call her "Our Katie", and well they may be, for she was class president as long as she lived. In 1891 she took her second degree, that of A.M., and in 1914 Middlebury College gave her the honorary degree of Litt.D.; two years later Oberlin did the same.

Her life as a teacher began at the Natick High School, from which she went to Dana Hall, a fine preparatory school, and later became an instructor in English at Wellesley College. She was long the honored and greatly beloved head of the English department of that college, so that she might well say, "I have been all my life a very busy teacher." However, she found time to travel and study abroad for four years and to write many books. Two that you would enjoy are "The Story of Chaucer's Canterbury Tales Retold" and "Sigurd, Our Golden Collie." On her retirement in 1925, Wellesley honored her with the title of Professor Emeritus. Her last years were spent in Wellesley village, where she passed away on March 28, 1929.

## AMERICA THE BEAUTIFUL

O beautiful for spacious skies,
    For amber waves of grain,
For purple mountain majesties
    Above the fruited plain!
      America! America!
    God shed His grace on thee
And crown thy good with brotherhood
    From sea to shining sea!

O beautiful for pilgrim feet,
   Whose stern, impassioned stress
A thoroughfare for freedom beat
   Across the wilderness!
      America! America!
   God mend thine every flaw,
Confirm thy soul in self-control,
   Thy liberty in law!

O beautiful for heroes proved
   In liberating strife,
Who more than self their country loved,
   And mercy more than life!
      America! America!
   May God thy gold refine
Till all success be nobleness
   And every gain divine!

O beautiful for patriot dream
   That sees beyond the years
Thine alabaster cities gleam
   Undimmed by human tears!
      America! America!
   God shed His grace on thee
And crown thy good with brotherhood
   From sea to shining sea!

### NOTES AND QUESTIONS ON "AMERICA THE BEAUTIFUL"

"America the Beautiful" was written in the summer of 1893 when Miss Bates made her first trip west, stopping at Chicago to attend the World's Fair and then going on to Colorado Springs "under the purple range of the Rockies." After a stay of about three weeks the party made a trip to Pikes Peak. Miss Bates tells the story best, so we quote: "Prairie wagons, their tail-boards emblazoned with

PIKE'S PEAK

the traditional slogan 'Pikes Peak or Bust', were pulled by horses up to the half-way house, where the horses were relieved by mules. We were hoping for half an hour on the summit, but two of our party became so faint in the rarefied air that we were bundled into the wagons again and started on our downward plunge so speedily that our sojourn on the peak remains in memory hardly more than one ecstatic gaze. It was then and there, as I was looking out over the sea-like expanse of fertile country spreading away so far under those ample skies, that the opening lines of the hymn floated into my mind. When we left Colorado Springs the four stanzas were penciled in my notebook, together with other memoranda, in verse and prose."

"America the Beautiful" was published first on the Fourth of July, 1895. Since then it has become one of the best-loved hymns of the generation, being sung by every class of American citizens. In 1922 it was adopted by the American Federation of Women's Clubs as their national song, which means that at every meeting of every club throughout the year this poem is sung. There have been over sixty original tunes composed for it, and it has been sung to many familiar ones; that which we find in most hymn-books is "Materna."

*Stanza 1.* The first four lines of this stanza give the picture which stamped itself on the memory of Miss Bates as she stood for that moment on Pikes Peak. What fine adjectives are used? Why did she use the metaphor "waves of grain"? Note how the explosive consonants in the first line and the liquid sounds in the second add to their beauty.

*Stanza 2.* Why is the expression "stern impassioned stress" used of the pioneers who settled the West? Can you think of any "flaw" which needs to be mended?

*Stanza 3.* Of whom is the poet speaking in this stanza? What is the purpose of refining a metal?

*Stanza 4.* This stanza looks forward into the future while the others have referred to the present and the past. "Alabaster" is a white marble; what effect is gained by the use of this word?

*In General.* The four stanzas are constructed on the same plan. Each sets forth a special beauty of America in the first four lines; then comes the refrain, and the last three lines voice a wish for our native land. All have the same rhyme-scheme and the seventh line, rhyming with no other, has a medial rhyme, *i.e.*, the last word rhymes with a word in the middle. Why did Miss Bates make this line prominent?

## TO SIGURD

Not one blithe leap of welcome?
Can you lie
Under this woodland mould,
More still
Than broken daffodil,
When I,
Home from too long a roving,
Come up the silent hill?
Dear, wistful eyes,
White ruff and windy gold
Of collie coat so oft caressed,
Not one quick thrill
In snowy breast,
One spring of jubilant surprise,
One ecstasy of loving?

Are all our frolics ended?   Never more
Those royal romps of old,
When one,
Playfellow of the sun,
Would pour
Adventures and romances
Into a morning run;
Off and away,
A flying glint of gold,
Startling to wing a husky choir
Of crows whose dun
Shadows would tire
Even that wild speed?   Unscared to-day
They hold their weird seances.

Ever you dreamed, legs twitching, you would catch
A crow, O leaper bold,
Next time,
Or chase to branch sublime
That batch
Of squirrels daring capture
In saucy pantomime;
Till one spring dawn,
Resting amid the gold
Of crocuses, Death stole on you
From that far clime
Where dreams come true,
And left upon the starry lawn
Your form without your rapture.

And was Death's whistle then so wondrous sweet
Across the glimmering wold
That you
Would trustfully pursue
Strange feet?
When I was gone, each morrow
You sought our old haunts through,
Slower to play,
Drooping in faded gold;
Now it is mine to grieve and miss
My comrade true
Who used to kiss
With eager tongue such tears away,
Coaxing a smile from sorrow.

I know not what life is, nor what is death,
Nor how vast Heaven may hold
All this
Earth-beauty and earth-bliss.

Christ saith
That not a sparrow falleth
— O songs of sparrow faith! —
But God is there.
May not a leap of gold
Yet greet me on some gladder hill,
A shining wraith,
Rejoicing still,
As in those hours we found so fair,
To follow where love calleth?

### NOTES AND QUESTIONS ON "SIGURD"

Sigurd is the name of the beautiful and intelligent collie once owned by Miss Bates and loved by every girl who attended Wellesley while he was alive. The story of his life is told by Miss Bates in her own inimitable style in the book "Sigurd, Our Golden Collie."

*Stanza 1.* What do you know about Sigurd after reading the first few lines? Select the details which make the description of him so true to life. Why is he compared to a daffodil?

*Stanza 2.* Select expressions in this stanza which you like especially. Why are the crows spoken of as "a husky choir"? Note the contrast in color here, "dun" meaning gloomy. Consult the dictionary to see why "seances" is used.

*Stanza 3.* What is true of a dog in this stanza? Why are the squirrels described as in "saucy pantomime"?

*Stanza 4.* Note how effective it is to speak of "Death's whistle."

*Stanza 5.* Why does Miss Bates not use the second person in this stanza? How do you know that she is a deeply religious woman? What is your answer to her question?

*In General.* Note how full of motion and quick joy the first two stanzas are; consult "Aids to Musical Sound in Poetry" in the Introduction to see how the vowels used help to produce this effect. The short lines of varying length also help. What color prevails throughout the poem and why? What have you learned about Miss Bates from reading this poem?

## REBECCA AND ABIGAIL

*When the Clans of the Open Hand convene*
  *And our valors are rehearsed,*
*Remember the year eighteen-fourteen*
  *And our proud September first.*
*When ye write the roll of our heroes down,*
  *Oh, be not the deed ignored*
*Of two little heroines, bonny and brown,*
  *Whose wit was sharp as a sword.*


Careless she sat in the lighthouse door,
  Lass of the laughing lip,
When there hove in sight off the Scituate shore
  The sails of a British ship.
Rebecca Bates was the merriest maid
  Between Cape Cod and Cape Ann,
But her quick breath sobbed, for, old fears allayed,
  The post had never a man.


Over her shoulder Abigail peered
  With the soft brown eyes of their race,
And the sisters watched as the frigate neared
  And anchored against the place
Where guards had been stationed till yestere'en,
  But now had no garrison more
Than the keeper's wife with her gentle mien,
  And the girls in the lighthouse door.


The work-worn mother, all unaware
  Of the blow about to fall,
Dozed in her faded rocking-chair,
  While the kitten teased the ball

That had rolled from her knitting, and not until
    Two barges in stealthy guise
Put off from the ship, had the girls a will
    To waken those weary eyes.

Then her dream was pierced by the shrilling fife
    And crushed by the rolling drum.
She swayed to her feet: "O Lord of Life,
    Is the hour of bloodshed come?"
White she sprang to the empty door
    And saw the redcoats, stayed
By that martial note, had raised the oar,
    Mistrusting an ambuscade.

A sullen gun from the ship warned back
    The boats, and with hurried stroke
They traversed again that foaming track
    To the shelter of British oak,
While "Yankee Doodle" rang out the fife,
    And the drum was calling to arms
As if mustering men for desperate strife
    From a hundred rebel farms.

Murmured the goodwife: "God be praised!"
    And next: "But how shall I feed
This patriot army Thou hast raised
    To succor us in our need?"
Then around the cottage, as large as life,
    She saw that army come —
Laughing Rebecca who waved the fife,
    And Abigail with the drum.

NOTES AND QUESTIONS ON "REBECCA AND ABIGAIL"

The story told in this poem is a true one, for a British ship was
actually frightened away from the Scituate shore in the War of 1812
by the quick wit of two young girls.

*Stanza 1.* What is the purpose of this stanza and what necessary information does it give? Where does the story itself begin?

*Stanza 2.* Note how the use of alliteration in the second line makes the description of Rebecca vivid. Where else in this stanza is it well used? Why was there no man at the post?

*Stanza 3.* What do you learn about the state of affairs from this stanza? Which of the girls is the older?

*Stanza 4.* What does Miss Bates imply as to the character of the girls?

*Stanza 5.* What fine use of adjectives do you find in this stanza? What picture is conveyed to the mind by the use of the verb "sway"?

*Stanza 6.* Select the well-chosen expressions which make the picture so clear. Notice that a poet can use much in painting a picture that an artist cannot.

*Stanza 7.* What shows that the girls piped and drummed with a will? Observe how the secret of who were responsible for routing the enemy is kept till the last stanza; is this a good thing to do?

*In General.* To what class of poetry does this poem belong? Are the metre and rhyme schemes the usual ones for this type of poem?

## THE DOGS OF BETHLEHEM

Many a starry night had they known,
Melampo, Lupina, and Cubilōn,
        Shepherd dogs, keeping
        The flocks, unsleeping,
Serving their masters for crust and bone.

Many a starlight, but never like this,
For star on star was a chrysalis
        Whence there went soaring
        A winged, adoring
Splendor outpouring a carol of bliss.

Sniffing and bristling the gaunt dogs stood,
Till the seraphs, who smiled at their hardihood,
        Calmed their panic
        With talismanic
Touches like wind in the underwood.

In the dust of the road like gold-dust blown,
Melampo, Lupina, and Cubilōn
      Saw strange kings, faring
      On camels, bearing
Treasures too bright for a mortal throne.

Shepherds three on their crooks a-leap
Sped after the kings up the rugged steep
      To Bethlehem; only
      The dogs, left lonely,
Stayed by the fold and guarded the sheep.

Faithful, grim hearts!  The marvelous glow
Flooded e'en these with its overflow,
      Wolfishness turning
      Into a yearning
To worship the highest a dog may know.

When dawn brought the shepherds, each to his own,
Melampo, Lupina, and Cubilōn
      Bounded to meet them
      Frolicked to greet them,
Eager to serve them for love alone.

NOTES AND QUESTIONS ON "THE DOGS OF BETHLEHEM"

Why was the starlight so much more beautiful than usual that even
the dogs felt its strange loveliness?  Who were the strange kings, and
why did the shepherds speed after them?  How is the faithfulness of
the dogs shown?  Express the thought of the next-to-the-last stanza
in your own words.  What makes the rhythm so unusual and so
lovely?

## THE FIRST VOYAGE OF JOHN CABOT

"He chases shadows," sneered the Bristol tars.
"As well fling nets to catch the golden stars
As climb the surges of earth's utmost sea;"
But for the Venice pilot, meagre, wan,
His swarthy sons beside him, life began
With that slipt cable, when his dream rode free.

And Henry, on his battle-wrested throne,
The Councils done, would speak in musing tone
Of Cabot, not the cargo he might bring.
"Man's heart, though morsel scant for hungry crow,
Is greater than a world can fill, and so
Fair fall the shadow-seekers!" quoth the king.

NOTES AND QUESTIONS ON "THE FIRST VOYAGE OF JOHN CABOT"

A Venetian pilot and the discoverer of the mainland of North America, John Cabot settled in Bristol, England, in 1472. For a time he was a merchant and then, fired by ambition, he obtained letters-patent from Henry the Seventh and, with two ships furnished by the King, and his three sons, the second of whom was the famous Sebastian, he set sail from Bristol in March, 1497, and sighted Cape Breton Island and Nova Scotia on June 24. This is the voyage referred to in the poem.

*Stanza 1.* Cabot was laughed at, you see, as all great dreamers and pioneers have been. The Bristol tars represent the average man who has no dreams. Why is Cabot described as "meagre, wan"? Picture to yourself how he felt when the cable slipped. Life truly begins only when a person begins to follow his vision.

*Stanza 2.* "Battle-wrested throne." Henry, an exile, had formed a wide conspiracy against Richard, who was king, and landed at Milford Haven. He advanced through Wales and met the royal army at Bosworth Field, where Richard was overpowered and killed. The crown which Richard had worn during the fight was found lying under a hawthorn bush and was placed on the head of the victorious Henry.

What in this stanza shows that Henry too "dreamed dreams and saw visions"?    What effect is gained by Henry's calling the Cabots "the shadow-seekers"?

## THE NEW CRUSADE

Life is a trifle;
   Honor is all;
Shoulder the rifle;
   Answer the call.
*"A nation of traders"!*
   *We'll show what we are,*
*Freedom's crusaders*
   *Who war against war.*

Battle is tragic;
   Battle shall cease;
Ours is the magic
   Mission of Peace.
*"A nation of traders"!*
   *We'll show what we are,*
*Freedom's crusaders*
   *Who war against war.*

Gladly we barter
   Gold of our youth
For Liberty's charter
   Blood-sealed in truth.
*"A nation of traders"!*
   *We'll show what we are,*
*Freedom's crusaders*
   *Who war against war.*

Sons of the granite,
   Strong be our stroke,
Making this planet
   Safe for the folk.

*"A nation of traders"!*
*We'll show what we are,*
*Freedom's crusaders*
*Who war against war.*

Life is but passion,
  Sunshine on dew.
Forward to fashion
  The old world anew!
*"A nation of traders"!*
*We'll show what we are,*
*Freedom's crusaders*
*Who war against war.*

### NOTES AND QUESTIONS ON "THE NEW CRUSADE"

The charm of this poem lies in the brevity with which the great thought in each stanza is expressed and in the refrain that makes the last half of the stanzas.

*Stanza 1.* Was this the spirit with which our boys went into the World War? "A nation of traders" only was what many European nations thought we were. Why is "crusaders" so fine a word to use as over against "traders"?

*Stanza 2.* This is a true statement of the real purpose of the United States in entering the war.

*Stanza 3.* What figure of speech in "barter the gold of our youth"? What does it add to the stanza?

*Stanza 4.* What figure in "sons of the granite"? Why is "planet" the best word to use here?

*Stanza 5.* This stanza illustrates the fact that poetry more than prose abounds in figures of speech; study the force of the one used.

*In General.* There are three metrical feet in each line, the last four lines being complete while many of the first four lack a syllable which is supplied by the marked pause at the end; in reading the poem aloud try to keep the rhythm perfect.

BLISS CARMAN

# BLISS CARMAN

During the Revolution a certain family of Tories or United Empire Loyalists, as they are called, left Connecticut and settled in Canada. These were the ancestors of (William) Bliss Carman, who was born in 1861 at Fredericton, New Brunswick. There he received his early education and attended the University, going later to Edinburgh and then coming to Harvard. More than forty years ago he took up his permanent residence in the United States at Canaan in the State from which his ancestors migrated more than a hundred years before. Like many other poets he served his apprenticeship in that wonderful trade of journalism, being editor of the *Independent* and of the *Chap Book*. Before his death in 1929 he had published more than thirty small volumes of poems.

## ROADSIDE FLOWERS

We are the roadside flowers,
    Straying from garden grounds;
Lovers of idle hours,
    Breakers of ordered bounds.

If only the earth will feed us,
    If only the wind be kind,
We blossom for those who need us,
    The stragglers left behind.

And lo, the Lord of the Garden,
    He makes His sun to rise,
And His rain to fall like pardon
    On our dusty paradise.

On us He has laid the duty —
    The task of the wandering breed —
To better the world with beauty,
    Wherever the way may lead.

Who shall inquire of the season,
    Or question the wind where it blows?
We blossom and ask no reason,
    The Lord of the Garden knows.

NOTES AND QUESTIONS ON "ROADSIDE FLOWERS"

*Stanza 1.* Is your attention attracted more by the use of the first person than it would be by that of the third? If so, why?

*Stanza 2.* Why will "The stragglers left behind" appreciate the flowers?

*Stanza 3.* Why is the figure of speech in line 3 a good one?

*Stanza 4.* Note how the mission of the flowers is brought out by the use of alliteration.

*Stanza 5.* What is the relation of the last line to the other three?

*In General.* What do you learn about Mr. Carman, the man, from this poem? Note the extreme simplicity of the poem, the directness, and the large proportion of words of one syllable. Does this detract from the beauty of the poem?

## THE JUGGLER

Look how he throws them up and up,
The beautiful golden balls!
They hang aloft in the purple air,
And there never is one that falls.

He sends them hot from his steady hand,
He teaches them all their curves;
And whether the reach be little or long,
There never is one that swerves.

Some, like the tiny red one there,
He never lets go far;
And some he has sent to the roof of the tent,
To swim without a jar.

So white and still they seem to hang,
You wonder if he forgot
To reckon the time of their return
And measure their golden lot.

Can it be that, hurried or tired out,
The hand of the juggler shook?
O never you fear, his eye is clear,
He knows them all like a book.

And they will home to his hand at last,
For he pulls them by a cord
Finer than silk and strong as fate,
That is just the bid of his word.

Was there ever such a sight in the world?
Like a wonderful winding skein, —
The way he tangles them up together
And ravels them out again!

He has so many moving now,
You can hardly believe your eyes;
And yet they say he can handle twice
The number when he tries.

You take your choice and give me mine,
I know the one for me,
It's that great bluish one low down
Like a ship's light out at sea.

It has not moved for a minute or more.
The marvel that it can keep
As if it had been set there to spin
For a thousand years asleep!

If I could have him at the inn
All by myself some night, —
Inquire his country, and where in the world
He came by that cunning sleight!

Where do you guess he learned the trick
To hold us gaping here,
Till our minds in the spell of his maze almost
Have forgotten the time of year?

One never could have the least idea.
Yet why be disposed to twit
A fellow who does such wonderful things
With the merest lack of wit?

Likely enough, when the show is done
And the balls all back in his hand,
He'll tell us why he is smiling so,
And we shall understand.

### NOTES AND QUESTIONS ON "THE JUGGLER"

*Stanza 1.* Why does it seem as if the balls never fall?

*Stanza 2.* What fine descriptive words in line 1?

*Stanza 3.* Note how picking out "the tiny red one" adds to the vividness of the picture.

*Stanza 4.* Have you ever thought this?

*Stanza 5.* Note how the use of the question and answer prevent monotony.

*Stanza 6.* What part of speech is "home" in line 1? What figure of speech in line 3?

*Stanza 7.* What consonant sounds prevail in this stanza? Consult "Aids to Musical Sound in Poetry", in the Introduction, for the effect produced by the consonants, and see if it is true here as you read the lines aloud.

*Stanzas 8, 9, and 10.* These stanzas help to keep the impression that we are watching the Juggler. What figures of speech also help?

*Stanza 11.* Is this a natural desire?

*Stanza 12.* Have you ever been so fascinated with anything that you forgot where you were, and the time?

*Stanza 14.* This stanza, with stanzas 5, 6, and 7, suggest that Mr. Carman was thinking of a wider application than the skill of the Juggler; can you think what it is?

## AN APRIL MORNING

Once more in misted April
The world is growing green.
Along the winding river
The plumy willows lean.

Beyond the sweeping meadows
The looming mountains rise,
Like battlements of dreamland
Against the brooding skies.

In every wooded valley
The buds are breaking through,
As though the heart of all things
No languor ever knew.

The golden-wings and bluebirds
Call to their heavenly choirs.
The pines are blue and drifted
With smoke of brushwood fires.

And in my sister's garden
Where little breezes run,
The golden daffodillies
Are blowing in the sun.

NOTES AND QUESTIONS ON "AN APRIL MORNING"

*Stanza 1.* Why is April called "misted"? Is "plumy" the right adjective to describe the willows in spring?

*Stanza 2.* Do you like the simile in line 3?

*Stanza 3.* Why are the last two lines of this stanza especially good?

*Stanza 4.* What does the poet add to the picture here which no artist could paint?

*Stanza 5.* This adds the personal note to the description; was that a wise thing to do?

*In General.* What do you consider the chief characteristic of the language used and of the manner of expressing the thought?

Photo by E. O. Hoppe
RUDYARD KIPLING

# RUDYARD KIPLING

Many to whom Rudyard Kipling is well known as a British poet, short-story writer and novelist, do not know of the early struggles and disappointments of this eminently successful author. Born in Bombay, India, where his father was professor of sculpture and architecture in a school of art, he was educated at the United Service College in Westward Ho, Devonshire, England. The novel, "Stalky

and Co.", well reflects his school life.   He entered upon literary work
as a reporter and later sub-editor of an Indian paper at Allahabad.
His poems he would slip furtively between advertisements and reading
matter.   He received a sharp reprimand and was told that "a sub-
editor was paid to edit, not to write verses."

His sole encouragement was received from the foreman of the
paper, *Rugn-Din*, who used to say, "Your paper very good, sir;
just coming proper length.   One-third column just proper; you giving
more, soon.   Always can take one-third page — just proper."   The
poems so grudgingly printed are now known the world over.   In 1932
he was made Honorary Fellow of Magdalene College, Cambridge,
England.

## GUNGA DIN

You may talk o' gin and beer
When you're quartered safe out 'ere,
An' you're sent to penny-fights an' Aldershot it;
But when it comes to slaughter
You will do your work on water,
An' you'll lick the bloomin' boots of 'im that's got it.
Now in Injia's sunny clime,
Where I used to spend my time
A-servin' of 'Er Majesty the Queen,
Of all them black-faced crew
The finest man I knew
Was our regimental bhisti, Gunga Din.
   He was "Din! Din! Din!
   You limping lump o' brick-dust, Gunga Din!
   Hi! slippery hitherao!
   Water, get it! Panee lao!
   You squidgy-nosed old idol, Gunga Din."

The uniform 'e wore
Was nothin' much before,
An' rather less than 'arf o' that be'ind,

For a piece o' twisty rag
An' a goatskin water-bag
Was all the field-equipment 'e could find.
When the sweatin' troop-train lay
In a sidin' through the day,
Where the 'eat would make your bloomin' eyebrows crawl,
We shouted "Harry By!"
Till our throats were bricky-dry,
Then we wopped 'im 'cause 'e couldn't serve us all.
    It was "Din! Din! Din!
    You 'eathen, where the mischief 'ave you been?
    You put some juldee in it
    Or I'll marrow you this minute
    If you don't fill up my helmet, Gunga Din!"

'E would dot an' carry one
Till the longest day was done,
And 'e didn't seem to know the use o' fear.
If we charged or broke or cut,
You could bet your bloomin' nut,
'E'd be waitin' fifty paces right flank rear.
With 'is mussick on 'is back,
'E would skip with our attack,
An' watch us till the bugles made "Retire."
An' for all 'is dirty 'ide
'E was white, clear white, inside
When 'e went to tend the wounded under fire!
    It was "Din! Din! Din!"
    With the bullets kickin' dust-spots on the green.
    When the cartridges ran out,
    You could 'ear the front-files shout,
    "Hi! ammunition-mules an' Gunga Din!"

I sha'n't forgit the night
When I dropped be'ind the fight,

With a bullet where my belt-plate should 'a' been.
I was chokin' mad with thirst,
An' the man that spied me first
Was our good old grinnin', gruntin' Gunga Din.
'E lifted up my 'ead,
An' 'e plugged me where I bled,
An' 'e guv me 'arf-a-pint o' water — green:
It was crawlin' and it stunk,
But of all the drinks I've drunk,
I'm gratefullest to one from Gunga Din.
    It was "Din! Din! Din!
    'Ere's a beggar with a bullet through 'is spleen;
    'E's chawin' up the ground,
    An' 'e's kickin' all around:
    For Gawd's sake git the water, Gunga Din!"

'E carried me away
To where a dooli lay,
An' a bullet came an' drilled the beggar clean.
'E put me safe inside,
An' just before 'e died:
"I 'ope you liked your drink," sez Gunga Din.
So I'll meet 'im later on
At the place where 'e is gone —
Where it's always double drill and no canteen;
'E'll be squattin' on the coals,
Givin' drink to poor damned souls,
An' I'll get a swig in Hell from Gunga Din!
    Din! Din! Din!
    You Lazarushian-leather Gunga Din!
    Though I've belted you and flayed you,
    By the livin' Gawd that made you,
    You're a better man than I am, Gunga Din!

### NOTES AND QUESTIONS ON "GUNGA DIN"

An English Tommy gives in his cockney dialect a character sketch of an Indian water carrier of his regiment. These servants were very necessary and often most devoted to the men, as was Gunga Din.

*Stanza 1.* "Aldershot it", Aldershot is a town not far from London, famous for its military camp; so the expression means "military training."

"A-servin' of 'Er Majesty the Queen"; most English soldiers were proud of serving Queen Victoria. "Bhisti", water-carrier. Note the fine word-picture of the hero in the second and last lines of the refrain. "Panee lao", according to Kipling's note, means "Bring water swiftly." Have you ever seen a picture of an Indian idol that would correspond to the description in the last line?

*Stanza 2.* The humorous description of his uniform completes the picture of Gunga Din; the rest of this stanza and the third give his character. "Harry By" means "O brother." Why is "bricky-dry" so effective? "Wopped" is the same as "whopped", which means to beat or strike. "juldee", speed. "Marrow you", hit you.

*Stanza 3.* "Dot an' carry one", used of any monotonous work. "Mussick", water-skins. Note the strong contrast between "dirty 'ide" and "white, clear white, inside." What was Kipling's purpose in coupling the call for the ammunition with that for Gunga Din?

*Stanzas 4 and 5* give the specific incident which proves Gunga Din's heroism. What is the climax of the incident? "Dooli", a kind of litter used in India. What does "no canteen" mean? "Belted you", struck you with my belt.

*In General.* The refrain "Din! Din! Din!" etc., is characteristic of many of Kipling's poems. What does it add to the effect? Is the order followed by the poet, namely, physical appearance, character, and specific incident, a good one for you to use in writing a character sketch? Would you enjoy it more if the poem were written in pure English? Do you agree with the statement in the last two lines?


# THE OVERLAND MAIL

## FOOT-SERVICE TO THE HILLS

In the name of the Empress of India, make way,
O Lords of the Jungle, wherever you roam.

The woods are astir at the end of the day —
  We exiles are waiting for letters from Home.
Let the robber retreat — and the tiger turn tail —
In the Name of the Empress, the Overland Mail!

With the jingle of bells as the dusk gathers in,
  He turns to the foot-path that heads up the hill —
The bags on his back and a cloth round his chin,
  And, tucked in his waistbelt, the Post Office bill;
"Despatched on this date, as received by the rail,
*Per* runner, two bags of the Overland Mail."

Is the torrent in spate?  He must ford it or swim.
  Has the rain wrecked the road?  He must climb by the
    cliff.
Does the tempest cry "halt"?  What are tempests to him?
  The service admits not a "but" or an "if."
While the breath's in his mouth, he must bear without fail,
In the Name of the Empress, the Overland Mail.

From aloe to rose-oak, from rose-oak to fir,
  From level to upland, from upland to crest,
From rice-field to rock-ridge, from rock-ridge to spur,
  Fly the soft-sandalled feet, strains the brawny brown
    chest.
From rail to ravine — to the peak from the vale —
Up, up through the night goes the Overland Mail.

There's a speck on the hill-side, a dot on the road —
  A jingle of bells on the foot-path below —
There's a scuffle above in the monkey's abode —
  The world is awake and the clouds are aglow.
For the great Sun himself must attend to the hail: —
"In the Name of the Empress, the Overland Mail!"

NOTES AND QUESTIONS ON "THE OVERLAND MAIL"

The central idea of this poem is the fact that nothing must be allowed to interfere with the delivery of the mail by the native runner. Since every stanza emphasizes this in a different way, and there is a distinct climax in the last stanza, of what principle of composition is the poem a fine example? Study every stanza to see what it adds to this central idea.

*Stanza 1.* "Empress of India", the title of Queen Victoria as ruler of that country. What does "Home" mean to these men who were waiting for their letters, and why does the word begin with a capital? What is accomplished by the use of alliteration in line 5?

*Stanza 2.* How is the time of starting indicated?

*Stanza 3.* "Spate", swollen with freshets. Note how the duty of the carrier is made clear by the questions and answers. What is the climax of this stanza?

*Stanza 4.* How is the runner's path indicated in this stanza? What do you think of the method? What words flash a picture of the man?

*Stanza 5.* What time of day is it when the carrier arrives and how long has he been running? Line 5 contains the climax of the poem; why?


# FUZZY–WUZZY

We've fought with many men acrost the seas,
  An' some of 'em was brave an' some was not:
The Paythan an' the Sulu an' Burmese;
  But the Fuzzy was the finest o' the lot,
We never got a ha'porth's change of 'im:
  'E squatted in the scrub an' 'ocked our 'orses,
'E cut our sentries up at Suakim,
  An' 'e played the cat an' banjo with our forces.
    So 'ere's to you, Fuzzy-Wuzzy, at your 'ome in the
      Soudan;
    You're a pore benighted 'eathen but a first-class fightin'
      man;

We gives you your certificate, an' if you want it
  signed
We'll come an' 'ave a romp with you whenever you're
  inclined.


We took our chanst among the Khyber 'ills,
  The Boers knocked us silly at a mile,
The Burman give us Irriwaddy chills,
  An' a Zulu impi dished us up in style:
But all we ever got from such as they
  Was pop to what the Fuzzy made us swaller;
We 'eld our bloomin' own, the papers say,
  But man for man the Fuzzy knocked us 'oller.
    Then 'ere's to you, Fuzzy-Wuzzy, and the missis and
      the kid;
    Our orders was to break you, an' of course we went an'
      did.
    We sloshed you with Martinis, an' it wasn't 'ardly
      fair;
    But for all the odds agin' you, Fuzzy-Wuz, you broke
      the square.


'E 'asn't got no papers of 'is own,
  'E 'asn't got no medals nor rewards,
So we must certify the skill 'e's shown
  In usin' of 'is long two-'anded swords:
When 'e's 'oppin' in an' out among the bush
  With 'is coffin-'eaded shield an' shovel-spear,
An 'appy day with Fuzzy on the rush
  Will last an 'ealthy Tommy for a year.
    So 'ere's to you, Fuzzy-Wuzzy, an' your friends which
      are no more,
    If we 'adn't lost some messmates we would 'elp you to
      deplore;

But give an' take's the gospel, an' we'll call the bargain
    fair,
For if you 'ave lost more than us, you crumpled up the
    square!

'E rushes at the smoke when we let drive,
  An', before we know, 'e's 'ackin' at our 'ead;
'E's all 'ot sand an' ginger when alive,
  An' 'e's generally shammin' when 'e's dead.
'E's a daisy, 'e's a ducky, 'e's a lamb!
  'E's a Injia-rubber idiot on the spree,
'E's the on'y thing that doesn't give a damn
  For a Regiment o' British Infantree!
    So 'ere's to you, Fuzzy-Wuzzy, at your 'ome in the
       Soudan;
    You're a pore benighted 'eathen but a first-class fightin'
       man;
    An' 'ere's to you, Fuzzy-Wuzzy, with your 'ayrick 'ead
       of 'air —
    You big black boundin' beggar — for you broke a
       British square!

### NOTES AND QUESTIONS ON "FUZZY–WUZZY"

The English Government was asked in 1924 to set free a
native of India, one Osman Digna, from imprisonment at Wady
Halfa, where he had been confined in a mild form of captivity since
1900. In the Sudan, Digna led his force of native soldiers, called
"Fuzzy-Wuzzies", against the trained British troops and put them
to rout in more than one of the battles which ensued. This inspired
Kipling's poem.

The British soldier here gives his tribute of respect to the native
soldier in the War in the Sudan. Though his methods of warfare
lacked all the skill and precision of the trained Englishman and his
weapons seemed clumsy, "the long two-handed sword, the coffin-
'eaded shield an' shovel spear", and though the last of the struggle was
terrific, yet blind courage knew no defeat and he fought on; at last

he accomplished what the Englishman regards as the supreme triumph — he broke the British formation.

Look up all the proper names in the poem. Can you explain: "We never got a ha'porth's change o' the lot"? "Was pop", etc.?

To what does the speaker give the credit for the poor native's success in "breaking the British square"?


## RECESSIONAL

God of our fathers, known of old,
   Lord of our far-flung battle line,
Beneath whose awful hand we hold
   Dominion over palm and pine —
Lord God of Hosts, be with us yet,
Lest we forget — lest we forget!

The tumult and the shouting dies;
   The captains and the kings depart:
Still stands Thine ancient sacrifice,
   An humble and a contrite heart.
Lord God of Hosts, be with us yet,
Lest we forget — lest we forget!

Far-called our navies melt away;
   On dune and headland sinks the fire:
Lo, all our pomp of yesterday
   Is one with Nineveh and Tyre!
Judge of the Nations, spare us yet,
Lest we forget — lest we forget!

If, drunk with sight of power, we loose
   Wild tongues that have not Thee in awe,
Such boastings as the Gentiles use,
   Or lesser breeds without the law —
Lord God of Hosts, be with us yet,
Lest we forget — lest we forget!

For heathen heart that puts her trust
  In reeking tube and iron shard,
All valiant dust that builds on dust,
  And guarding, calls not Thee to guard,
For frantic boast and foolish word —
Thy mercy on Thy people, Lord!

### NOTES AND QUESTIONS ON "RECESSIONAL"

At Queen Victoria's diamond jubilee in 1897, celebrating the sixtieth year of her reign, all the poets read their elaborate tributes to her goodness and greatness and then, at the close of the ceremony, came the thrilling "Recessional", expressing in its majestic, scriptural language the spirit of the race. The effect was tremendous, not only in England but all over the civilized world. The poem has been beautifully set to music by Reginald de Koven.

*Stanza 1.* This stanza expresses the extent of England's power and a deep humility because of the responsibility involved. "Far-flung" attracts our attention because of the alliteration, as does "palm and pine." Since "palm" stands for the south and "pine" for the north, what other figure of speech does the expression contain?

*Stanza 2.* Note the contrast between the first and the last two lines.

*Stanza 3.* Nineveh, an ancient city of vast extent, the capital of the great Assyrian Empire. Tyre, a famous city of antiquity, on the coast of Phœnicia, frequently mentioned in the Old Testament because of its beauty, strength, and wealth, and threatened with destruction on account of its arrogance. Why did Kipling make the fifth line of this stanza differ from that of the first, second, and fifth?

*Stanza 4.* Explain the meaning of the metaphor in the first two lines. "Gentiles" used with the Biblical meaning, not belonging to the chosen people of God.

*Stanza 5.* This is the climax of the poem, culminating in the fifth line, which is totally unlike the same line of any other stanza. Note also the effectiveness of the petition in the last line. "Shard" as used here means shell.

*In General.* The structure of the poem is the same throughout; trace the rhyme-scheme. The metre is that of many of our hymns, namely, iambic tetrameter, which means that there are four metrical feet in each line, and these feet consist of a short syllable followed by a long one. Most noticeable are the long vowel sounds, giving solemnity and dignity to the lines. Consult "Symbolic Value of Vowel Sounds" in the Introduction, and select words and expressions in the poem which illustrate this. Nothing could be finer or simpler than the repeated "Lest we forget." Is this poem applicable in any way to America? If so, how? Have you personally any responsibility?

WILLIAM BUTLER YEATS

# WILLIAM BUTLER YEATS

William Butler Yeats belongs to that group of young Irish poets who have done so much to revive Irish folk-lore and old-wives'-tales from the oblivion into which they had sunk. His father was a brilliant student at Trinity College, Dublin, and later became an artist of note. William was born at Dublin in 1865 and spent most of his childhood at Sligo. At first he studied art, but decided not to follow

92

his father's profession, and having, while at Sligo, become thoroughly familiar with the native folk-lore, delightful fairy stories and old-wives'-tales of the peasantry, he decided to devote himself to producing poetry and dramas written in English but Irish in spirit, and to this end he identified himself with a "Young Ireland" society.   In a few years he was recognized as one of the leaders of the Celtic revival and, with J. M. Synge and Lady Gregory, has done much toward the production of truly Irish dramas acted by Irish players.   He has written several splendid one-act plays of which "The Land of Heart's Desire" is noteworthy.   He is a senator in the Irish Parliament at Dublin and was awarded the Nobel Prize in Literature for 1923, the year in which his "Collected Poems" were published.

## THE BALLAD OF FATHER GILLIGAN

The old priest Peter Gilligan
Was weary night and day,
For half his flock were in their beds,
Or under green sods lay.

Once, while he nodded on a chair,
At the moth-hour of eve,
Another poor man sent for him,
And he began to grieve.

"I have no rest, nor joy, nor peace,
For people die and die";
And after cried he, "God forgive!
My body spake, not I!"

He knelt, and leaning on the chair
He prayed and fell asleep;
And the moth-hour went from the fields,
And stars began to peep.

They slowly into millions grew,
And leaves shook in the wind;

And God covered the world with shade,
And whispered to mankind.


Upon the time of sparrow chirp
When the moths came once more,
The old priest Peter Gilligan
Stood upright on the floor.


"Mavrone, mavrone! the man has died,
While I slept on the chair";
He roused his horse out of its sleep,
And rode with little care.


He rode now as he never rode,
By rocky lane and fen;
The sick man's wife opened the door:
"Father! you come again!"


"And is the poor man dead?" he cried.
"He died an hour ago."
The old priest Peter Gilligan
In grief swayed to and fro.


"When you were gone, he turned and died
As merry as a bird."
The old priest Peter Gilligan
He knelt him at that word.


"He who hath made the night of stars
For souls, who tire and bleed,
Sent one of His great angels down
To help me in my need.

"He who is wrapped in purple robes,
With planets in his care,
Had pity on the least of things
Asleep upon a chair."

From "Poems" by William Butler Yeats.  By permission of **The Macmillan**
Company.

### NOTES AND QUESTIONS ON "FATHER GILLIGAN"

This is a typical ballad in the form of most of the early Scotch and
Irish ballads and consists of stanzas of four lines, the second and fourth
rhyming, and the lines alternating long and short.   The language is
simple and quaint and yet in many instances of great beauty.   In
this connection what is the way of indicating the time?   The incident is related without introduction and the supernatural element
is prominent, thus fulfilling all the requirements of a ballad.

## THE SONG OF THE OLD MOTHER

I rise in the dawn, and I kneel and blow
Till the seed of the fire flicker and glow.
And then I must scrub, and bake, and sweep,
Till the stars are beginning to blink and peep;
But the young lie long and dream in their bed
Of the matching of ribbons, the blue and the red,
And their day goes over in idleness,
And they sigh if the wind but lift up a tress.
While I must work, because I am old
And the seed of the fire gets feeble and cold.

From "Poetical Works" by William Butler Yeats.   By permission of The Macmillan Company.

### NOTES AND QUESTIONS ON "THE SONG OF THE OLD MOTHER"

This is a poem built on contrast.   Do you know any mothers who
have to work as this one did, or any young people like these?   Where
is the fire, if she has to kneel and blow to rekindle it?   How long are
this woman's days?   Is there any similarity between the fire and the
old mother?

# RICHARD LE GALLIENNE

Although he is now considered an American poet, Richard Le Gallienne was born in Liverpool in 1866, was educated at Liverpool College, and had been engaged in business seven years before he took up his residence in the United States. He was also recognized as a critic, a poet, and a novelist at that time. He has since published many books of essays and verse and has written many newspaper and magazine articles. His home is at Rowayton, Connecticut. He has a gifted daughter, Eva Le Gallienne, who is considered one of the leading actresses of the day.

## BALLADE OF QUEEN'S LACE

Go not to marts of costly show
  To clothe those limbs so round and fair,
But let us to the woodlands go —
  I'll find you prettier things to wear,
  Hung in a magic wardrobe there;
Garlands to frame your fairy face,
  And misty lawns as fine as air,
And for your petticoat Queen's Lace.

Soft draperies of virgin snow,
  If you must hide that bosom rare,
Whiter than Helen's long ago —
  'Twere kinder, love, to leave it bare,
  Dimmed only by your falling hair, —
Yet, if you must deny that grace,
  Lo! veils of filmiest gossamer —
And for your petticoat Queen's Lace.

And flounce and frill and furbelow,
   Quaint dimity and diaper,
The fairy artists shape and sew ;
   Here's silk-weed for your stomacher

QUEEN'S LACE

   And round that sweet diameter
Yclept your waist this girdle place —
   Diana wore the same I swear!
And for your petticoat Queen's Lace.

*Envoi*

Princess, and ladies everywhere,
Fashion but ill your form displays;
Nature's your best costumier —
And for your petticoat Queen's Lace.

### NOTES AND QUESTIONS ON "BALLADE OF QUEEN'S LACE"

The *ballade* is very different from the ballad, though the words are so very much alike, for the former is a lyric and the latter is a narrative poem. The *ballade* is a French form and always consists of three stanzas, all of which have exactly the same rhyme-scheme and rhyme-sound, and an "envoi" or postcript addressed to an imaginary prince which repeats two of the rhyme-sounds of the other stanzas. Note that each of the four stanzas ends with the same line. Trace the rhyme-scheme of this poem and compare it with that of the "Ballade of the Road Unknown."

*Stanza 1.* In what sense can the woodlands be a "wardrobe"? How does this metaphor help to carry out the idea of the poem? "Queen's Lace", sometimes called "Queen Anne's Lace", is a common summer flower growing in great profusion in the meadows of New England. The tiny white flowers grow in little clusters on a slender stem, and these clusters in turn form larger clusters three to four inches in diameter. The whole effect is very like that of fine lace.

*Stanza 2.* Can you suggest what the poet was thinking of as "veils of filmiest gossamer"? . . . Helen, the most beautiful woman in the world and the cause of the Trojan War.

*Stanza 3.* What does the use of alliteration in lines 1 and 2 add to the musical effect? "Stomacher" is a garment worn on the upper part of the body and often richly embroidered with jewels. "Yclept" is an obsolete word, the passive participle of the Anglo-Saxon verb "clepen", meaning "to call."

*Envoi.* Why is this ballade addressed to a princess rather than to a prince, as is usual? "Costumier" has four syllables; with what does the last one rhyme?

This is a very easy poem to divide into metrical feet, for it is more regular than many of the modern poems. You can readily see that every line has four feet, each consisting of a short syllable followed by a long one, except that once in a while a foot has a long syllable followed by a short one; therefore, the metre is iambic tetrameter.

# BALLADE OF THE ROAD UNKNOWN

Let others keep to the beaten track,
   The straight and narrow paths of fears,
Like timid travellers looking back
   At any sound that meets their ears;
   Shall I, because some neighbor jeers,
Follow the same dull road as he;
   Or steer the coward course he steers? —
The lure of the road unknown for me.

A hickory stick, a shouldered pack,
   Bread and a book, the wine that cheers,
The sun and moon for almanack,
   The planets leaning on their spears,
   A bush for inn as twilight nears,
And somewhere through it all the sea;
   Afoot again as morning peers —
The lure of the road unknown for me.

When comes the fatal click and clack
   Of Time's relentless iron shears,
When the thin ice of life goes crack,
   And the black gulf beneath uprears,
   And all the kind world disappears;
Still, as of old, my cry shall be,
   Somewhere high up amid the spheres —
The lure of the road unknown for me.

### *Envoi*

Dear Prince, the old romantic years
   Were filled with glory, girls and glee;
But, though I love them through my tears —
   The lure of the road unknown for me.

NOTES AND QUESTIONS ON "BALLADE OF THE ROAD UNKNOWN"

For the characteristics of a *ballade* and the difference between it and a ballad see notes on "Ballade of Queen's Lace."

*Stanza 1.* What sort of person does Le Gallienne show himself to be?

*Stanza 2.* Would you enjoy a trip of this sort? The traditional tramp always carried a hickory stick. Do you agree with the poet in line 7?

*Stanza 3.* What aids to the musical sound do you find in the first three lines? Is the poet afraid of death?

*Envoi.* Why is alliteration used in line 2? What other poets have written about roads?

# AS IN THE WOODLAND I WALK

As in the woodland I walk, many a strange thing I learn —
How from the dross and the drift the beautiful things return,
And the fires quenched in October in April reburn;

How foulness grows fair with the stern lustration of sleets
     and snows,
And rottenness changes back to the breath and the cheek of
     the rose,
And how gentle the wind that seems wild to each blossom
     that blows;

How the lost is ever found, and the darkness the door of
     light,
And how soft the caress of the hand that to shape must not
     fear to smite,
And how the dim pearl of the moon is drawn from the gulf
     of night;

How, when the great tree falls, with its empire of rustling
     leaves,
The earth with a thousand hands its sunlit ruin receives,
And out of the wreck of its glory each secret artist weaves

AS IN THE WOODLAND I WALK

Splendours anew and arabesques and tints on his swaying
    loom,
Soft as the eyes of April, and black as the brows of doom,
And the fires give back in blue-eyed flowers the woodland
    they consume;

How when the streams run dry, the thunder calls on the hills,
And the clouds spout silver showers in the laps of the little
    rills,
And each spring brims with the morning star, and each
    thirsty fountain fills;

And how, when the songs seemed ended, and all the music
    mute,
There is always somewhere a secret tune, some string of a
    hidden lute,
Lonely and undismayed that has faith in the flower and the
    fruit.

So I learned in the woods — that all things come again,
That sorrow turns to joy, and that laughter is born of pain,
That the burning gold of June is the gray of December's rain.

NOTES AND QUESTIONS ON "AS IN THE WOODLAND I WALK"

What relation to the first line has all the rest of the poem except
the last stanza? Can you, therefore, account for the punctuation?
What is the office of the last stanza?

Why is "lustration" so expressive a word to use in the second stanza
and what figure of speech is involved in its use? Find some lines that
are unusually melodious because of the frequent use of the liquid
sounds of "l" and "r". Is the sound of these lines expressive of
their meaning?

Find some fine examples of simile and metaphor and note how much
force and beauty they lend to the poem.

The structure of this lyric is especially good; as you read it aloud,
try to keep the cadence of the lines, which you can easily do if you
observe the pauses. Note how the three rhyming lines, called trip-
lets, bind the thought of each stanza together.

## TO A MOUNTAIN SPRING

Strange little spring, by channels past our telling,
Gentle, resistless, welling, welling, welling;
Through what blind ways, we know not whence
You darkling come to dance and dimple —
Strange little spring!
Nature has no such innocence,
And no more secret thing —
So mysterious and so simple;
Earth has no such fairy daughter
Of all her witchcraft shapes of water.
When all the land with summer burns,
And brazen noon rides hot and high,
And tongues are parched and grasses dry,
Still are you cool as some old sanctuary;
Still are you brimming o'er with dew
And stars that dipped their feet in you.
And I believe when none is by,
Only the young moon in the sky —
The Greeks of old were right about you —
A naiad, like a marble flower,
Lifts her lovely shape from out you,
Swaying like a silver shower.

So in old years dead and gone
Brimmed the spring on Helicon,
Just a little spring like you —
Ferns and moss and stars and dew —
Nigh the sacred Muses' dwelling,
Dancing, dimpling, welling, welling.

NOTES AND QUESTIONS ON "TO A MOUNTAIN SPRING"

Do you know a spring like this one, and have you ever thought of
its mystery and in what that mystery consists? Why are the liquid

Photo. by E. P. Tinkham.

A PLACE TO LOITER

The little stream, too indolent to pass,
Loiters below the cloudy willow boughs.
"Noon."   RICHARD LE GALLIENNE

sounds of "l" and "w" used in the first four lines so appropriate?
What figure of speech adds vividness and force to lines 9 and 10?
Name some other "witchcraft shapes of water." What lines seem
to you very quiet and peaceful? What contrasting lines increase this
effect? See if you can account in part for the delicate beauty of the
last two lines of the first stanza.

Explain naiad, Helicon, Muses' dwelling.

## NOON

Noon like a naked sword lies on the grass,
    Heavy with gold, and Time itself doth drowse;
The little stream, too indolent to pass,
    Loiters below the cloudy willow boughs,
    That build amid the glare a shadowy house,
And with a Paradisal freshness brims
    Amid cool-rooted reeds with glossy blade;
The antic water-fly above it skims,
    And cows stand shadow-like in the green shade,
    Or knee-deep in the grassy glimmer wade.

The earth in golden slumber dreaming lies,
    Idly abloom, and nothing sings or moves,
Nor bird, nor bee; and even the butterflies,
    Languid with noon, forget their painted loves,
    Nor hath the woodland any talk of doves.
Only at times a little breeze will stir,
    And send a ripple o'er the sleeping stream,
Or run its fingers through the willows' hair,
    And sway the rushes momently agleam —
    Then all fall back again into a dream.

### NOTES AND QUESTIONS ON "NOON"

In these two stanzas the poet gives a remarkable picture with
charmed words. Select the expressions which give an almost photographic clearness to the picture without any of the sharp outlines of a
photograph. What does the poem portray that no artist could paint?

EDWIN ARLINGTON ROBINSON

# EDWIN ARLINGTON ROBINSON

Edwin Arlington Robinson was of the group of writers whose work proves that American literature did not cease with the death of that great New England group of the late Nineteenth Century. He was born in 1869 in the village of Head Tide, Maine, near the town of Gardiner, to which place his family soon moved and which figures in many of his poems as "Tillbury Town." While yet in Harvard College he wrote many poems, and leaving his course uncompleted, in the next year, 1896, he privately printed a volume of his poems. This was followed in 1897 by "The Children of the Night", which showed promise of the work he afterward accomplished. After five years he published "Captain Craig" and since then "The Town Down the River", a series of short poems, and in 1916 "The Man Against the Sky", his strongest effort.

Mr. Robinson did not concern himself with problems or social questions. He dealt with men and women, their lives, their motives, their ideals. Though sometimes psychological, he was always optimistic, hopeful. In advance of his time, his works were not at first appreciated. After thirteen years the public awoke to his worth and thrice he was given the Pulitzer Prize. The American Institute of Arts and Letters awarded him the Gold Medal in 1929. His brilliant work was ended by his death in 1935. At heart he was a reformer, seeking to substitute joy for gloom, sunshine for shadow. His poems have been well pictured in the words, "His work is like a May day in his old boyhood town, not balmy but bracing, with the sparkle of the sea and the taste of the east wind through it all."

## THE HOUSE ON THE HILL

They are all gone away,
    The House is shut and still,
There is nothing more to say.

Through broken walls and gray
    The winds blow bleak and shrill:
They are all gone away.

Nor is there one to-day
    To speak them good or ill:
There is nothing more to say.

Why is it then we stray
    Around the sunken sill?
They are all gone away.

And our poor fancy-play
  For them is wasted skill:
There is nothing more to say.

There is ruin and decay
  In the House on the Hill:
They are all gone away,
There is nothing more to say.

### NOTES AND QUESTIONS ON "THE HOUSE ON THE HILL"

The picture of the deserted house is made more desolate by the allusion to its former occupants, apparently forgotten by all.   "They are all gone away", and no one remembers aught of them.

Note that the three-line stanza changes at the end to four lines — what is gained by that?

Find the proportion of two-or-more-syllable words to those of one used in the poem, and then write a good, clear sentence characterizing the kind of words employed and their effectiveness.


## THE TOWN DOWN THE RIVER

### I

Said the Watcher by the Way
To the young and the unladen,
To the boy and to the maiden,
"God be with you both to-day,
First your song came ringing,
Now you come, you two, —
Knowing naught of what you do,
Or of what your dreams are bringing.

"O you children who go singing
To the Town down the River,
Where the millions cringe and shiver,
Tell me what you know to-day;

Tell me how far you are going,
Tell me how you find your way.
O you children who go dreaming,
Tell me what you dream to-day."

"He is old and we have heard him,"
Said the boy then to the maiden;
"He is old and heavy laden
With a load we throw away.
Care may come to find us,
Age may lay us low;
Still, we seek the light we know,
And the dead we leave behind us.

"Did he think that he would blind us
Into such a small believing
As to live without achieving,
When the lights have led so far?
Let him watch or let him wither, —
Shall he tell us where we are?
We know best who go together,
Downward, onward, and so far."

## II

Said the Watcher by the Way
To the fiery folk that hastened
To the loud and the unchastened,
"You are strong, I see, to-day.
Strength and hope may lead you
To the journey's end, —
Each to be the other's friend
If the Town should fail to need you.

"And are ravens there to feed you
In the Town down the River,
Where the gift appalls the giver
And youth hardens day by day?
O you brave and you unshaken,
Are you truly on your way?
And are sirens in the River,
That you come so far to-day?"

"You are old, and we have listened,"
Said the voice of one who halted;
"You are sage and self-exalted,
But your way is not our way.
You that cannot aid us
Give us words to eat.
Be assured that they are sweet,
And that we are as God made us.

"Not in vain have you delayed us,
Though the River still be calling
Through the twilight that is falling
And the Town be still so far.
By the whirlwind of your wisdom
Leagues are lifted as leaves are;
But a king without a kingdom
Fails us, who have come so far."

### III

Said the Watcher by the Way
To the slower folk who stumbled,
To the weak and the world-humbled,
"Tell me how you fare to-day.

Some with ardor shaken,
All with honor scarred,
Do you falter, finding hard
The far chance that you have taken?

"Or, do you at length awaken
To an antic retribution,
Goading to a new confusion
The drugged hopes of yesterday?
O you poor mad men that hobble,
Will you not return, or stay?
Do you trust, you broken people,
To a dawn without the day?"

"You speak well of what you know not,"
Muttered one; and then a second:
"You have begged and you have beckoned,
But you see us on our way.
Who are you to scold us,
Knowing what we know?
Jeremiah, long ago,
Said as much as you have told us.

"As we are, then, you behold us:
Derelicts of all conditions,
Poets, rogues, and sick physicians,
Plodding forward from afar;
Forward now into the darkness
Where the men before us are;
Forward, onward, out of grayness,
To the light that shone so far."

## IV

Said the Watcher by the Way
To some aged ones who lingered,

To the shrunken, the claw-fingered,
"So you come for me to-day." —
"Yes, to give you warning;
You are old," one said;
"You have old hairs on your head,
Fit for laurel, not for scorning.

"From the first of early morning
We have toiled along to find you;
We, as others, have maligned you,
But we need your scorn to-day.
By the light that we saw shining,
Let us not be lured alway;
Let us hear no River calling
When to-morrow is to-day."

"But your lanterns are unlighted
And the Town is far before you:
Let us hasten, I implore you,"
Said the Watcher by the Way.
"Long have I waited,
Longer have I known
That the Town would have its own,
And the call be for the fated.

"In the name of all created,
Let us hear no more, my brothers;
Are we older than all others?
Are the planets in our way?" —
"Hark," said one; "I hear the River,
Calling always, night and day." —
"Forward, then! The lights are shining,"
Said the Watcher by the Way

This poem illustrates the author's simple directness, his use of iambic measures and conventional style. It is interesting, also, in that it marks the stages of his progress in writing, as well as a change in the poetry-reading public. The poem illustrates the joy and hope of youth, the courage that perseveres through the years in spite of discouragements and dismal prophecies, and the exultation as the end approaches and Faith cries "Forward, then! Her lights are shining."

Explain the reference in "Are ravens there to feed you?" Part II.

Explain "Jeremiah" in Part III; also "antic retributions." What is symbolized by the River?

Select the fine expressions used to picture the four stages of life — youth, young manhood, middle age, and old age.

How many feet of two syllables (iambic) are in each line?

Note how the rhyme-scheme divides each stanza into two parts of four lines each, and find on what principle the division is made.

## STAFFORD'S CABIN

Once there was a cabin here, and once there was a man;
And something happened here before my memory began.
Time has made the two of them the fuel of one flame
And all we have of them is now a legend and a name.

All I have to say is what an old man said to me,
And that would seem to be as much as there will ever be.
"Fifty years ago it was we found it where it sat." —
And forty years ago it was old Archibald said that.

"An apple tree that's yet alive saw something, I suppose,
Of what it was that happened there, and what no mortal
    knows.
Some one on the mountain heard far off a master shriek,
And then there was a light that showed the way for men to
    seek.

"We found it in the morning with an iron bar behind,
And there were chains around it; but no search could ever
    find,
Either in the ashes that were left, or anywhere,
A sign to tell of who or what had been with Stafford there.

"Stafford was a likely man with ideas of his own —
Though I could never like the kind that likes to live alone;
And when you met, you found his eyes were always on
    your shoes,
As if they did the talking when he asked you for the news.

"That's all, my son.  Were I to talk for half a hundred years
I'd never clear away from there the cloud that never clears.
We buried what was left of it, — the bar, too, and the
    chains;
And only for the apple tree there's nothing that remains."

Forty years ago it was I heard the old man say,
"That's all, my son." — And here again I find the place
    today,
Deserted and told only by the tree that knows the most,
And overgrown with golden-rod as if there were no ghost.

From "Collected Poems" by Edwin Arlington Robinson.  By special permission
of The Macmillan Company.

### NOTES AND QUESTIONS ON "STAFFORD'S CABIN"

The poem pictures a spot such as is often to be found in remote
country regions, a spot where some tragedy occurred, avoided for a
time, neglected, at last fallen to decay and forgotten.  Observe how
the time is marked as nearly a century ago by the words, "Fifty years
ago we found it", and "Forty years ago it was Old Archibald said
that."   Also note how the scene is relieved by the closing picture of the
place overgrown with golden-rod, its gloom relieved by "the beauty
Nature loves to share."

DENIS A. McCARTHY Photo. J. E. Purdy & Co.

# DENIS A. McCARTHY

A valuable American citizen was lured to the United States, the land of promise, when Denis A. McCarthy at the age of fifteen left Carrick, County Tipperary, Ireland, where he was born in 1870. He had received his education at the Christian Brothers' school in his native town, but he had no trade or profession and no friends in the new land. By his own unaided efforts he worked his way up until he became associate editor of a Catholic paper, which position he held for fifteen years.

He came to love America as much as he did his native land, and by his lectures, readings from his poems, and magazine articles he made a warm place for himself in the hearts of the American people. He was special editorial writer for the *Boston Herald* and other publications, but the strongest proof of his loyalty and service to his adopted land is the fact that he was Lecturer for the Massachusetts Department of Education for Americanization. He died at Arlington, Massachusetts, in 1931, sincerely mourned by his adopted country.

## AH, SWEET IS TIPPERARY

Ah, sweet is Tipperary in the springtime of the year,
    When the hawthorn's whiter than the snow,
When the feather folks assemble and the air is all a-tremble
    With their singing and their winging to and fro;
When queenly Slieve-na-mon puts her verdant vesture on,
    And smiles to hear the news the breezes bring;
When the sun begins to glance on the rivulets that dance —
    Ah, sweet is Tipperary in the spring!

Ah, sweet is Tipperary in the springtime of the year,
    When the mists are rising from the lea,
When the Golden Vale is smiling with a beauty all beguiling
    And the Suir goes crooning to the sea;
When the shadows and the showers only multiply the flowers
    That the lavish hand of May will fling;
When in unfrequented ways, fairy music softly plays —
    Ah, sweet is Tipperary in the spring!

Ah, sweet is Tipperary in the springtime of the year,
    When life like the year is young,
When the soul is just awaking like a lily blossom breaking,
    And love words linger on the tongue;

When the blue of Irish skies is the hue of Irish eyes,
  And love dreams cluster and cling
Round the heart and round the brain, half of pleasure, half
    of pain —
  Ah, sweet is Tipperary in the spring!

NOTES AND QUESTIONS ON "TIPPERARY"

*Stanza 1.* Tipperary is an inland county of Ireland lying chiefly
in the valley of the Suir (pronounced Shure). Its soil is singularly
rich and productive, especially in the district called "The Golden
Vale", in which stands the town of Tipperary. Why is "feather folks"
more poetic than "birds"? "Queenly Slieve-na-mon" — a mountain
three miles southwest from Tipperary. How many rhymes within the
lines themselves has this stanza? Notice how you anticipate them
and how disappointed you would be if you did not find them. How much
music is added by alliteration? What kind of consonants do you find
in line 6? Why? Line 7 fairly dances of itself; what makes it?
What does the pause after "glance" add?

*Stanza 2.* What kind of noise is described by "crooning"? The
repetition of "sh" in lines 5 and 6 is a marked addition to the music of
the lines. "Fairy music" is to be understood literally, for all true
Irishmen are supposed to believe in fairies. Have you ever seen or
heard any?

*Stanza 3.* What examples of simile do you find here? Notice the
liquid consonants in lines 3 and 4. What prevents the lines from being
flat? Why does line 5 stand out?

*In General.* This poem has been set to music, as you may infer, for
it almost sings itself. Its lilt and flow are characteristic of most of
Mr. McCarthy's poems, for he has the music-loving quality of the true
Celt. Read the poem aloud again and observe the fine effect of the
pauses in the alternating long lines.

## THE FIELDS O' BALLYCLARE

I've known the Spring in England —
  And, oh, 'tis pleasant there
When all the buds are breaking
  And all the land is fair!

But all the time the heart of me,
The better, sweeter part of me,
  Was sobbin' for the robin
    In the fields o' Ballyclare!

I've known the Spring in England —
  And, oh, 'tis England's fair!
With Springtime in her beauty,
  A queen beyond compare!
But all the while the soul of me,
Beyond the poor control of me,
  Was sighin' to be flyin'
    To the fields o' Ballyclare!

I've known the Spring in England —
  And now I know it here;
This many a month I've longed for
  The openin' of the year.
But, ah, the Irish mind of me
(I hope 'tis not unkind of me)
  Is turnin' back with yearnin'
    To the fields o' Ballyclare!

NOTES AND QUESTIONS ON "THE FIELDS O' BALLYCLARE"

*Stanza 1.* The spring in England is wonderfully beautiful; is it more so in Ireland? If not, why did the poet long to be there?

*Stanza 2.* Why is the "g" dropped in the next to the last line?

*Stanza 3.* Where is "here"? Purpose of the remark in the parenthesis?

*In General.* Trace the rhyme-scheme and note again the use of the internal rhyme and the rhyme including several words as "part of me" and "heart of me."

CARRICK–ON–SUIR
Birthplace of Denis A. McCarthy

## THE CHILDHER

### (An Irish Mother Speaks)

Ah, sure, without the childher, now, I don't know what
    I'd do at all,
'Twould be the same old story, every day, an' nothing new
    at all!
'Tis thrue, they are a throuble, an' I'm often almost wild
    with them —
But what about the times when I am just another child
    with them?
When all their fun an' frolic makes the very rafters ring
    again,
An' I, with all my years, am led to join them when they
    sing again?
When Patsy (that's the eldest) — he that has the roguish
    glance with him —

He fairly dhrags me in to show the girls how I can dance
  with him?
When Mary (that's my second) plays the tunes of other
  days to me —
An' she not knowing half the things, poor child, the music
  says to me? —
When I can see around me every youthful face love-lit for
  me,
An' feel that all their merriment's intended, every bit for
  me? —
Ah, then, in spite of all the work, the worry and bewildher-
  ment,
I'm thanking God He gave me this: to know what little
  childher meant!

Ah, sure, without the childher, 'tis myself might take it
  aisier;
But would I be much better off because I might be lazier?
My hand it might be whiter, an' I'd have more rings to
  wear on it,
But would my heart be lighter if I had no mother-care on it?
An' tell me how I'd spend the day — I'm thinkin' 'twould
  be weary, now,
If I could not be lookin' out for Patsy an' for Mary, now,
Or some one or another of the little lives so dear to me,
An' thinkin' are they safe an' sound? an' wishin' they were
  near to me;
An' kissin' them when they come in, an' layin' lovin' hands
  on them,
An' askin' if they're wet, for fear they'd maybe have a cold
  on them.
An' smilin' to see Michael draw each lovin' little one to him,
An' laughin' when the youngest one, the toddler, tries to
  run to him.

'Tis thrue, the world is filled with care, we suffer every day
  from it,
But, ah, the little childher, sure, they lure our hearts away
  from it!

The house that has the childher is the house that has the
  joy in it;
To me 'tis the only house that has a girleen or a boy in
  it;
An' every one that's added only makes the place the cheer-
  ier;
If childher are the gifts of God, the more He sends the
  merrier:
Sure, every little one I've had gave something to my bliss
  the more,
An' every little baby face my lips were drawn to kiss the
  more,
An' though I know the throuble an' the thrial an' the care
  they are,
An' though I know how often wild, how wayward an' how
  quare they are,
An' though 'tis many a night I've watched beside the little
  beds of them,
An' held their little hands an' cooled the fevered little heads
  of them;
An' though I know the surly moods that fall upon the best
  of them —
Can one who is unkind outweigh the love of all the rest of
  them?
No, no, the throuble that I've had, through them I'll never
  rue at all,
An' sure, without the childher, now, I don't know what
  I'd do at all!

NOTES AND QUESTIONS ON "THE CHILDHER"

*Stanza 1.* What kind of person does the mother show herself to be? Would her children be likely to love her?

*Stanza 2.* What additional reasons for happiness are given here? Do most mothers enjoy what this one does? Who is Michael?

*Stanza 3.* What faults does she see in her children? Does she love them the less on that account? Has her life been one of ease?

*In General.* What qualities of style characteristic of Mr. McCarthy do you find in this poem? Consider rhyme and dialect especially. Pronounce the "i" in "childher" short, as in children.


## BANNER OF AMERICA

Banner of America! Oh, banner of the west-land!
   Banner of a nation great and generous and young!
Banner of a land we deem the dearest and the best land,
   Lights eternal be the stars that shine your folds among!

Banner of America! Oh, banner of the mountains!
   Banner of the prairie-lands outspreading lone and far!
Banner of the mighty streams, the lakes, the falls, the
     fountains —
   Love to you, and greeting, every stripe and every star!

Banner of America! Oh, banner of the cowboys!
   Banner of the pioneers that break the virgin soil,
Banner of the country-bred, the reapers and the plough-
     boys —
   None to you more loyal than the sons who watch and
     toil.

Banner of America! Oh, banner of the street-folk —
   Are they lost in trafficking, in selfish plot and plan?
Nay, let danger threaten you, and, squalid folk or neat folk,
   Banner of the roaring mart, they'll answer to a man!

*Photograph by F. J. Mortimer, F.R.P.S.*
BANNER OF AMERICA

Banner of America!   Oh, banner of the people
  In the love we bear you let all class distinction die,
Wave from towr'ing city spire or tiny village steeple,
  Every eye is glad to see your splendor in the sky!

Banner of America!   Oh, gonfalon of glory!
  Many a soldier son for you has suffered death's eclipse,

Many a sailor lad whose name is lost to song or story,
   Gladly gave his life to see you shine above the ships!

Banner of a freedom that the centuries have sighed for,
   Banner of a land that gives the soaring spirit scope,
Ever-sacred symbol of a dream that men have died for,
   Wave above a nation where the humblest heart may hope!

### NOTES AND QUESTIONS ON "BANNER OF AMERICA"

*Stanza 1.* This stanza serves as the introduction, in which the theme is expressed in general terms. Express the thought of line 4 in your own words.

*Stanzas 2 to 4.* What relation do these stanzas bear to the theme as given in stanza 1?

*Stanza 5.* What makes line 3 forceful? This stanza sums up the thought of the three preceding.

*Stanza 6.* A "gonfalon" is a small pennon, usually with two or three streamers and fixed to a revolving frame or a crossyard. Note the alliteration gained by using this word. Where else in the stanza do you find this figure? How is the word "eclipse" used in line 2?

*Stanza 7.* How does this stanza differ from the rest? What is meant by "freedom that the centuries have sighed for"? What fine uses of alliteration here?

*In General.* This poem owes much of its musical quality to assonance; see "Aids to Musical Sound" in the Introduction. In stanza 1, line 1, the same sound of "a" in banner and land; in line 2, same sound of "a" in nation and great; same sound of "ou" in generous and young; in line 3, same sound of "e" in we and deem; in line 4, same sound of "i" in lights and shine; same sound of "e" in eternal and be. Read the other stanzas aloud slowly and see how many more instances of assonance you can find. Could the poem be set to music?

What prevents the repetition of "Banner of America" from becoming tiresome? Words of how many syllables prevail? What is the effect?

# THOMAS AUGUSTINE DALY

The sympathetic interpretation of loyal, lovable immigrants living among us to a generally unsympathetic and too often hostile American public is the chief contribution of Thomas Augustine Daly to our poetry of to-day. He was born in Philadelphia in 1871 and after attending Villanova College he went to Fordham University, but left at the end of his second year to go into newspaper work, like many other present-day poets. Because of his charming lyrics portraying "Americans of the first generation", and his equally delightful Irish poems, he became very popular; Fordham conferred upon him the degree of Doctor of Literature (Litt.D.), the American Press Humorists' Association made him their president, and the "Players'" and the "Authors' Club" of New York welcomed him as a distinguished addition to their membership. He gives recitals of his own poems which delight his audiences and he is considered one of the cleverest of humorous speakers. His home is in Philadelphia.

*Photo. by Bachrach.*

THOMAS A. DALY

126

## DA LEETLA BOY

Da spreeng ees com'! but oh, da joy
   Eet ees too late!
He was so cold, my leetla boy,
   He no could wait.

I no can count how manny week,
How manny day, dat he ees seeck;
How manny night I seet an' hold
Da leetla hand dat was so cold.
He was so patience, oh, so sweet!
Eet hurts my throat for theenk of eet:
An' all he evra ask ees w'en
Ees gona com' da spreeng agen.
Wan day, wan brighta sunny day,
He see, across da alleyway,
Da leetla girl dat's livin' dere
Ees raise her window for da air,
An' put outside a leetla pot
Of — w'at you call? — forgat-me-not.
So smalla flower, so leetla theeng!
But steel eet mak' hees hearta seeng:
"Oh, now, at las', ees com' da spreeng!
Da leetla plant ees glad for know
Da sun ees com' for mak' eet grow.
So, too, I am grow warm and strong."
So lika dat he seeng hees song.
But, Ah! da night com' down an' den
Da winter ees sneak back agen,
An' een da alley all da night
Ees fall da snow, so cold, so white,
An' cover up da leetla pot
Of — wa't-you-call? — forgat-me-not.

All night da leetla hand I hold
Ees grow so cold, so cold, so cold!

Da spreeng ees com'; but oh, da joy
Eet ees too late!
He was so cold, my leetla boy,
He no could wait.

From "Carmina", by T. A. Daly, by permission of Harcourt, Brace & Co., Inc.

NOTES AND QUESTIONS ON "DA LEETLA BOY"

This is one of the most beautiful and touching of Daly's poems. Did you ever think that an Italian immigrant might be just as fond of his child as your father is of you? What sort of child was the little boy? Why is the incident of the forget-me-not introduced? Why is the short stanza repeated at the end? What difference do you find in its rhythm and rhyme from those of the long stanza? Can you see why this is so?

## THE OULD APPLE WOMAN

With her basket of apples comes Nora McHugh,
  Wid her candies an' cakes an' wan thing an' another,
But the best thing she brings to commind her to you
  Is the smile in her eyes that no throuble can smother.
An' the wit that's at home on the tip of her tongue
  Has a freshness unknown to her candy and cake;
Though her wares had been stale since ould Nora was
      young,
  There is little complaint you'd be carin' to make.
Well I mind, on a day, I complained of a worm
  That I found in an apple, near bitten in two,
"But suppose ye had bit it, an' where'd be the harm?
  For, shure, this isn't Friday," said Nora McHugh.

O Nora McHugh, you've the blarneyin' twist in you,
Where is the anger could drame o' resistin' you?
 Faix, we'll be sp'ilin' you,
 Blind to the guile in you,
 While there's a smile in you,
  Nora McHugh.


It was Mistress De Vere, that's so proud of her name,
 Fell to boastin' wan day of her kin in the peerage —
Though there's some o' thim, years ago whin they came
 To this glorious land, was contint wid the steerage —
An' she bragged of her ancistry, Norman an' Dane,
 An' the like furrin ancients that's thought to be swell.
"Now, I hope," said ould Nora, "ye'll not think me vain,
 Fur it's little I care fur ancistry mesel';
  But wid all o' your pedigree, ma'am, I believe
  'Tis mesel' can go back a bit further than you,
  Fur in me you perceive a descindant of Eve,
  The first apple woman," said Nora McHugh.


O Nora McHugh, sich owdacious frivolity!
How can you dare to be jokin' the quality?
 Still, we'll be sp'ilin' you,
 Blind to the guile in you,
 While there's a smile in you,
  Nora McHugh.

From "Carmina", by T. A. Daly, by permission of Harcourt, Brace & Co., Inc.


NOTES AND QUESTIONS ON "THE OULD APPLE WOMAN"

*Stanza 1.* Do you know any old woman peddler like Nora? In
what does the wit of her reply about the worm consist?
*The Refrain.* "Blarneyin' twist." There is a stone near the top
of Blarney Castle, Blarney, Ireland, which is said to give to those who
kiss it the peculiar kind of persuasive flattery supposed to belong to the

natives of Ireland.   Can you explain now what Daly means by "blarneyin' twist"?

*Stanza 2.*   Why the high-sounding name in the first line?   Is line
4 true?   Normans and Danes were early settlers of the British Isles.
Why does Daly call them "furrin ancients"?   In what does the wit
lie in Nora's reply in this stanza?   Why does she call Eve "the first
apple woman"?

*The Refrain.*   Why is Mistress De Vere called "the quality"?

*In General.*   Does this poem remind you of any written by another
Irishman?

## W'EN SPREENG EES COM'

Oh! 'scusa, lady, 'scusa, pleass',
For dat I stop an' stare;
I no can halpa do like dees
W'en Spreeng ees een da air.

I s'pose you know how moocha joy
Ees feell da heart of leetla boy,
W'en beeg parade ees passa by,
Eef he can climb da pole so high;
Or find on window-seell a seat
Where he can see da whola street,
An' watch da soldiers marcha 'way
An' hear da sweeta music play.
Ah! lady, eef dees joy you know,
You would no frown upon me so.
For, like da boy dat climb da pole,
From deep eensida me my soul —
My hongry, starva soul — ees rise
Onteell eet looka from my eyes
At all dat com' so sweet an' fair
W'en now da Spreeng ees een da air;
At greena grass, at buddin' trees
Dat wave deir branches een da breeze,

At leetla birds dat hop an' seeng
Baycause dey are so glad for Spreeng —
An' dat you look so pure, so sweet,
O, lady, you are part of eet!

So, 'scusa, lady, 'scusa, pleass',
For dat I stop an' stare;
I no can halpa do like dees
W'en Spreeng ees een da air.

From "Madrigali", by T. A. Daly, by permission of Harcourt, Brace & Co., Inc.

NOTES AND QUESTIONS ON " W'EN SPREENG EES COM' "

*Stanza 1.* Do you see anything characteristic of an Italian in this stanza?

*Stanza 2.* What shows that Mr. Daly understands the heart of a boy? Does that help him to understand the Italian? Why is the soul of the Italian "hongry, starva" and why does he more than others welcome the spring?

*Stanza 3.* Note how much more these words mean now than they did in stanza 1 before they were explained by the intervening lines.

Compare the form, rhythm, and rhyme of this poem with that of "Da Leetla Boy."

## TWO 'MERICANA MEN

Beeg Irish cop dat walks hees beat
    By dees peanutta stan',
First two, t'ree week w'en we are meet
    Ees call me "Dagoman."
An' w'en he see how mad I gat,
    Wheech eesa pleass heem, too,
Wan day he say: "W'at's matter dat,
    Ain't 'Dago' name for you?
Dat's 'Mericana name, you know,
    For man from Eetaly;
Eet ees no harm for call you so,
    Den why be mad weeth me?"

First time he talka deesa way
    I am too mad for speak,
But nexta time I justa say:
    "All righta, Meester Meeck!"

O! my, I nevva hear bayfore
    Sooch langwadge like he say;
An' he don't look at me no more
    For mebbe two, t'ree day.
But pretta soon agen I see
    Das beeg poleeceaman
Dat com' an' growl an' say to me:
    "Hallo, Eyetalian!
Now, mebbe so you gon' deny
    Dat dat's a name for you."
I smila back, an' mak' reply:
    "No, Irish, dat's a true."
"Ha! Joe," he cry, "you theenk dat we
    Should call you 'Merican?"
"Dat's gooda 'nough," I say, "for me,
    Eef dat's w'at you are, Dan."

So now all times we speaka so
    Like gooda 'Merican:
He say to me, "Good morna, Joe,"
    I say, "Good morna, Dan."

From "Carmina", by T. A. Daly, by permission of Harcourt, Brace & Co., Inc.

### NOTES AND QUESTIONS ON "TWO 'MERICANA MEN"

In this poem we have a study of both the Italian and the Irish nature. Is it natural for one foreigner who has been in the country longer than another to look down on the newcomer? Are foreigners usually anxious to be called Americans soon after their arrival? Is Mr. Daly fair to both?

Photo. by Bachrach.

WALTER DE LA MARE

# WALTER DE LA MARE

Walter de la Mare's ancestors were of mingled Huguenot, Scotch, and English blood — the Huguenots, of course, giving him his French name. He was born at Charlton, Kent, England, in 1873, and received his education at St. Paul's Cathedral Choir School. He did not begin to write until he was nearly thirty years old and at first published his poems under the pseudonym of Walter Ramal.

In 1916 he came to America and lectured and read many of his own poems. He is a modest, unassuming man with a quiet, beautiful voice and has a great love for and understanding of children. He possesses the power of imparting a sense of the mysterious to his poems and is, as someone has said, "an astonishing joiner of words." His poem "The Return" won the Edmond de Polignac Prize for 1910, and "Peacock Pie, a Book of Rhymes" ranks with "The Jungle Books" by Kipling in the delight it affords old and young alike. His collection of fairy stories in rhyme, entitled "Down-adown-Derry", you would enjoy. He is also recognized as a novelist of note.

## NOD

Softly along the road of evening,
  In a twilight dim with rose,
Wrinkled with age, and drenched with dew
  Old Nod, the shepherd goes.

His drowsy flock streams on before him,
  Their fleeces charged with gold,
To where the sun's last beam leans low
  On Nod the shepherd's fold.

The hedge is quick and green with briar,
  From their sand the conies creep;
And all the birds that fly in heaven
  Flock singing home to sleep.

His lambs outnumber a noon's roses,
  Yet when night's shadows fall,
The blind old sheep dog, Slumber-soon,
  Misses not one of all.

His are the quiet steeps of dreamland,
  The waters of no-more-pain;
His ram's bell rings 'neath an arch of stars,
  "Rest, rest, and rest again."

The gently swinging rhythm with the alternating long and short lines and the quiet words used in this slumber song make it very pleasing to the ear, and the use of personification adds life and interest. In stanza 3 "quick" means live. "Conies" are rabbits.

*Stanza 5.* "His ram's bell", the bell worn by the wether of the flock, whereby the sheep can be located. Note the English pronunciation of "again" to rhyme with "pain."

*In General.* Select expressions which illustrate the poet's whimsical imagination. Which stanza do you like best and why?


# JIM JAY

Do diddle di do,
    Poor Jim Jay
Got stuck fast
    In Yesterday.
Squinting he was
    On cross-legs bent,
Never heeding
    The wind was spent.
Round veered the weathercock,
    The sun drew in —
And stuck was Jim
    Like a rusty pin. . . .
We pulled and we pulled
    From seven till twelve,
Jim too frightened
    To help himself.
But all in vain.
    The clock struck one,
And there was Jim
    A little bit gone.
At half-past five
    You scarce could see

A glimpse of his flapping
  Handkerchee.
And when came noon,
  And we climbed sky-high,
Jim was a speck
  Slip-slipping by.
Come to-morrow,
  The neighbors say,
He'll be past crying for;
  Poor Jim Jay.

NOTES AND QUESTIONS ON "JIM JAY"

This is one of De la Mare's poems described by Mr. Louis Untermeyer as "reading like lyrics by William Shakespeare rendered by Mother Goose." "Do diddle di do" at the beginning is just in the style of that lady. The poem itself describes the fate of reactionary people and warns us that it is wise to change with the times. Notice that most of the lines contain but two metrical feet and none more than three; do you know any Mother Goose rhymes in the same metre?

## LOB LIE-BY-THE-FIRE

He squats by the fire
  On his three-legged stool,
When all in the house
  With slumber are full.

And he warms his great hands,
  Hanging loose from each knee.
And he whistles as soft
  As the night wind at sea.

For his work now is done;
  All the water is sweet;
He has turned each brown loaf,
  And breathed magic on it.

The milk in the pan,
  And the bacon on beam
He has "spelled" with his thumb,
  And bewitched has the dream.

Not a mouse, not a moth,
  Not a spider but sat,
And quaked as it wondered
  What next he'd be at.

But his heart, O, his heart —
  It belies his great nose;
And at gleam of his eye
  Not a soul would suppose

He had stooped with great thumbs
  And big thatched head, ·
To tuck his small mistress
  More snugly in bed.

Who would think, now, a throat
  So lank and so thin
Might make birds seem to warble
  In the dream she is in!

Now hunched by the fire,
  While the embers burn low,
He nods until daybreak,
  And at daybreak he'll go.

Soon the first cock will 'light
  From his perch and point high
His beak at the Ploughboy
  Grown pale in the sky;

And crow will he shrill;
  Then meek as a mouse,
Lob will rouse up and shuffle
  Straight out of the house.

His supper for breakfast;
  For wages his work;
And to warm his great hands
  Just an hour in the mirk.

### NOTES AND QUESTIONS ON "LOB LIE-BY-THE-FIRE"

Lob, a Scotch brownie or house-elf, who haunts homesteads by
night and does menial labor; also called "lubber fiend." Two characteristics of Lob are emphasized in this poem, his awkwardness and
his service for man. Follow the poem through and find the descriptive
words that picture his appearance. Do the same for his kindly acts.
Select the stanza which sets forth prominently the contrast between
these two characteristics of Lob.

*Stanza 2.* Why are the last two lines of this stanza remarkable for
sound?

*Stanza 11.* What part of speech is "shrill"?

*Stanza 12.* "Mirk", a Scotch word for darkness; why is it appropriate to use here?

## SILVER

Slowly, silently, now the moon
Walks the night in her silver shoon;
This way, and that, she peers, and sees
Silver fruit upon silver trees;
One by one the casements catch
Her beams beneath the silvery thatch;
Couched in his kennel, like a log,
With paws of silver sleeps the dog;
From their shadowy cote the white breasts peep
Of doves in a silver-feathered sleep.

A harvest mouse goes scampering by,
With silver claws and a silver eye;
And moveless fish in the water gleam,
By silver reeds in a silver stream.

### NOTES AND QUESTIONS ON "SILVER"

This little descriptive poem is a color study in silver.   What does
the poet portray in it that no artist could paint?   The rhythm, which
is cool and smooth, aids in making the picture perfect.   Note the large
number of words containing "s"; not a line in which the sound is not
prominent.

Have you seen a night like this?  What objects mentioned would
you not see in an American landscape?

# ANNA HEMPSTEAD BRANCH

Anna Hempstead Branch attracted favorable notice by winning the first of the *Century* prizes offered to college graduates in a best-poem contest. The successful poem, "The Road 'Twixt Heaven and Hell", gave the author a recognized place among American poets.

Miss Branch was born in New London, Connecticut, was educated at Adelphi Academy, Brooklyn, Smith College, and the American Academy of Dramatic Art.

Her poems include three volumes, "The Shoes that Danced", "The Heart of the Road", and "Nimrod and Other Poems." They show deep thought, great lyric value and poetic revelation. Her "Rose of the Wind", a play, was successfully presented in 1907.

## TO A NEW YORK SHOP–GIRL DRESSED FOR SUNDAY

To-day I saw the shop-girl go
Down gay Broadway to meet her beau.

Conspicuous, splendid, conscious, sweet,
She spread abroad and took the street.

And all that niceness would forbid,
Superb, she smiled upon and did.

Let other girls, whose happier days
Preserve the perfume of their ways,

Go modestly. The passing hour
Adds splendor to their opening flower.

But from this child too swift a doom
Must steal her prettiness and bloom,

140

Toil and weariness hide the grace
That pleads a moment from her face.

So blame her not if for a day
She flaunts her glories while she may.

She half perceives, half understands,
Snatching her gifts with both her hands.

That little strut beneath the skirt
That lags neglected in the dirt,

The indolent swagger down the street —
Who can condemn such happy feet!

Innocent! vulgar — that's the truth!
Yet with the darling wiles of youth!

The bright, self-conscious eyes that stare
With such hauteur, beneath such hair!
Perhaps the men will find me fair!

Charming and charmed, flippant, arrayed,
Fluttered and foolish, proud, displayed,
Infinite pathos of parade!

The bangles and the narrowed waist —
The tinseled boa — forgive the taste!
Oh, the starved nights she gave for that,
And bartered bread to buy her hat!

She flows before the reproachful sage
And begs her woman's heritage.

Dear child, with the defiant eyes,
Insolent with the half surmise
We do not quite admire, I know
How foresight frowns on this vain show!

And judgment, wearily sad, may see
No grace in such frivolity.

Yet which of us was ever bold
To worship Beauty, hungry and cold!

Scorn famine down, proudly expressed
Apostle to what things are best.

Let him who starves to buy the food
For his soul's comfort find her good,

Nor chide the frills and furbelows
That are the prettiest things she knows.

Poet and prophet in God's eyes
Make no more perfect sacrifice.

Who knows before what inner shrine
She eats with them the bread and wine?

Poor waif!   One of the sacred few
That madly sought the best they knew!

Dear — let me lean my cheek to-night
Close, close to yours.   Ah, that is right.

How warm and near!   At last I see
One beauty shines for thee and me.

So let us love and understand —
Whose hearts are hidden in God's hand.

And we will cherish your brief Spring
And all its fragile flowering.

God loves all prettiness, and on this
Surely his angels lay their kiss.

NOTES AND QUESTIONS ON "TO A NEW YORK SHOP-GIRL
DRESSED FOR SUNDAY"

The shop-girl, gayly flaunting the cheap finery her lack of refined taste has prompted her to buy with the money she has "bartered bread" to have for the purpose, represents an effort to possess and enjoy that which in her judgment is best.   She is really a kindred spirit with the one who, on a higher plane, makes sacrifices to gain "food for his soul's good", — books, education, perhaps.

The pathos of her lot is in the fleeting nature of that which stands as "the best" to her — the adorning of the quickly passing beauty of youth, with no thought of developing permanent enjoyment in high character.

Define "strut", "flippant", "bangles", "tinseled", "sage." Why is the sage reproachful?

What is the final reason why the shop-girl is not to be entirely condemned?

Can you think of a better ambition she might have?

Has every one a right to happiness?

What use of contrast do you find here?

What relation do the last six stanzas bear to the rest?


# MY MOTHER'S WORDS

My mother has the prettiest tricks
  Of words and words and words.
Her talk comes out as smooth and sleek
  As breasts of singing birds.

She shapes her speech all silver fine
  Because she loves it so.
And her own eyes begin to shine
  To hear her stories grow.

And if she goes to make a call
  Or out to take a walk,
We leave our work when she returns
  And run to hear her talk.

We had not dreamed these things were so
  Of sorrow and of mirth.
Her speech is as a thousand eyes
  Through which we see the earth.

God wove a web of loveliness,
  Of clouds and stars and birds,
But made not anything at all
  So beautiful as words.

They shine around our simple earth
  With golden shadowings,
And every common thing they touch
  Is exquisite with wings.

There's nothing poor and nothing small
  But is made fair with them.
They are the hands of living faith
  That touch the garment's hem.

They are as fair as bloom or air,
  They shine like any star,
And I am rich who learned from her
  How beautiful they are.


NOTES AND QUESTIONS ON "MY MOTHER'S WORDS"

This little poem presents most charmingly the beauty and power
of the well-chosen word and the wonderful gift of the mother to the
child in showing that "speech is as a thousand eyes, through which we
see the earth."

Find words which give pictures, light, beauty, glory. What is
the child's idea of the value of the mother's gift to her in teaching her
the value of words?

THE PETRIFIED FERN

# MARY L. B. BRANCH

## THE PETRIFIED FERN

In a valley, centuries ago,
   Grew a little fern-leaf, green and slender,
   Veining delicate and fibres tender,
Waving when the wind crept down so low;
Rushes tall and moss and grass grew round it,
Playful sunbeams darted in and found it,
Drops of dew stole down by night and crowned it,
   But no foot of man e'er trod that way,
   Earth was young and keeping holiday.

145

Monster fishes swam the silent main,
  Stately forests waved their giant branches,
  Mountains hurled their snowy avalanches,
Mammoth creatures stalked across the plain;
Nature reveled in great mysteries,
But the little fern was not of these,
Did not number with the hills and trees,
  Only grew and waved its sweet wild way,
  No one came to note it day by day.

Earth, one time, put on a frolic mood,
  Heaved the rocks and changed the mighty motion
  Of the deep, strong currents of the ocean,
Moved the hills and shook the haughty wood,
Crushed the little fern in soft moist clay,
Covered it and hid it safe away.
Oh! the long, long centuries since that day!
  Oh! the changes! Oh! life's bitter cost
  Since the little useless fern was lost!

Useless? lost? There came a thoughtful man
  Searching nature's secrets far and deep;
  From a fissure in a rocky steep
He withdrew a stone o'er which there ran
Fairy pencilings, a quaint design,
Leafage, veinings, fibres, clear and fine,
And the fern's life lay in every line!
  So I think God hides some souls away
  Sweetly to surprise us the Last Day!

### NOTES AND QUESTIONS ON "THE PETRIFIED FERN"

This poem, "The Petrified Fern", was written by Mrs. Mary L. B. Branch, the mother of Anna Hempstead Branch. It has a fitting place with the daughter's tribute to her mother in the poem which precedes, a tribute which finds response in filial affection everywhere.

The poem beautifully tells the story of a little fern which in prehistoric times grew in a sheltered valley.  A great convulsion of nature overturned the hills, filled the valleys, and buried the little fern in soft, moist clay which slowly petrified or became stone.  Long afterward a geologist searching among the rocks found in a fissure a rock on which was the perfect imprint of the little fern which ages before had seemed to be destroyed.

The moral speaks for itself : many who lack the power of expression, and seem perhaps dull and uninteresting, may be discovered at last to have developed wondrous beauty of character.

If there is near you a museum you can readily visit, try to see a petrified fern.  Also read in Physical Geography and Geology the explanation of fossils.

What interests you in the story?  When do you find a suggestion of promise for the fern?

# ROBERT W. SERVICE

Robert W. Service, "the American Kipling" as he is often called since, though an Englishman, his poems are household words in America, was born in Preston, England, Jan. 16, 1874, the son of a banker whose name he bears. The boy was educated at Hillhead Public School in Glasgow, Scotland, and then apprenticed to the Commercial Bank of Glasgow. He emigrated to Canada and settled for a time on a farm

ROBERT W. SERVICE

in Vancouver, but gave up farming for the rough life of the explorer, and for eight years travelled up and down the Pacific Coast and the Yukon region. He saw service as an ambulance driver in the World War. The varied scenes of his life are reflected in his poems. No writer has better depicted the courage and endurance of the miners of the Yukon, and his own bravery and sympathy are reflected in his matchless poems of the World War. His poems comprise several volumes: "Rhymes of a Rolling Stone", "Songs of a Sourdough", "Ballads of a Cheechako", "The Trail of '98", "The Pretender", and "Rhymes of a Red Cross Man."

## YOUNG FELLOW MY LAD

"Where are you going, Young Fellow My Lad,
On this glittering morn of May?"
    "I'm going to join the Colours, Dad;
They're looking for men, they say."
"But you're only a boy, Young Fellow My Lad;
You aren't obliged to go."
"I'm seventeen and a quarter, Dad,
And ever so strong, you know."

       \*    \*    \*    \*    \*    \*    \*

"So you're off to France, Young Fellow My Lad,
And you're looking so fit and bright."
"I'm terribly sorry to leave you, Dad,
But I feel that I'm doing right."
"God bless you and keep you, Young Fellow My Lad,
You're all of my life, you know."
"Don't worry.  I'll soon be back, dear Dad,
And I'm awfully proud to go."

       \*    \*    \*    \*    \*    \*    \*

"Why don't you write, Young Fellow My Lad?
I watch for the post each day;
And I miss you so, and I'm awfully sad,
And it's months since you went away.
And I've had the fire in the parlour lit,
And I'm keeping it burning bright
Till my boy comes home; and here I sit
Into the quiet night."

       \*    \*    \*    \*    \*    \*    \*

"What is the matter, Young Fellow My Lad?
No letter again to-day.
Why did the postman look so sad,
And sigh as he turned away?

I hear them tell that we've gained new ground,
But a terrible price we've paid:
God grant, my boy, that you're safe and sound;
But oh I'm afraid, afraid."

YOUNG FELLOW MY LAD

"They've told me the truth, Young Fellow My Lad:
You'll never come back again:
(Oh God! the dreams and the dreams I've had,
And the hopes I've nursed in vain!)
For you passed in the night, Young Fellow My Lad,
And you proved in the cruel test
Of the screaming shell and the battle hell
That my boy was one of the best.

"So you'll live, you'll live, Young Fellow My Lad,
In the gleam of the evening star,
In the wood-note wild and the laugh of the child,
In all sweet things that are.
And you'll never die, my wonderful boy,
While life is noble and true;
For all our beauty and hope and joy
We will owe to our lads like you."

From " Rhymes of a Red Cross Man", by Robert W. Service, author of " Spell of
the Yukon ", " Ballards of a Cheechako ", and " Ballads of a Bohemian ", published
by Barse & Hopkins, New York.

NOTES AND QUESTIONS ON "YOUNG FELLOW MY LAD"

This poem vividly pictures the spirit of the World War — young
men left education, business, whatever occupied them.  In each case,
as the young soldier said, "I feel I am doing right."  And when, often
after weeks of anxiety and waiting, sad news came, friends comforted
themselves with the thought that these soldiers would live in all things
beautiful and noble, and that the world would owe  them a debt of
gratitude.
Memorize the last stanza.  Find three reasons why the young man
joined the colours.

## THE OUTLAW

A wild and woven race he ran
    Of lust and sin by land and sea;
Until, abhorred of God and man,
    They swung him from the gallows-tree.
And then he climbed the Starry Stair,
    And dumb and naked and alone,
With head unbowed and brazen glare,
    He stood before the Judgment Throne.

The Keeper of the Records spoke:
    "This man, O Lord, has mocked thy name.

The weak have wept beneath his yoke,
  The strong have fled before his flame.
The blood of babes is on his sword;
  His life is evil to the brim;
Look down, decree his doom, O Lord!
  Lo! there is none will speak for him."

The golden trumpets blew a blast
  That echoed in the crypts of Hell,
For there was Judgment to be passed,
  And lips were hushed and silence fell.
The man was mute; he made no stir,
  Erect before the Judgment stood. . . .
When all at once a mongrel cur
  Crept out and cowered and licked his feet.

It licked his feet with whining cry,
  Come Heaven, come Hell, what did it care?
It leapt, it tried to catch his eye;
  Its master, yea, its God was there.
Then, as a thrill of wonder sped
  Through throngs of shining seraphim,
The Judge of ALL looked down and said:
  "Lo! here is ONE who pleads for him.

"And who shall love of these the least,
  And who by word or look or deed
Shall pity show to bird or beast,
  By Me shall have a friend in need.
Aye, though his sin be black as night,
  And though he stand mid men alone,
He shall be softened in My sight,
  And find a pleader by My Throne.

"So let this man the glory win;
　From life to life salvation glean;
By pain and sacrifice and sin,
　Until he stand before Me — clean.
For he who loves the least of these
　(And here I say and here repeat)
Shall win himself an angel's pleas
　For Mercy at My Judgment Seat."

From "Ballads of a Bohemian", by Robert W. Service, author of "Spell of the Yukon", "Ballads of a Cheechako", and "Rhymes of a Red Cross Man", published by Barse & Hopkins, New York.

### NOTES AND QUESTIONS ON "THE OUTLAW"

A dramatic picture of one who in life had violated the laws of God and man, and had come to a shameful death at last. No word of any good in his life could be spoken. All were silent when a poor cur crept in and plainly showed his joy at seeing his master, and the Judge of all the earth granted another chance to the man who, though so sinful, had shown pity to dumb animals.

Compare the idea of this poem with the lines in "The Ancient Mariner":

He prayeth well who loveth well
Both man and bird and beast.
He prayeth best who loveth best
All things both great and small. . .


## JEAN DESPREZ

Oh ye whose hearts are resonant, and ring to War's romance,
Hear ye the story of a boy, a peasant boy of France;
A lad uncouth and warped with toil, yet who, when trial
　　came,
Could feel within his soul upleap and soar the sacred flame;
Could stand upright, and scorn and smite, as only heroes
　　may:
Oh, hearken! Let me try to tell the tale of Jean Desprez.

With fire and sword the Teuton horde was ravaging the
land,
And there was darkness and despair, grim death on every
hand;
Red fields of slaughter sloping down to ruin's black
abyss:
The wolves of war ran evil-fanged, and little did they
miss.
And on they came with fear and flame, to burn and loot
and slay,
Until they reached the red-roofed croft, the home of Jean
Desprez.


"Rout out the village, one and all!" the Uhlan Captain
said.
"Behold!  Some hand has fired a shot.  My trumpeter is
dead.
Now shall they Prussian vengeance know; now shall they
rue the day,
For by this sacred German slain, ten of these dogs shall
pay."
They drove the cowering peasants forth, women and babes
and men,
And from the last, with many a jeer, the Captain chose
the ten;
Ten simple peasants, bowed with toil; they stood, they
knew not why,
Against the grey wall of the church, hearing their children
cry;
Hearing their wives and mothers wail, with faces dazed
they stood.
A moment only. . . Ready!  Fire!  They weltered in
their blood.

But there was one who gazed unseen, who heard the fren-
    zied cries,
Who saw these men in sabots fall before their children's
    eyes;
A Zouave wounded in a ditch, and knowing death was nigh,
He laughed with joy: ".Ah! here is where I settle ere I die."
He clutched his rifle once again, and long he aimed and
    well. . . .
A shot! Beside his victims ten the Uhlan Captain fell.

They dragged the wounded Zouave out; their rage was
    like a flame.
With bayonets they pinned him down, until their Major
    came.
A blonde, full-blooded man he was, and arrogant of eye;
He stared to see with shattered skull his favourite Captain
    lie.
"Nay, do not finish him so quick, this foreign swine," he
    cried;
"Go nail him to the big church door: he shall be crucified."

With bayonets through hands and feet they nailed the
    Zouave there,
And there was anguish in his eyes, and horror in his stare;
"Water! A single drop!" he moaned; but how they
    jeered at him,
And mocked him with an empty cup, and saw his sight
    grow dim;
And as in agony of death with blood his lips were wet.
The Prussian Major gaily laughed, and lit a cigarette.

But mid the white-faced villagers who cowered in horror by,
Was one who saw the woeful sight, who heard the woeful
    cry:

"Water!   One little drop, I beg!   For love of Christ who
    died . . ."
It was the little Jean Desprez who turned and stole aside;
It was the little barefoot boy who came with cup abrim
And walked up to the dying man, and gave the drink to him.

A roar of rage!   They seize the boy; they tear him fast
    away.
The Prussian Major swings around; no longer is he gay.
His teeth are wolfishly agleam; his face all dark with spite:
"Go, shoot the brat," he snarls, "that dare defy our Prus-
    sian might.
Yet stay!   I have another thought.   I'll kindly be, and
    spare;
Quick!   give the lad a rifle charged, and set him squarely
    there,
And bid him shoot, and shoot to kill.   Haste!   Make him
    understand
The dying dog he fain would save shall perish by his hand.
And all his kindred they shall see, and all shall curse his
    name,
Who bought his life at such a cost, the price of death and
    shame."

They brought the boy, wild-eyed with fear; they made
    him understand;
They stood him by the dying man, a rifle in his hand.
"Make haste!" said they; "the time is short, and you
    must kill or die."
The Major puffed his cigarette, amusement in his eye.
And then the dying Zouave heard, and raised his weary
    head:
"Shoot, son, 'twill be the best for both; shoot swift and
    straight," he said.

"Fire first and last, and do not flinch; for lost to hope am I;
And I will murmur: Vive la France! and bless you ere
    I die."

Half-blind with blows the boy stood there; he seemed to
    swoon and sway;
Then in that moment woke the soul of little Jean Desprez,
He saw the woods go sheening down; the larks were sing-
    ing clear;
And oh! the scents and sounds of spring, how sweet they
    were! how dear!
He felt the scent of new-mown hay, a soft breeze fanned
    his brow;
O God! the paths of peace and toil! How precious were
    they now!
The summer days and summer ways, how bright with hope
    and bliss!
The autumn such a dream of gold . . . and all must end
    in this:
This shining rifle in his hand, that shambles all around;
The Zouave there with dying glare; the blood upon the
    ground;
The brutal faces round him ringed, the evil eyes aflame;
That Prussian bully standing by, as if he watched a game.
"Make haste and shoot," the Major sneered; "a minute
    more I give;
A minute more to kill your friend, if you yourself would
    live."

They only saw a barefoot boy, with blanched and twitch-
    ing face;
They did not see within his eyes the glory of his race;
The glory of a million who for fair France have died,
The splendour of self-sacrifice that will not be denied.

Yet . . . he was but a peasant lad, and oh! but life was
    sweet. . . .

"Your minute's nearly gone, my lad," he heard a voice
    repeat.

"Shoot! Shoot!" the dying Zouave moaned; "Shoot!
    Shoot!" the soldiers said.

Then Jean Desprez reached out and shot . . . *the Prussian
    Major dead!*

From "The Rhymes of a Red Cross Man", by Robert W. Service, author of "Spell
of the Yukon", "Ballads of a Cheechako", and "Ballads of a Bohemian", published
by Barse & Hopkins, New York.

### NOTES AND QUESTIONS ON "JEAN DESPREZ"

The heroism of youth, often sung by the poets, has rarely been more
vividly presented than in this poem of Robert Service.  In a German
invasion of France a Captain, enraged because one of his trumpeters
had been shot, ordered that ten of the French peasants be ranged in
line and shot.  A French Zouave, lying mortally wounded near by,
raised his rifle and shot the Captain.  A Major, succeeding to the
Captain's command, ordered that the Zouave be crucified by being
nailed to the church door.  In anguish the Zouave begged for "water,
a single drop."  Then little Jean Desprez, a barefoot lad, quietly
stole away and brought a cup of water to the dying man.  In rage the
Major ordered that a rifle be given the boy, and that with his own hand
he should shoot the Zouave whom he had befriended — or himself be
shot.  Life had never seemed so sweet to the boy.  "One minute,"
shouted the Major, and at the word, Jean Desprez raised the rifle and
"shot the Prussian Major dead."

What was the motive which prompted Jean's act of kindness?
What the act of shooting the Major?  Have you read of other acts
of heroism on the part of boys?  Read Browning's "Incident of the
French Camp."

Define: Zouave, Prussian, bully, Teuton, Uhlan, sabots.

Would this make a good motion-picture?  Why?  What is the
climax?

Note that the lines consist of seven metrical feet of two syllables
each, and that after the first four feet there is a pause; what is the
effect of this?  What is the name of the metre, since there are seven
feet in a line?

AMY LOWELL    *Copyright, Moffett, 1916.*

# AMY LOWELL

Like Virgil's hero, Miss Lowell was indeed "born of noble ancestry" and the heritage of poesy is hers. James Russell Lowell, of the Nineteenth Century group of poets, was a cousin of her grandfather. Her maternal grandfather was Abbott Lawrence, minister to England.

Abbott Lawrence Lowell, President Emeritus of Harvard, is her brother, as was also the late Professor Percival Lowell, the astronomer.

When extensive study and travel, both in her own and in foreign lands, had prepared her to choose a field for her talents, she decided to devote herself to poetry.  Like Milton, who cared not to come early into the work of life, but only to come "fit", Miss Lowell studied the best models among the master writers, the technique of poetry, and wrote much without publishing any of her work.  Her first published poem appeared in the *Atlantic Monthly* in 1910.  Her writings comprise several volumes of poetry, two of critical essays on French and American Poetry, one of Chinese translations, and one long biography.  She died at her home in Brookline, Massachusetts, in 1925.

Miss Lowell's vision of the greater possibilities of poetry in freedom from set poetic form had given her marked prominence.  In the use of such forms as *vers libre* and "polyphonic prose" she had broken away from conventionality.  But it is a mistake to consider Miss Lowell as a practitioner of the free forms of poetry alone.  She wrote quite as much verse in regular metre; in fact, she was thoroughly *eclectic* in her choice of medium, believing that the content of a poem determines its form.

Not only in America, but in England, Miss Lowell was appreciated. An English writer described her as "an explorer . . . offering of her own vision to unobservant eyes the breaking of innumerable barriers." In her clear vision, simplicity of style, and masterly choice and arrangement of words, Miss Lowell gave to her readers a picture which she had used "eyes, ears and heart" to discover.

## WINTER'S TURNING

Snow is still on the ground,
But there is a golden brightness in the air.
Across the river,
Blue,
Blue,
Sweeping widely under the arches
Of many bridges,
Is a spire and a dome.

Clear as though ringed with ice-flakes,
Golden, and pink, and jocund.
On a near-by steeple,
A golden weather-cock flashes smartly,
His open beak "Cock-a-doodle-dooing"
Straight at the ear of Heaven.
A tall apartment house,
Crocus-coloured,
Thrusts up from the street
Like a new-sprung flower.
Another street is edged and patterned
With the bloom of bricks,
Houses and houses of rose-red bricks,
Every window a-glitter.
The city is a parterre,
Blowing and glowing,
Alight with the wind,
Washed over with gold and mercury.
Let us throw up our hats,
For we are past the age of balls
And have none handy.
Let us take hold of hands,
And race along the sidewalks,
And dodge the traffic in crowded streets.
Let us whir with the golden spoke-wheels
Of the sun.
For to-morrow Winter drops into the waste-basket,
And the calendar calls it March.

NOTES AND QUESTIONS ON "WINTER'S TURNING"

Perhaps this little poem may at first seem to you to be prose. Try reading it aloud, as prose. You cannot quite do it. Study it a little more and you will find it has not regular metre but "cadence."

Select lines which present pictures. Define jocund, patterned, parterre.

Is there a touch of humor in the last line?
What other poems in this book express the joy of spring?   Which
do you like best?

## AN OPERA HOUSE

Within the gold square of the proscenium arch,
A curtain of orange velvet hangs in stiff folds,
Its tassels jarring slightly when someone crosses the stage
    behind.
Gold carving edges the balconies,
Rims the boxes,
Runs up and down fluted pillars.
Little knife-stabs of gold
Shine out whenever a box door is opened.
Gold clusters
Flash in soft explosions
On the blue darkness,
Suck back to a point,
And disappear.
Hoops of gold
Circle necks, wrists, fingers,
Pierce ears,
Poise on heads
And fly up above them in coloured sparkles.
Gold!
Gold!
The opera house is a treasure-box of gold;
Gold in a broad smear across the orchestra pit:
Gold of horns, trumpets, tubas;
Gold — spun-gold, twittering-gold, snapping-gold
Of harps.
The conductor raises his baton,
The brass blares out
Crass, crude,

Parvenu, fat, powerful,
Golden.
Rich as the fat, clapping hands in the boxes.
Cymbals, gigantic, coin-shaped,
Crash.
The orange curtain parts
And the prima-donna steps forward.
One note,
A drop: transparent, iridescent,
A gold bubble,
It floats . . . floats . . .
And bursts against the lips of a bank president
In the grand tier.

### NOTES AND QUESTIONS ON "AN OPERA HOUSE"

The wonderfully beautiful opera house with all its ornamentation profusely gilded, the orchestra with their "golden" instruments, make a fitting setting for the famous prima donna as she steps forward through the parted orange curtains. Do you think the allusion to the "one note", the "gold bubble", is a reference to the rare power and beauty of the singer's voice, or is it perhaps a bit of irony referring to the fabulous sums received by opera singers?

Does the latter suggestion add any favor to the idea of the note falling on the lips of a bank-president? Does the gorgeous opera house seem at all like any you have seen?

## THE PAINTER ON SILK

There was a man
Who made his living
By painting roses
Upon silk.

He sat in an upper chamber
And painted,
And the noises of the street
Meant nothing to him.

When he heard bugles, and fifes, and drums,
He thought of red, and yellow, and white roses
Bursting in the sunshine,
And smiled as he worked.

He thought only of roses,
And silk.
When he could get no more silk
He stopped painting
And only thought
Of roses.

The day the conquerors
Entered the city,
The old man
Lay dying.
He heard the bugles and drums,
And wished he could paint the roses
Bursting into sound.

### NOTES AND QUESTIONS ON "THE PAINTER ON SILK"

The poem presents a beautiful, almost pathetic picture of a painter whose work was always the painting of roses on silk.

Because he was absorbed in his work, the sounds of the outside world were unnoticed, or were interpreted by his mind in terms of his task. The music of the passing drum corps reminded him of red, yellow, and white roses, and he smiled.

War came and he could get no more silk. Though he could no longer paint, he still thought of roses. At last the conquerors were entering the city. The painter lay dying. As he heard the bugles and drums his last thought was a wish that he might paint the roses the music represented to him.

How do you explain the painter's concentrated interest in his work? Is such concentration a good thing? Do you think it might make a man become more narrow-minded?

What is beautiful in the picture of the painter?

SEVENELS, BIRTHPLACE AND HOME OF AMY LOWELL

## PURPLE GRACKLES

The grackles have come.
The smoothness of the morning is puckered with their
   incessant chatter.
A sociable lot, these purple grackles,
Thousands of them strung across a long run of wind,
Thousands of them beating the air-ways with quick wing-
   jerks,
Spinning down the currents of the South.
Every year they come,
My garden is a place of solace and recreation evidently,
For they always pass a day with me.
With high good nature they tell me what I do not want
   to hear.
The grackles have come.

I am persuaded that grackles are birds;
But when they are settled in the trees

I am inclined to declare them fruits
And the trees turned hybrid blackberry vines.
Blackness shining and bulging under leaves,
Does not that mean blackberries, I ask you?
Nonsense!   The grackles have come.

Nonchalant highwaymen, pickpockets, second-story bur-
      glars,
Stealing away my little hope of Summer.
There is no stealthy robbing in this.
Who ever heard such a gabble of thieves' talk!
It seems they delight in unmasking my poor pretense.
Yes, now I see that the hydrangea blooms are rusty;
That the hearts of the golden glow are ripening to lustreless
      seeds;
That the garden is dahlia-coloured,
Flaming with its last over-hot hues;
That the sun is pale as a lemon too small to fill the picking-
      ring.
I did not see this yesterday,
But today the grackles have come.

They drop out of the trees
And strut in companies over the lawn,
Tired of flying, no doubt;
A grand parade to limber legs and give wings a rest.
I should build a great fish-pond for them,
Since it is evident that a bird-bath, meant to accommodate
      two gold-finches at most,
Is slight hospitality for these hordes.
Scarcely one can get in,
They all peck and scrabble so,
Crowding, pushing, chasing one another up the bank with
      spread wings.

"Are we ducks, you, owner of such inadequate comforts,
That you offer us lily-tanks where one must swim or drown,
Not stand and splash like a gentleman?"
I feel the reproach keenly, seeing them perch on the edges
    of the tanks, trying the depth with a chary foot,
And hardly able to get their wings under water in the bird-
    bath.
But there are resources I had not considered,
If I am bravely ruled out of count.
What is that thudding against the eaves just beyond my
    window?
What is that spray of water blowing past my face?
Two — three — grackles bathing in the gutter,
The gutter providentially choked with leaves.
I pray they think I put the leaves there on purpose;
I would be supposed thoughtful and welcoming
To all guests, even thieves.
But considering that they are going South and I am not,
I wish they would bathe more quietly,
It is unmannerly to flaunt one's good fortune.

They rate me of no consequence,
But they might reflect that it is my gutter.
I know their opinion of me,
Because one is drying himself on the window-sill
Not two feet from my hand.
His purple neck is sleek with water,
And the fellow preens his feathers for all the world as if I
    were a fountain statue.
If it were not for the window,
I am convinced he would light on my head.
Tyrian-feathered freebooter,
Appropriating my delightful gutter with so extravagant
    an ease,

You are as cool a pirate as ever scuttled a ship,
And are you not scuttling my Summer with every **peck of**
    your sharp bill?

But there is a cloud over the beech-tree,
A quenching cloud for lemon-livered suns.
The grackles are all swinging in the tree-tops,
And the wind is coming up, mind you.
That boom and reach is no Summer gale,
I know that wind,
It blows the Equinox over seeds and scatters them,
It rips petals from petals, and tears off half-turned leaves.
There is rain on the back of that wind.
Now I would keep the grackles,
I would plead with them not to leave me.
I grant their coming, but I would not have them **go.**
It is a milestone, this passing of grackles.
A day of them, and it is a year gone by.
There is magic in this and terror,
But I only stare stupidly out of the window.
The grackles have come.

Come! Yes, they surely came.
But they have gone.
A moment ago the oak was full of them,
They are not there now.
Not a speck of a black wing,
Not an eye-peep of a purple head.
The grackles have gone,
And I watch an Autumn storm
Stripping the garden,
Shouting black rain challenges
To an old, limp Summer
Laid down to die in the flower-beds.

### NOTES AND QUESTIONS ON "PURPLE GRACKLES"

The purple grackle, a bird of the starling or blackbird species, migrates to the South in the late Autumn months. Great flocks of grackles settle upon gardens and fields and make a clean sweep of any small fruits and berries. They are handsome birds, about the size of a robin, with beautiful iridescent coloring on neck and wings. They keep up an incessant chattering, a sharp note which somehow suggests the name, grackle. They are quite tame, alighting on the steps or window ledge without fear. In a day they disappear, continuing their journey southward.

The unpleasant thing about their appearance, as the poem so cleverly tells us, is that they tell by their presence what we do not like to hear — "Summer is gone."

What is meant by "the trees turned hybrid blackberry vines"? "The garden is dahlia coloured"?

Explain "equinox."

Explain "It is a milestone, this passing of the grackles."

JOHN MASEFIELD

# JOHN MASEFIELD

John Masefield, England's Poet Laureate, often called the "Chaucer of to-day", was born in Ledbury, Hertfordshire, England, in 1874. His father was a lawyer and wished his son to have an education, but John did not like school, though he loved books, and at the age of fifteen he ran away, shipped as a cabin boy aboard a sailing vessel, and followed the sea for three years. Realizing at last that life on the sea did not satisfy his intellectual craving, he came ashore at New York, for he had heard that in America "one could become almost anything one wished." After a long and disappointing search for work in the great city, he secured a position as a handy man in Luke O'Connor's saloon, the Columbia Hotel, at the corner of Sixth Avenue and Greenwich Avenue, at a salary of thirty dollars a month.   Here he stayed but a short time and then entered a carpet factory in the Bronx.   One day, with seventy-five cents to spare, he purchased a copy of Chaucer's "Canterbury Tales" and read far into the night.   He had always longed to write, and then and there he resolved to be a poet.   He returned to England where he met William Butler Yeats and J. M. Synge, the great Irish poets, from whom he received encouragement to develop his talent.   In 1911 he published his long narrative poem, "The Everlasting Mercy", and the next year "The Widow in the Bye Street" and "The Dauber."   That year he received the Edmond de Polignac prize of $500.

During the war Masefield was very active, serving with the Red Cross in France, where he sold his manuscripts and originals to raise money for a field hospital of his own.   Later, in the Gallipoli campaign, he did heroic work under shell fire.   His story of that disastrous campaign in the Dardanelles is a great prose epic, hardly to be read with dry eyes.

The five poems which follow are taken from the copyrighted volumes "Salt Water Poems and Ballads" and "The Story of a Round-House" and are used by permission of The Macmillan Company.


## A BALLAD OF JOHN SILVER

We were schooner-rigged and rakish, with a long and lissome
　　hull,
And we flew the pretty colours of the cross-bones and the
　　skull;
We'd a big black Jolly Roger flapping grimly at the fore,
And we sailed the Spanish Water in the happy days of yore.

We'd a long brass gun amidships, like a well conducted ship,
We had each a brace of pistols and a cutlass at the hip;
It's a point which tells against us, and a fact to be deplored,
But we chased the goodly merchant-men and laid their ships
　　aboard.

Then the dead men fouled the scuppers and the wounded
　　filled the chains,
And the paint-work all was spatter-dashed with other
　　people's brains,
She was boarded, she was looted, she was scuttled till she
　　sank,
And the pale survivors left us by the medium of the plank.

O! then it was (while standing by the taffrail on the poop)
We could hear the drowning folk lament the absent chicken-
　　coop;
Then, having washed the blood away, we'd little else to do
Than to dance a quiet hornpipe as the old salts taught us to.

O! the fiddle on the fo'c's'le, and the slapping naked soles,
And the genial "Down the middle, Jake, and curtsey when
　　she rolls!"
With the silver sea around us and the pale moon overhead,
And the look-out not a-looking and his pipe-bowl glowing
　　red.

Ah! the pig-tailed, quidding pirates and the pretty pranks
　　we played,
All have since been put a stop to by the naughty Board of
　　Trade;
The schooners and the merry crews are laid away to rest,
A little south the sunset in the Islands of the Blest.

NOTES AND QUESTIONS ON "A BALLAD OF JOHN SILVER"

"Ballad" is used here in the sense of a short poem, chiefly narrative
in nature, suited to be sung; *i.e.* a song of John Silver.

*Stanza 1.* "Lissome", corrupted form of lithesome. What does
it mean as applied to a hull? What about the sound of the first line
attracts immediate attention? "Spanish Water", the sea about the
circular bank of islands forming the northern and eastern boundaries
of the Caribbean Sea.

*Stanza 2.* The guns of Spanish pirates were commonly of brass, but what color effect is added by mentioning the metal?

*Stanza 3.* How is the care-free spirit of the pirates set forth in this stanza and the following?

*Stanza 4.* "Taffrail", a rail around the after deck. Is the ship moving or standing still? How do you know?

*Stanza 5.* What bits of humor do you find here? Why are they so effective? What makes lines 1 and 2 fine examples of onomatopœia?

*Stanza 6.* "Quidding", dropping food while eating; what does this show about the manners of the pirates?

*In General.* The merry, rollicking rhythm of the lines is particularly adapted to the character of the poem. The abrupt pause in the middle of the lines adds to this effect. In the midst of the gay and care-free lines there are some of surpassing beauty; find them and see how they stand out by contrast.

## SEA–FEVER

I must down to the seas again, to the lonely sea and the sky,
And all I ask is a tall ship and a star to steer her by,
And the wheel's kick and the wind's song and the white
    sail's shaking,
And a grey mist on the sea's face and a grey dawn breaking.

I must down to the seas again, for the call of the running
    tide
Is a wild call and a clear call that must not be denied;
And all I ask is a windy day with the white clouds flying,
And the flung spray and the blown spume, and the sea-gulls
    crying.

I must down to the seas again to the vagrant gypsy life,
To the gull's way and the whale's way where the wind's like
    a whetted knife;
And all I ask is a merry yarn from a laughing fellow-rover,
And quiet sleep and a sweet dream when the long trick's
    over.

NOTES AND QUESTIONS ON "SEA-FEVER"

This lyric voices Masefield's yearning for the sea and is written in a form or pattern of which he is very fond; namely, stanzas of four lines (quatrains) rhyming 1, 2; 3, 4, with a pause in the middle of each line. This pause is important to the music of the poem; be sure to give it full value in reading the poem aloud.

Try to visualize the picture in the first stanza. What expressions in the other stanzas are particularly fine? Pick out the expressions which are repeated, and note the effect of this repetition. Do you, too, love the sea? What would you give as your reasons if you were writing a sea poem? Why not try it?

Read the poem aloud many times, listening carefully to see how much of its beauty is due to the skillful use of consonants and the musical succession of vowel sounds. In what lines do long vowels predominate and in what do you find chiefly short ones? Why is this? Do you think that the form which Masefield has used is suited to the theme?

## TEWKESBURY ROAD

It is good to be out on the road, and going one knows not
    where,
  Going through meadow and village, one knows not whither
    nor why;
Through the grey light drift of the dust, in the keen, cool
    rush of the air,
  Under the flying white clouds, and the broad blue lift of
    the sky.

And to halt at the chattering brook, in the tall green fern
    at the brink
  Where the harebell grows, and the gorse, and the fox-
    gloves purple and white;
Where the shy-eyed, delicate deer troop down to the brook
    to drink
  When the stars are mellow and large at the coming on of
    the night.

O, to feel the beat of the rain, and the homely smell of the
    earth,
  Is a tune for the blood to jig to, a joy past power of words ;
And the blessed green comely meadows are all a-ripple with
    mirth
  Of the noise of the lambs at play and the dear wild cry of
    the birds.

By permission of The Macmillan Company.

### NOTES AND QUESTIONS ON "TEWKESBURY ROAD"

How does the rhyme-scheme of this lyric differ from that of the two
preceding? This is one of the most musical of Masefield's short
poems. Observe that the vowel sounds employed are largely short;
consult "Symbolic Value of Vowel Sounds" (in this book) to see what
gives it its delicate, joyous beauty. How much do alliteration and
onomatopœia help? How much the pauses? Do you see that the
poet has adhered strictly to the pattern he set for himself in the first
stanza? How do you like the constant use of double adjectives?
Words of how many syllables prevail? Note how this causes the
longer words to stand out.

## THE WEST WIND

It's a warm wind, the west wind, full of birds' cries ;
I never hear the west wind but tears are in my eyes.
For it comes from the west lands, the old brown hills,
And April's in the west wind, and daffodils.

It's a fine land, the west land, for hearts as tired as mine,
Apple orchards blossom there, and the air's like wine.
There is cool green grass there, where men may lie at rest,
And the thrushes are in song there, fluting from the nest.

'Will ye not come home, brother? ye have been long away,
It's April, and blossom time, and white is the may ;
And bright is the sun, brother, and warm is the rain, —
Will ye not come home, brother, home to us again?

'The young corn is green, brother, where the rabbits run,
It's blue sky, and white clouds, and warm rain and sun.
It's song to a man's soul, brother, fire to a man's brain,
To hear the wild bees and see the merry spring again.

'Larks are singing in the west, brother, above the green
        wheat,
So will ye not come home, brother, and rest your tired
        feet?
I've a balm for bruised hearts, brother, sleep for aching
        eyes,'
Says the warm wind, the west wind, full of birds' cries.

It's the white road westward is the road I must tread
To the green grass, the cool grass, and rest for heart and
        head,
To the violets and the warm hearts and the thrushes'
        song,
In the fine land, the west land, the land where I belong.

NOTES AND QUESTIONS ON "THE WEST WIND"

This poem expresses Masefield's love for England. Compare its rhyme and rhythm with that of the preceding lyrics.

*Stanza 1.* Where must the poet have been for the west wind to blow from England? Daffodils grow wild in England; in this connection look up Wordsworth's poem "Daffodils."

*Stanza 2.* What instance of skillful repetition do you find here?

*Stanza 3.* Who is speaking in this stanza and the next two? Consult the dictionary to see why "may" does not begin with a capital.

*Stanza 4.* Trace the fine metaphors in line 3 which add beauty and force to this stanza.

*Stanza 5.* Line 3 of this stanza also contains fine metaphors. The repetition of the first line of stanza 1 with the change of two words is very effective.

How do you think this poem compares with Masefield's other lyrics for beauty of thought and musical expression?

## THE YARN OF THE 'LOCH ACHRAY'

The 'Loch Achray' was a clipper tall  
With seven-and-twenty hands in all.  
Twenty to hand and reef and haul,  
A skipper to sail and mates to bawl  
'Tally on to the tackle-fall,  
Heave now 'n' start her, heave 'n' pawl!'  
    Hear the yarn of a sailor,  
    An old yarn learned at sea.

Her crew were shipped, and they said 'Farewell,  
So-long, my Tottie, my lovely gell;  
We sail to-day if we fetch to hell,  
It's time we tackled the wheel a spell.'  
    Hear the yarn of a sailor,  
    An old yarn learned at sea.

The dock-side loafers talked on the quay  
The day that she towed down to sea:  
'Lord, what a handsome ship she be!  
Cheer her, sonny boys, three times three!'  
And the dock-side loafers gave her a shout  
As the red-funnelled tug-boat towed her out;  
They gave her a cheer as the custom is,  
And the crew yelled 'Take our loves to Liz —  
Three cheers, bullies, for old Pier Head  
'N' the bloody stay-at-homes!' they said.  
    Hear the yarn of a sailor,  
    An old yarn learned at sea.

In the grey of the coming on of night  
She dropped the tug at the Tuskar Light,  
'N' the topsails went to the topmast head  
To a chorus that fairly awoke the dead.

She trimmed her yards and slanted South
With her royals set and a bone in her mouth.
  Hear the yarn of a sailor,
  An old yarn learned at sea.

She crossed the Line and all went well,
They ate, they slept, and they struck the bell
And I give you gospel truth when I state
The crew didn't find any fault with the Mate,
But one night off the River Plate.
  Hear the yarn of a sailor,
  An old yarn learned at sea.

It freshened up till it blew like thunder
And burrowed her deep, lee-scuppers under.
The old man said, 'I mean to hang on
Till her canvas busts or her sticks are gone' —
Which the blushing looney did, till at last
Overboard went her mizzen-mast.
  Hear the yarn of a sailor,
  An old yarn learned at sea.

Then a fierce squall struck the 'Loch Achray'
And blowed her down to her water-way;
Her main-shrouds gave and her forestay,
And a green sea carried her wheel away;
Ere the watch below had time to dress
She was cluttered up in a blushing mess.
  Hear the yarn of a sailor,
  An old yarn learned at sea.

She couldn't lay-to nor yet pay-off,
And she got swept clean in the bloody trough;
Her masts were gone, and afore you knowed
She filled by the head and down she goed.

Her crew made seven-and-twenty dishes
For the big jack-sharks and the little fishes,
And over their bones the water swishes.
    Hear the yarn of a sailor,
    An old yarn learned at sea.

The wives and girls they watch in the rain
For a ship as won't come home again.
'I reckon it's them head-winds,' they say,
'She'll be home to-morrow, if not to-day.
I'll just nip home 'n' I'll air the sheets
'N' buy the fixings 'n' cook the meats
As my man likes 'n' as my man eats.'

So home they goes by the windy streets,
Thinking their men are homeward bound
With anchors hungry for English ground,
And the bloody fun of it is, they're drowned!
    Hear the yarn of a sailor,
    An old yarn learned at sea.

By permission of The Macmillan Company.

NOTES AND QUESTIONS ON "THE YARN OF THE 'LOCH ACHRAY'"

*Stanza 1.* "Clipper", a sailing vessel with fine lines and built for speed. "Tackle", pronounced by sailors "taykle", a combination of pulleys for obtaining artificial power; "tackle-fall", the rope that connects the blocks of a tackle. "Heave 'n' pawl", a cry of encouragement at the capstan.

*Stanza 3.* What is very true to life in this stanza? "Pier Head", wharf.

*Stanza 4.* "Tuskar Light", the lighthouse, one hundred and ten feet high, on Tuskar Rock on the coast of Ireland, whose light can be seen for fifteen miles. Why the shout when the tug left them?

*Stanza 5.* This gives the monotony of the ship routine which Masefield knew so well. What bit of sarcasm do you find?

*Stanza 6.* "Lee-scuppers", holes in the sides of the ship on a level with the deck. Who is "the old man"?

*Stanza 7.* Why is the color of the wave effective here?

*Stanza 8.* What picture do you get from the second line? Why do lines 5, 6, 7 end in "ishes"? Note the stark brutality of the description.

*Stanza 9.* Note the swift change of the scene. What is given here by direct quotation which could not be given in any other way? How can this be applied in your theme work?

*Stanza 10.* In spite of the rough joke in the fourth line, this stanza is very pathetic; what makes it so? What figure of speech in line 3?

*In General.* The refrain is in keeping with the ballad form of the poem. Observe that Masefield varies the length of the stanzas just as he would paragraphs in prose. On what principle is this done? Note the increased number of lines having the same rhyme in certain stanzas and see if you can discover the reason.

# ABBIE FARWELL BROWN

Poems, plays, and stories fell in quick succession from the pen of Abbie Farwell Brown, though she was most widely known as a writer of verse.

Miss Brown was born in Boston in 1875, and was educated at the Girls' Latin School and Radcliffe College. She spent much time in travel, both in her own country and in foreign lands.

Among her works are: "The Book of Saints and Friendly Beasts", "The Lonesomest Doll", "In the Days of the Giants", "The Flower Princess", "The Star Jewels", "Brothers and Sisters", "The Christmas Angel", "Fresh Posies", "The Song of Sixpence", "A Pocketful of Posies", and several plays and librettos. She died March 5, 1927.

## THE VIGIL

Through the long dark I watch and wake
   Beside my armor bright,
For tomorrow's dawning sun shall make
   Me, too, a belted Knight.

The silent hours drag slow and long,
   The chapel floor is cold
My weary eyes are faint, but strong
   My heart to win and hold.

No kin may help, no friend draw nigh,
   And all the world's asleep;
For this one night my soul and I
   Alone must vigil keep.

Yet thro' yon oriel's tinted wheel,
　　Of stars a silent throng
Watch over me and wish my weal, —
　　Knights who were brave and strong.

In silver armor clad, like mine,
　　They throng the blessed field,
Bright on my helm and corselet shine,
　　And bless my sword and shield.

THE VIGIL

They nobly strove in war's alarms,
　　They died to keep their vow;
But first they watched to win their arms
　　As I am watching now.

May their noblesse me too inspire,
　　Who long like them to fight
When I, who now am but a squire,
　　Shall rise a belted Knight.

Look up the ancient custom of Knighthood under which the young squire, about to be made a knight, watches all night in prayer and fasting beside his armor. Try to find some good pictures illustrating the custom.

Who are "the silent throng"? Why do they help him? Explain: "belted knight", "oriel", "corselet", "noblesse."

Read Lowell's "The Vision of Sir Launfal", and from Tennyson's "The Idylls of the King", to explain the young squire's vigil.


## GREEN CROSSES

At the back of the pompous houses,
Above the beautiful river way,
A row of squalid barrels
Blush at themselves in the morning light.
From one grotesquely leaning
Dusty and scarred
Amid the dead, forgotten slag and ashes,
A fir-tree thrusts its live, protesting fingers —
Crosses of green.
About it still cling a few silver cobwebs,
Rags of its brief splendor.
It was the Christmas Tree
That graced the cheerful drawing-room
A little while;
That blessed the comfortable house with its fragrance,
And with its symbols of love,
The small green crosses.

A pinched, pale child with hungry eyes,
Ragged and wolfish, but with wisps of glory
Still haloing her hair,
Comes with her bag of rubbish.

Her eyes brighten;
She sets down her heavy burden,
She forgets the cold as she picks at the little tree,
Plucks eagerly at the fragile cobwebs;
They are so silvery few!
But they do not go into the heavy sack.
Her thin, blue fingers snap one of the green crosses;
She twists the tinsel thread about it,
And sticks it in her breast.
Then she shoulders her bundle of trash,
And stumbles away, smiling.

The green crosses, alive in the dust!
The Christmas Tree!
The evergreen tree whose roots are cut —
On the dump it will die!

The Christmas Tree!
What if this ornament of brief holidays,
This plaything of the favored few,
This strong, slow-murdered creature of pure woods,
With its green crosses,
Were really growing!
If it were rooted in the hearts
Of Christendom!
How different a world would see this sunny morning!
No war; no hate;
No want nor selfishness;
No ragged children, starved for tinsel joys,
Furtively clutching at rejected beauty
On a forgotten cross,
The green cross of Love.

#### NOTES AND QUESTIONS ON "GREEN CROSSES"

*Stanza 1.* At the back of the magnificent houses on Beacon Street, Boston, runs the beautiful Charles River with its wide embankment.

In the morning one may see the ash barrels filled with rubbish placed outside the garden gates waiting to be emptied by the ash man.   What details of the description of the tree are especially forceful?   How can the poet speak of "protesting fingers" of the tree?   What uses of contrast make the stanza appeal to you?   In what sense are the fir tree's twigs "green crosses"?

*Stanza 2.*   Miss Brown, who lives near the river way, witnessed the incident she describes.   Many other persons in that vicinity have told of just such little scavengers who come from the West End of Boston and search the ash-barrels for treasures.   What makes the picture of the child so pathetic?   What shows how little of the joy and beauty which are every child's right had come into her life?

*Stanza 3.*   What contrast in line 1?   Miss Brown is almost as sorry for the poor tree as she is for the sad little child.

*Stanza 4.*   Why is line 4 so fine?   In the rest of the stanza the poet shows her wider, deeper sympathy for the world's troubles.   What does she mean by "really growing"?   Why would there be "no war; no hate"?   Notice how the last four lines tie the thoughts of stanzas 3 and 4 to the incident of the child, thereby securing unity.   Why is the Christmas tree called "The green cross of love"?   Would you like the poem better if it were written in rhyme?

## A BARGAIN

What for an amethyst sea
    And a turquoise sky?
Blind canyons of misery
    Where pale children cry.

What for the languorous breath
    Of lemon or lily?
A tenement reeking of death,
    Crowded and chilly.

What for a league of green sward
    On the slope of a valley?
Ten foot of brick yard
    At the end of an alley.

What for an olive-arched lane,
   With friendly bells ringing?
Din, confusion and pain,
   Dust choking and clinging.

Innocence, ragged and gay
   In Eden's delight,
Sold for a miserly day
   And a homesick night.

Reprinted from *The Gleam*, a magazine of verse for high schools.

### NOTES AND QUESTIONS ON "A BARGAIN"

*Stanza 1.* To get the full effect recall just what the colors are that are used in lines 1 and 2. In calling the narrow streets between high houses "canyons", what figure of speech is used? How do you know immediately that the first half of each stanza refers to the country and the last half to the city?

*Stanza 2.* What is the purpose of the two instances of alliteration in this stanza?

*Stanza 3.* What makes the last half of this stanza so good?

*Stanza 4.* Note the effect of the pauses in the last two lines as you read them aloud.

*Stanza 5.* What relation does this stanza bear to the rest of the poem? What would be the reverse order? How does it differ in form from the others? Try to compose some stanzas giving the other side of the question.

Compare the thought with that expressed by James Russell Lowell in "The Vision of Sir Launfal":

"For a cap and bells our lives we pay,
   Bubbles we buy with a whole soul's tasking:
'Tis heaven alone that is given away,
   'Tis only God may be had for the asking."

JOSEPHINE PRESTON PEABODY

# JOSEPHINE PRESTON PEABODY

"America's Dramatic Poet" was the title given Josephine Preston Peabody when her play "The Piper" won the Stratford-on-Avon prize in 1910, a prize of $1500 offered by one of the governors of the Shakespeare Memorial Theatre for the best play submitted for the festival to be given in honor of the great poet. She had written "The Piper" the year before with no thought of entering the contest, and her first knowledge of the offered prize came to her through a news-

paper clipping sent to her by a friend.  The play was sent to Stratford
and, after a long period of waiting, she learned that of the three
hundred and fifteen plays submitted, the decision lay between hers
and one other.  Again there was a long delay and when the news
of her victory finally came Miss Peabody was ill in a hospital, but
she recovered in time to be present at the presentation of her play
in Shakespeare's native town and receive the prize in person.

Although Miss Peabody was born in New York, her family soon
moved to Massachusetts and she was educated in Boston where she
attended the Girls' Latin School; later she graduated from Radcliffe College.  Her first poem was published when she was but fourteen years old and, encouraged by some of the most distinguished men
of the day, she steadily grew in power until she was recognized as
one of the foremost women poets of America.

In 1906, resigning from her position as instructor in English at
Wellesley College, she married Professor Lionel Marks of the engineer-
ing department at Harvard, an Englishman born at Birmingham, whose
family now live in Warwickshire near Stratford.  During the stay
at Stratford when "The Piper" was given, Lionel Marks, Jr., was
christened in the church which Shakespeare attended.  On their
return the family settled at Cambridge where they lived an idyllic
life of usefulness and happiness, surrounded by hosts of friends, until
after a long illness this gifted and charming woman passed on, leaving her devoted husband and children to miss her love and care but
to cherish her memory with pride and satisfaction.


## THE HOUSE AND THE ROAD

The little Road says, Go,
The little House says, Stay:
And O, it's bonny here at home,
But I must go away.

The little Road, like me,
Would seek and turn and know;
And forth I must, to learn the things
The little Road would show!

And go I must, my dears,
And journey while I may,
Though heart be sore for the little House
That had no word but Stay.

Maybe, no other way
Your child could ever know
Why a little House would have you stay,
When a little Road says, Go.

### NOTES AND QUESTIONS ON "THE HOUSE AND THE ROAD"

This short lyric was written when Miss Peabody was leaving her
teaching at Wellesley College to be married to Professor Marks, and
expresses the conflict most persons experience in leaving that with
which they are familiar to enter upon entirely new interests.  In no
other way, however, can we grow in knowledge and widen our horizon.
Notice how much is gained by the use of personification throughout
the poem.  What difference do you find in length of lines in each
stanza?  Observe the effect of this as you read the poem aloud.

## THE STAY–AT–HOME

I have waited, I have longed —
   I have longed as none can know,
All my spring and summer time,
   For this day to come and go ;
And the foolish heart was mine,
Dreaming I could see them shine, —
*Harlequin and Columbine*
                    *And Pierrot!*

Now the laughing has gone by,
   On the highway from the inn ;
And the dust has settled down,
   And the house is dead within.

And I stay — who never go —
Looking out upon the snow,
*Columbine and Pierrot*
　　　　　　*And Harlequin!*

All the rainbow things you see
　　Understream are not so fine;
And their voices weave and cling
　　Like my honeysuckle vine,
Lovely as a Violin! —
Mellow gold and silver-thin:
*Pierrot and Harlequin*
　　　　　　*And Columbine!*

Oh, the people that have seen,
　　They forget that it was so!
They, who never stay at home,
　　Say, "'Tis nothing but a show."
— And I keep the passion in:
And I bide: and I spin.
*Columbine . . . Harlequin*
　　　　　　*. . . Pierrot!*

NOTES AND QUESTIONS ON "THE STAY-AT-HOME"

Miss Peabody as a girl longed to see the world but feared that she never would. In this poem she sets forth her own feelings under the guise of one who is forced to stay at home from a long anticipated show which all the rest of the town has been able to see.

*Stanza 1.* How long has she been looking forward to this day? Harlequin in the British pantomime is a sprite invisible to all except his sweetheart Columbine, who also is invisible. He dances through the world and outwits the clown, Pierrot, who is in love with Columbine.

*Stanza 2.* What time of day is it, and what has happened?

*Stanza 3.* Have you ever seen "rainbow things understream" and thought them beautiful? Why does the poet represent the disappointed one as hearing the voices of the players?

*Stanza 4.* What makes this stanza so touching? What great truth does it set forth? Was the poet's longing ever satisfied?

HOME OF JOSEPHINE PRESTON PEABODY MARKS

## TO A DOG

So, back again?
    — And is your errand done,
  Unfailing one?
How quick the gray world, at your morning look,
Turns wonder-book!
Come in, — O guard and guest:
Come, O you breathless, from a life-long quest!
Search here my heart; and if a comfort be,
Ah, comfort me.
You eloquent one, you best
Of all diviners, so to trace
The weather-gleams upon a face;
With wordless, querying paw,
Adventuring the law!

You shaggy Loveliness,
What call was it? — What dream beyond a guess,
Lured you, gray ages back,
From that lone bivouac
Of the wild pack? —
Was it your need or ours?   The calling trail
Of faith that should not fail?
Of hope dim understood? —
That you should follow our poor humanhood,
Only because you would!
To search and circle, — follow and outstrip,
Men and their fellowship;
And keep your heart no less,
Your to-and-fro of hope and wistfulness,
Through all world-weathers and against all odds!

Can you forgive us, now? —
Your fallen gods?

### NOTES AND QUESTIONS ON "TO A DOG"

This poem is a proof of Miss Peabody's love and appreciation of
a dog.  Notice that she begins with a question without any introduction.  What does she gain by this?  What do you think the dog
is seeking in his "life-long quest"?  What does she mean by "morning look" in line 4?  How can a dog be spoken of as "eloquent"?
"Weather-gleams" means signs of approval or disapproval on his
master's face.  Is "wordless querying paw", etc., an accurate
description of a dog's ways?  "What was it" etc., refers to the fact
that in the dim ages of the past dogs were not domesticated animals;
read Jack London's "The Call of the Wild" in this connection.
"Your to-and-fro of hope and wistfulness" is a fine description of a
dog asking for something.  The last few lines are a fine tribute to the
love and faithfulness of dogs; do the last two imply that sometimes
their faith in their masters has been disappointed?  Did you ever
think that man stands in place of God to animals?

## THE PIPER

"Piper, wherefore wilt thou roam?
  Piper, wilt thou bide?
Here thou shalt have hearth and home,
  And neighbors at thy side;
Many flocks we'll give thee, too,
  Piper, an thou bide."

"Nay and nay!  For one unheard
  Calleth me to follow.
All I ask, a brother bird
  Singing thro' the hollow;
And a friendly star at night,
  And a brook to follow."

#### NOTES AND QUESTIONS ON "THE PIPER"

Miss Peabody wrote two poems entitled "The Piper."  What do
you know about the other?
*Stanza 1.*  Who speaks in this stanza?  Why should the villagers
offer the Piper so much to stay?  "An", old-fashioned word for "if."
*Stanza 2.*  Why will he not stay?  Does this poem remind you of
any others in this book setting forth the same wanderlust?

## RETURN

Soldier-boy, soldier-boy,
  Now the war is done,
Are you not a happy lad
  To see the world at one?
Home again — home again,
  Living in the sun!

"Oh, the faces smiled on us
  While the faces passed;

And the cannon hailed the flags
    Waving from the mast.
It was good, it was good, —
    Ah, too good to last.


"Now the streets are still again,
    Still enough to fret,
Though the hurts you do not see
    May be aching yet,
What we gave, what we won,
    Most of you forget.


"For however much I pay
    There is more to owe;
And I must be doing still,
    And choose my yes and no!
But friend to me or enemy, —
    Who wears aught to show?


"Taking orders from myself
    Leaves me many ways;
And there isn't much to choose
    When a man obeys!
But a bullet keeps its word
    When a kiss betrays."


Soldier-boy, soldier-boy,
    Tell me what you bring
From the wisdom of the war
    Years and nations sing.
"What is death?   A bitter sting!
    Life's the hardest thing."

NOTES AND QUESTIONS ON "RETURN"

*Stanza 1.* This is the way most persons think a returned soldier must feel. Note the soldier's answer which follows.

*Stanza 2.* What about the war did the lad enjoy?

*Stanza 3.* What does he miss? What hurts his feelings?

*Stanza 4.* This means that however much he has already given, he must still fight on; what must he now struggle against?

*Stanza 5.* Express lines 1–4 in your own words.

*Stanza 6.* What lesson has he learned? Express his answer in another way.

ROBERT FROST

# ROBERT FROST

Robert Frost was born in San Francisco in 1875 and lived there until he was nine years old, when the family moved to Lawrence, Massachusetts. His father was a newspaper man, being editor-in-charge of both the *San Francisco Bulletin* and the *Post*. Robert graduated from the Lawrence High School and went to work in the mills of that city after the death of his father.  He also worked on a newspaper there.  He wanted more education so he went to Dartmouth College, but did not graduate, though he later studied a short time at Harvard.  He so hated everything academic that he never received a degree; and it may be encouraging to you to know that this youth, who was destined to become one of the recognized American poets, hated to write the formal compositions required of him as much as you ever did.  He tried business for a while but, as it had become clear that he would never be a success at it, and since he had married and needed some source of income, his grandfather bought him a small farm in Derry, New Hampshire, and there he lived for ten years in the simplest fashion.  Frost was never much of a success as a farmer, but was assistant in the English Department of Pinkerton Academy in Derry for a time, "teaching school on the side", as he says, meanwhile writing many poems which were never published.  Then he sold the farm, which was mortgaged, and with what was left he and his wife, who never once lost faith in her husband, and the children, moved to Beaconsfield, England, where he secured a small place, still practised writing poetry, and met many people of note.  One day he made a collection of about twenty poems and found a publisher for them. This collection was entitled "A Boy's Will" and met with the heartiest enthusiasm in England.  He returned to America in 1915 and lived in Franconia, New Hampshire, and from 1916 to 1919 he taught in Amherst College.  Later he moved to South Shaftsbury, Vermont, where he again lived on a farm with his faithful wife and their four children.  In 1915 he published "North of Boston", a larger and more mature collection of poems.  The University of Michigan conferred upon him a resident fellowship in poetry and he again became connected with Amherst College, an honor which is still his.

In 1924, after seven years of silence, he published "New Hampshire", which was followed by "West Running Brook" in 1928, "Collected Poems" in 1930, and "A Lone Striker" in 1933.

Though born in the West, Robert Frost is essentially of New England, and no one more sympathetically describes New England landscapes or interprets New England life.

## BROWN'S DESCENT

### or

## THE WILLY–NILLY SLIDE

Brown lived at such a lofty farm
  That everyone for miles could see
His lantern when he did his chores
  In winter after half past three.

And many must have seen him make
  His wild descent from there one night,
'Cross lots, 'cross walls, 'cross everything,
  Describing rings of lantern light.

Between the house and barn the gale
  Got him by something he had on
And blew him out on the icy crust
  That cased the world, and he was gone!

Walls were all buried, trees were few:
  He saw no stay unless he stove
A hole in somewhere with his heel.
  But though repeatedly he strove

And stamped and said things to himself,
  And sometimes something seemed to yield,
He gained no foothold, but pursued
  His journey down from field to field.

Sometimes he came with arms outspread
  Like wings, revolving in the scene
Upon his longer axis, and
  With no small dignity of mien.

Faster or slower as he chanced,
  Sitting or standing as he chose,

According as he feared to risk
  His neck, or thought to spare his clothes.

He never let the lantern drop.
  And some exclaimed who saw afar
And figures he described with it,
  "I wonder what those signals are

Brown makes at such an hour of night!
  He's celebrating something strange.
I wonder if he's sold his farm,
  Or been made Master of the Grange."

He reeled, he lurched, he bobbed, he checked:
  He fell and made the lantern rattle
(But saved the light from going out),
  So half-way down he fought the battle

Incredulous of his own bad luck.
  And then becoming reconciled
To everything, he gave it up
  And came down like a coasting child.

"Well — I — be — " that was all he said,
  As standing in the river road,
He looked back up the slippery slope
  (Two miles it was) to his abode.

Sometimes as an authority
  On motor-cars, I'm asked if I
Should say our stock was petered out,
  And this is my sincere reply:

Yankees are what they always were.
  Don't think Brown ever gave up hope
Of getting home again because
  He couldn't climb that slippery slope;

Or even thought of standing there
  Until the January thaw
Should take the polish off the crust.
  He bowed with grace to natural law,

And then went round it on his feet,
  After the manner of our stock;
Not much concerned for those to whom,
  At that particular time o'clock,

It must have looked as if the course
  He steered was really straight away
From that which he was headed for —
  Not much concerned for them, I say;

No more so than became a man —
  *And* politician at odd seasons.
I've kept Brown standing in the cold
  While I invested him with reasons;

But now he snapped his eyes three times;
  Then shook his lantern saying, "Ile's
'Bout out!" and took the long way home
  By road, a matter of several miles.

NOTES AND QUESTIONS ON "BROWN'S DESCENT"

"Willy-nilly", whether he would or not.   This is a simple narrative poem, typical of Frost, and has the ballad form and rhyme.   It illustrates two characteristics of Frost's work, economy in the use of words and the conversational style.   Observe the few descriptive adjectives and find expressions exactly like those you use every day.   In stanzas 3 and 4 we have marked alliteration.   Why are stanzas 5 and 6 particularly good?   Are the verbs in stanza 10 noteworthy?   Notice how the two remarks which Brown makes indicate that he belongs to New England.   How does Mr. Frost prove that New England stock has not "petered out"?

BIRCHES

Photo. by Alton H. Blackinton.

# BIRCHES

When I see birches bend to left and right
Across the line of straighter darker trees,
I like to think some boy's been swinging them.
But swinging doesn't bend them down to stay.
Ice-storms do that.   Often you must have seen them
Loaded with ice a sunny winter morning
After a rain.   They click upon themselves
As the breeze rises, and turn many-colored
As the stir cracks and crazes their enamel.
Soon the sun's warmth makes them shed crystal shells
Shattering and avalanching on the snow-crust —
Such heaps of broken glass to sweep away
You'd think the inner dome of heaven had fallen.
They are dragged to the withered bracken by the load,
And they seem not to break; though once they are bowed
So low for long, they never right themselves:
You may see their trunks arching in the woods
Years afterwards, trailing their leaves on the ground
Like girls on hands and knees that throw their hair
Before them over their heads to dry in the sun.
But I was going to say when Truth broke in
With all her matter-of-fact about the ice-storm,
I should prefer to have some boy bend them
As he went out and in to fetch the cows —
Some boy too far from town to learn baseball,
Whose only play was what he found himself,
Summer and winter, and could play alone.
One by one he subdued his father's trees
By riding them down over and over again
Until he took the stiffness out of them,
And not one but hung limp, not one was left
For him to conquer.   He learned all there was

To learn about not launching out too soon
And so not carrying the tree away
Clear to the ground.   He always kept his poise
To the top branches, climbing carefully
With the same pains you use to fill a cup
Up to the brim, and even above the brim.
Then he flung outward, feet first, with a swish,
Kicking his way down through the air to the ground.

So was I once myself a swinger of birches;
And so I dream of going back to be.
It's when I'm weary of considerations,
And life is too much like a pathless wood
Where your face burns and tickles with the cobwebs
Broken across it, and one eye is weeping
From a twig's having lashed across it open.
I'd like to get away from earth awhile
And then come back to it and begin over.
May no fate willfully misunderstand me
And half grant what I wish and snatch me away
Not to return.   Earth's the right place for love:
I don't know where it's likely to go better.
I'd like to go by climbing a birch tree,
And climb black branches up a snow-white trunk
*Toward* heaven, till the tree could bear no more,
But dipped its top and set me down again.
That would be good both going and coming back.
One could do worse than be a swinger of birches.

### NOTES AND QUESTIONS ON "BIRCHES"

"Birches" is written in blank verse, but the cadence is that of conversation rather than that of ordinary rhythm.  Find expressions exactly like those used in everyday speech.  Do these detract from the interest of the poem?  From its beauty?  What lines show that Frost is a close observer of nature?  Notice the beauty of the description of the effect of ice-storms, beginning, "Often you must have seen them." What lines in this description are especially fine because of their sound? Which because of the accuracy of the picture? How do you like the simile about the girls? Do you think the digression about the ice-storm injures the poem? What shows that Frost knows and sympathizes with boys? Note the accuracy of the description of how a boy climbs birches. Have you ever tried to travel "a pathless wood"? If so, you will appreciate Frost's description. Does the poet love life? Is his desire at times to get away from the world for a little time and then come back a natural one? In what way is it like swinging birches?

# THE TUFT OF FLOWERS

I went to turn the grass once after one
Who mowed it in the dew before the sun.

The dew was gone that made his blade so keen
Before I came to view the levelled scene.

I looked for him behind an isle of trees;
I listened for his whetstone on the breeze.

But he had gone his way, the grass all mown,
And I must be, as he had been, — alone,

"As all must be," I said within my heart,
"Whether they work together or apart."

But as I said it, swift there passed me by
On noiseless wing a 'wildered butterfly,

Seeking with memories grown dim o'er night
Some resting flower of yesterday's delight.

And once I marked his flight go round and round,
As where some flower lay withering on the ground.

And then he flew as far as eye could see,
And then on tremulous wing came back to me.

I thought of questions that have no reply,
And would have turned to toss the grass to dry;

But he turned first, and led my eye to look
At a tall tuft of flowers beside a brook,

A leaping tongue of bloom the scythe had spared
Beside a reedy brook the scythe had bared.

I left the place to know them by their name,
Finding them butterfly-weed when I came.

The mower in the dew had loved them thus,
By leaving them to flourish, not for us,

Nor yet to draw one thought of ours to him,
But from sheer morning gladness at the brim.

The butterfly and I had lit upon,
Nevertheless, a message from the dawn,

That made me hear the wakening birds around,
And hear his long scythe whispering to the ground,

And feel a spirit kindred to my own;
So that henceforth I worked no more alone;

But glad with him, I worked as with his aid,
And weary, sought at noon with him the shade;

And dreaming, as it were, held brotherly speech
With one whose thought I had not hoped to reach.

"Men work together," I told him from the heart,
"Whether they work together or apart."

NOTES AND QUESTIONS ON "THE TUFT OF FLOWERS"

"The Tuft of Flowers" is unlike most of Robert Frost's poems in
that it is written in rhyming couplets; nevertheless it keeps to the
cadences of conversation.  Find evidence of this.  What fine descriptive expressions do you find in the first five stanzas?  What figure of
speech in "an isle of trees"?  In what sense must we all be alone,
whether we work together or apart?  Have you ever seen a bewildered
butterfly act as described in stanzas 6 to 9?  Note how much is said
in "some resting flower of yesterday's delight."  What made Frost
think of questions that have no reply?  Of what value is the metaphor
in stanza 12?  What is the effect of "the scythe had spared" and "the
scythe had bared"?  Why had the mower spared the tuft of flowers?
In what way did the tuft of flowers unite the mower, the butterfly, and
the poet?  What fine expression in stanza 17?  Does the statement
in stanza 21 contradict that in stanza 5?

*In General.*  Do you think that the rhyme adds to the beauty of
the poem?  Select lines that seem especially musical and consult
"Aids to Musical Sound in Poetry" (in this book) to see what makes
them so.

# THE ROAD NOT TAKEN

Two roads diverged in a yellow wood,
And sorry I could not travel both
And be one traveler, long I stood
And looked down one as far as I could
To where it bent in the undergrowth;

Then took the other, as just as fair,
And having perhaps the better claim,
Because it was grassy and wanted wear;
Though as for that the passing there
Had worn them really about the same,

And both that morning equally lay
In leaves no step had trodden black.
Oh, I kept the first for another day!
Yet knowing how way leads on to way,
I doubted if I should ever come back.

I shall be telling this with a sigh
Somewhere ages and ages hence:
Two roads diverged in a wood, and I —
I took the one less traveled by,
And that has made all the difference.

### NOTES AND QUESTIONS ON "THE ROAD NOT TAKEN"

This poem should not be taken literally only; it signifies as well a choice of two lines of action.

*Stanza 1.* What time of year is indicated in this stanza? Have you ever felt about two roads as Frost did?

*Stanza 2.* Why did he take the other road? Of two lines of action would Frost choose the usual or the unusual?

*Stanza 3.* What in this stanza shows that he is a close observer of nature?

*Stanza 4.* Might a choice of one of two lines of action affect one's destiny for all eternity?

*In General.* What is the rhyme-scheme and is it a common one? Note that the poet uses the conversational style as usual. Find marked instances of this. Express in one clear sentence the central thought of the poem.

## THE BLACK COTTAGE

We chanced in passing by that afternoon
To catch it in a sort of special picture
Among tar-banded ancient cherry-trees,
Set well back from the road in rank lodged grass,
The little cottage we were speaking of,
A front with just a door between two windows,
Fresh painted by the shower a velvet black.
We paused, the minister and I, to look.
He made as if to hold it at arm's length
Or put the leaves aside that framed it in.
"Pretty," he said. "Come in. No one will care."

ROBERT FROST                     209

The path was a vague parting in the grass
That led us to a weathered window-sill.
We pressed our faces to the pane.   "You see," he said,
"Everything's as she left it when she died.
Her sons won't sell the house or the things in it.
They say they mean to come and summer here
Where they were boys.   They haven't come this year.

THE BLACK COTTAGE

They live so far away — one is out West —
It will be hard for them to keep their word.
Anyway they won't have the place disturbed.
A buttoned hair-cloth lounge spread scrolling arms
Under a crayon portrait on the wall
Done sadly from an old daguerreotype.
That was the father as he went to war.
She always, when she talked about war,
Sooner or later came and leaned, half knelt

Against the lounge beside it, though I doubt
If such unlifelike lines kept power to stir
Anything in her after all the years.
He fell at Gettysburg or Fredericksburg,
I ought to know — it makes a difference which:
Fredericksburg wasn't Gettysburg, of course.
But what I'm getting to is how forsaken
A little cottage this has always seemed;
Since she went more than ever, but before —
I don't mean altogether by the lives
That had gone out of it, the father first,
Then the two sons, till she was left alone.
(Nothing could draw her after those two sons.
She valued the considerate neglect
She had at some cost taught them after years.)
I mean by the world's having passed it by —
As we almost got by this afternoon.
It always seems to me a sort of mark
To measure how far fifty years have brought us.
Why not sit down if you are in no haste?
These doorsteps seldom have a visitor.
The warping boards pull out their own old nails
With none to tread and put them in their place.
She had her own idea of things, the old lady.
And she liked talk.   She had seen Garrison
And Whittier, and had her story of them.
One wasn't long in learning that she thought
Whatever else the Civil War was for
It wasn't just to keep the States together,
Nor just to free the slaves, though it did both.
She wouldn't have believed those ends enough
To have given outright for them all she gave.
Her giving somehow touched the principle
That all men are created free and equal.

And to hear her quaint phrases — so removed
From the world's view to-day of all those things.
That's a hard mystery of Jefferson's.
What did he mean?   Of course the easy way
Is to decide it simply isn't true.
It may not be.   I heard a fellow say so.
But never mind, the Welshman got it planted
Where it will trouble us a thousand years.
Each age will have to reconsider it.
You couldn't tell her what the West was saying,
And what the South to her serene belief.
She had some art of hearing and yet not
Hearing the latter wisdom of the world.
White was the only race she ever knew.
Black she had scarcely seen, and yellow never.
But how could they be made so very unlike
By the same hand working in the same stuff?
She had supposed the war decided that.
What are you going to do with such a person?
Strange how such innocence gets its own way.
I shouldn't be surprised if in this world
It were the force that would at last prevail.
Do you know but for her there was a time
When to please younger members of the church,
Or rather say non-members in the church,
Whom we all have to think of nowadays,
I would have changed the Creed a very little?
Not that she ever had to ask me not to;
It never got so far as that; but the bare thought
Of her old tremulous bonnet in the pew,
And of her half asleep was too much for me.
Why, I might wake her up and startle her.
It was the words 'descended into Hades'
That seemed too pagan to our liberal youth.

You know they suffered from a general onslaught.
And well, if they weren't true why keep right on
Saying them like the heathen? We could drop them.
Only — there was the bonnet in the pew.
Such a phrase couldn't have meant much to her.
But suppose she had missed it from the Creed
As a child misses the unsaid Good-night,
And falls asleep with heartache — how should I feel?
I'm just as glad she made me keep hands off,
For, dear me, why abandon a belief
Merely because it ceases to be true.
Cling to it long enough, and not a doubt
It will turn true again, for so it goes.
Most of the change we think we see in life
Is due to truths being in and out of favour.
As I sit here, and oftentimes, I wish
I could be monarch of a desert land
I could devote and dedicate forever
To the truths we keep coming back and back to.
So desert it would have to be, so walled
By mountain ranges half in summer snow,
No one would covet it or think it worth
The pains of conquering to force change on.
Scattered oases where men dwelt, but mostly
Sand dunes held loosely in tamarisk
Blown over and over themselves in idleness.
Sand grains should sugar in the natal dew
The babe born to the desert, the sand storm
Retard mid-waste my cowering caravans —

"There are bees in this wall." He struck the clapboards,
Fierce heads looked out; small bodies pivoted.
We rose to go. Sunset blazed on the windows.

On a New Hampshire hillside, sloping to the west, stood the cottage which time and storm had painted black.

The owner, widowed by the Civil War, lived on in the little home; her two boys grew up, and went their way out in the wide world. She, unselfish ever, urged them not to spend their money in travel, and so saw them but rarely. Living alone, she allowed nothing to be changed in the house; all remained much as when the young soldier left it for the last time — all having a quaint look to-day. The world seemed to have passed by and left the little house behind. Just so the aged owner held her opinions unchanged. She felt sure the War must have been for something more than just to free the slaves, or hold the States together, since it took *him*. She held fast to the great principles of the Constitution and to the truths of the Bible, and in her simplicity she was yet an influence. The author indulges in a playful wish that there might be an island of lost beliefs, which after being discarded for a time are restored to favor.

## THE COW IN APPLE TIME

Something inspires the only cow of late
To make no more of a wall than an open gate,
And think no more of wall-builders than fools.
Her face is flecked with pomace and she drools
A cider syrup. Having tasted fruit,
She scorns a pasture withering to the root.
She runs from tree to tree where lie and sweeten
The windfalls spiked with stubble and worm-eaten.
She leaves them bitten when she has to fly.
She bellows on a knoll against the sky.
Her udder shrivels and the milk goes dry.

Select brief statements which say a great deal or give a vivid picture. What kind of weather has it been, and how do you know? Why has the cow "to fly"? Note the picture in the single line next to the last. What variation do you find in the rhyme-scheme? What are the chief points of excellence in this brief sketch?

# CHARLES HANSON TOWNE

Another journalist turned poet is "Charley" Towne, as he is familiarly called. Though born in the South, in Louisville, he was educated in the public schools of New York, attended New York City College one year, and has spent most of his life in that city; in fact, he is a true "New Yorker" and is interested in everything pertaining to city life and activity. As he tells you in his sonnet, "The City", he would not be contented to live in the country. He has been at different times editor of *The Smart Set*, *The Delineator*, *McClure's Magazine*, and *Harper's Bazaar*. He now conducts a literary column in the *New York American*.

CHARLES HANSON TOWNE

## CITY ROOFS

Roof-tops, roof-tops, what do you cover?
Sad folks, bad folks, and many a glowing lover;
Wise people, simple people, children of despair —
Roof-tops, roof-tops, hiding pain and care.

Roof-tops, roof-tops, O what sin you're knowing,
While above you in the sky the white clouds are blowing;
While beneath you, agony and dolor and grim strife
Fight the olden battle, the olden war of Life.

Roof-tops, roof-tops, cover up their shame —
Wretched souls, prisoned souls too piteous to name;
Man himself hath built you all to hide away the stars —
Roof-tops, roof-tops, you hide ten million scars.

Roof-tops, roof-tops, well I know you cover
Many solemn tragedies and many a lonely lover;
But ah, you hide the good that lives in the throbbing
   city —
Patient wives, and tenderness, forgiveness, faith, and pity.

Roof-tops, roof-tops, this is what I wonder:
You are thick as poisonous plants, thick the people under;
Yet roofless, and homeless, and shelterless they roam,
The driftwood of the town who have no roof-top and no
   home!

NOTES AND QUESTIONS ON "CITY ROOFS"

*Stanza 1.* Is there some high building in your city or town from which you have looked out over the house-tops of the inhabitants? Is the question in the first line a natural one? Note the difference in the sound of the first and the last half of each line and see if you can tell what causes it.

*Stanza 2.* Why did Mr. Towne write the second line?

*Stanza 3.* Can you think of some kinds of people who might be described by line 2?

*Stanza 4.* Do you think there is more bad than good in the average city or town?

*Stanza 5.* What is especially good in the simile of line 2? Are there any persons in your city or town who might be called "the drift-wood of the town"? What makes this metaphor so expressive? Why is this new thought stated so briefly?

*In General.* What is the effect of the whole poem's being written in the second person?  Note in reading it aloud that the difference in sound in the first and last half of the lines pointed out in stanza 1 is characteristic of the poem as a whole.

## THE TIME–CLOCK

### I

"Tick-tock!  Tick-tock!"
Sings the great time-clock.
And the pale men hurry
And flurry and scurry
To punch their time
Ere the hour shall chime.
"Tick-tock!  Tick-tock!"
Sings the stern time-clock.


"It — is — time — you — were — come!"
Says the pendulum.
"Tick-tock!  Tick-tock!"
Moans the great time-clock.
They must leave the heaven
Of their beds. . . . It is seven,
And the sharp whistles blow
In the city below.
They can never delay —
If they're late, they must pay.
"God help them!"  I say.
But the great time-clock
Only says, "Tick-tock!"


They are chained, they are slaves
From their birth to their graves!

And the clock
Seems to mock
With its awful "Tick-tock!"
There it stands at the door
Like a brute, as they pour
Through the dark little way
Where they toil night and day.
They are goaded along
By the terrible song
Of whistle and gong,
And the endless "Tick-tock!"
Of the great time-clock.
"Tick-tock!  Tick-tock!"
Runs the voice of the clock.

## II

Some day it will cease!
They will all be at peace,
And dream a new dream
Far from shuttle and steam.
And whistles may blow
And whistles may scream —
They will smile — even so,
And dream their new dream.

But the clock will tick on
When their bodies are gone;
And others will hurry,
And scurry and worry,
While "Tick-tock!  Tick-tock!"
Whispers the clock.

"Tick-tock!  Tick-tock!
Tick-tock!  Tick-tock!"
Forever runs on the song of the clock!

NOTES AND QUESTIONS ON "THE TIME-CLOCK"

The first thing you will notice when reading this poem aloud is that it is written in exactly the time of the ticking of a great clock which ticks once every second.

*Part I*. Has a clock ever seemed "stern" to you? In what kind of work do men still have to be ready for the day's labor at seven o'clock? Is time usually deducted if they are late? In what sense are these workers "slaves from their birth"? Why is "goaded" in the third stanza an expressive word as used here?

*Part II*. When only will these laborers be at peace? What effect is produced by the second stanza?

From this poem we must infer that Mr. Towne has deep sympathy with the workers of the world. What other poets have you read who feel the same?

## A BALLAD OF THE CIRCUS

When we went to the circus
　　We had seats by the door,
Where the clowns made their entrance,
　　And a coach and four.

A shabby old carriage,
　　Trying to be grand,
Painted up with gold figures,
　　Painted to beat the band.

In it sat a "princess",
　　In cheap, tawdry lace,
A gorgeous wig upon her head,
　　And powder on her face.

I could see the clowns waiting
　　For their cues to come in.
How solemn were their faces
　　In that strange, hellish din!

Great elephants stood near them,
   Trained seals, and giraffes.
Together they were waiting
   For five thousand laughs.

Together they were waiting
   For the signal to begin.
One face haunts me yet,
   A boyish harlequin,

With a grave, sad expression
   Even beneath that paint;
The deep eyes of a poet,
   The thin cheeks of a saint.

Suddenly the band played,
   And every one was off;
But somehow, through the rush and roar
   I heard a little cough,

And I saw a tiny smile come
   Around his lips and eyes.
But to me there was a tragedy
   Beneath that pale disguise.

He pranced and cavorted,
   And the children screamed with joy;
But I lost him in the mêlée.
   What was one sad boy

When three rings were crowded
   With tableaux and fun,
And the loud band was playing
   "Johnny, Get Your Gun!"

The chariots were racing
  Around the outer track,
And a marvelous French juggler
  Held a pole on his back,

And a girl like an angel
  Dropped from a trapeze,
And I looked with wonder
  At a young Japanese,

Who twirled a bright barrel
  Lightly on his toes?
Far down the arena
  Loud laughter arose,

And my young clown was making
  The people expire
As he danced like a fool
  On a long, thin wire.

They roared at his antics,
  And clapped for awhile,
And then grew weary
  Of his smooth, fixed smile,

And turned to the others
  Who romped in the ring,
And I lost my taste
  For the whole silly thing.

I was glad it was over,
  The false, foolish show.
But one face haunts me —
  A sad, mad Pierrot;

A boy with the soul
     Of a poet and saint,
Smiling in public
     Beneath his cheap paint,

Yet looking so grave
     When no one could see
The ache in his eyes
     But a fool like me!

### NOTES AND QUESTIONS ON "A BALLAD OF THE CIRCUS"

*Stanza 1.* This stanza gives the time and the place, in other words, the setting of the poem.

*Stanzas 2 to 5.* What details of the scene are familiar to you? What unusual word to describe clowns in stanza 4? How large was the audience?

*Stanzas 6 to 10.* These give the picture of the central figure of the ballad, the boy harlequin or Pierrot. Select the expressions which give the idea of sadness. What did the tiny cough show? Explain the simple forcefulness of line 4, stanza 10.

*Stanzas 11 to 17.* How many of these sights have you seen at the circus? Why did the crowd grow weary of the boyish clown?

*Stanzas 18 to 20.* Why was the poet glad when the circus was over? Note the combination of strong monosyllables in line 4 of stanza 18. Why does the poet call himself a fool?

*In General.* This is a very fine example of skillful use of contrast, for the pathos of the situation lies in the fact that the boy who had the soul of a saint and a poet was obliged to play the part of a fool in the most sordid surroundings to an audience utterly incapable of appreciating his fineness.

## RENEWAL

April, when I heard
Your lyrical low word,
And when upon the hawthorn hedge your first white blossom
     stirred,

Something strangely came —
Something I cannot name —
And touched my heart, and cleansed my soul with a reviving
    flame.

When the yellow gleam
Of your hosts that stream —
Jonquil, buttercup, and crocus — made the world a golden
    dream,

Something, April, said
To my heart that bled —
Bled with old remembrances — "Lo, the grief-strewn days
    are fled!"

*Sursum corda!*   Now,
When blooms the apple-bough,
April, of your pity, let your light rain kiss my brow;

Heal me, if you will;
Bathe my heart until
I am one with your first primrose or the shining daffodil!

### NOTES AND QUESTIONS ON "RENEWAL"

*Stanza 1.*   What about line 2 attracts your attention, and what
did the poet have in mind?

*Stanza 2.*   This sets forth the mystery of the message of spring;
have you heard it?   What figure of speech in "reviving flame"?

*Stanza 3.*   Have you ever noticed how many yellow flowers there
are in April?   Has Mr. Towne named them all?

*Stanza 4* contains the message as a grown person somewhat sad-
dened by the years hears it.   Try writing a similar stanza telling
what April says to you.

*Stanza 5.*   "*Sursum corda*" is the old exhortation of the Church
and means "Lift up your hearts!"

*Stanza 6.*   What characteristics of the first primrose or the daffodil would the poet like to share?

## THE CITY

When sick of all the sorrow and distress
  That flourish in the City like foul weeds,
    I sought blue rivers and green, opulent meads,
And leagues of unregarded loneliness
Whereon no foot of man had seemed to press,
  I did not know how great had been my needs,
    How wise the woodland's gospel and her creeds,
How good her faith to one long comfortless.

But in the silence came a Voice to me ;
  In every wind it murmured, and I knew
    It would not cease though far my heart might roam.
It called me in the sunrise and the dew,
  At noon and twilight, sadly, hungrily,
    The jealous City, whispering always — "Home !"

### NOTES AND QUESTIONS ON "THE CITY"

This poem is a sonnet; look up the definition of a sonnet in the Introduction and find what the first part is called, and what the second.

*The Octet.* The City is New York, hence the capital letter. What figure do you find in the second line? What is gained by its use? What was the first effect of the visit to the country?

*The Sestet.* Why does "Voice" begin with a capital? Note how much vividness is gained by this personification; also how effective is the single brief word "Home." Do you think Mr. Towne's feelings would be shared by most persons living in the city?

Express the thought of the first eight lines in one short sentence. Do the same for the last six lines and with the help of the two express the central thought of the sonnet in one good, clear, crisp sentence.

# WILFRED WILSON GIBSON

Wilfred Wilson Gibson, an English poet, has been styled "the Twentieth Century Thomas Hood." His poems arouse sympathy for the wage earner, the one who struggles for daily bread. For some years he lived in the East End, the slum district of London. Like Dickens he has known and sympathized with the sufferings, the hardships and the thwarted ambitions of the poor, but unlike Dickens he gives not the individual but the type. His poems are mainly narrative. Several volumes have been published under the title "Daily Bread." Though somewhat too realistic, Gibson interprets the character and life of the laborer in terms of sweetness and real dignity.

## OLD MAN JOBLING

### (A Catch for Singing)

*Old man, old man, whither are you hobbling?*
*Old man Jobling, whither are you going —*
*Battered hat and tattered coat, and clogs in want of cobbling —*
*And the snell wind lowing and the mirk lift snowing?*

Young man Catchieside, and if I go a-fairing,
Who's declaring I'm too old for going —
Dressed in Sunday-best and all: and why should I be caring
For the snell wind lowing and the mirk lift snowing?

*Ay, but what will come of you as drifts get deep and deeper —*
*Steep roads steeper, and your shanks too numb for going?*
Happen I shall nap — I was ever a good sleeper
With the snell wind lowing and the mirk lift snowing.

*Deep will be your sleep.* . . . It's truth you are declaring —
After fairing, whichever way we're going,
Deep will be the sleep of all; so why should I be caring
For the snell wind lowing and the mirk lift snowing?

NOTES AND QUESTIONS ON "OLD MAN JOBLING"

A catch is a song in which different voices take up the air. The
two speakers are Old Man Jobling and Young Man Catchieside,
catchie being the Scotch for merry.

*Stanza 1.* How does the poet produce so vivid a picture in this
stanza? "Snell", Scotch for keen, sharp; "mirk", Scotch for dull,
gloomy; "lift", provincial English for air, heavens; "a-fairing", fair,
a verb, obsolete form of fare, to go forth.

*Stanza 4.* What great truth does the old man express?

*In General.* Note every instance of rhyme and half-rhyme and
listen for their effect as you read the poem aloud. Look up some old
catches and see if this is characteristic of most of them.

## THE VOICE

At sunrise striking out to sea,
I heard a clear voice calling me
From the little oaks whose branches lean
Over the restless water —
I heard, half-dreaming that I heard
The voice of some enchanted bird;
And glancing back, among the green
I saw my little daughter.

When I must breast the stiller sea
That stretches everlastingly
Beneath the starless unknown night,
The darkness round me falling,
May it be given me to hear
Life calling me as crystal-clear —
To glance back once through failing light
And answer that sweet calling.

NOTES AND QUESTIONS ON "THE VOICE"

How does stanza 1 help you to interpret the deeper meaning of stanza 2?

Read Tennyson's "Crossing the Bar", as an example of a radiant view of death.

# KATHERINE VEITCH

He fell at Loos : and when she heard
The tidings, though she did not stir,
Some light within her at the word
Was darkened; and it seemed to her
Death sought to snatch her bairn from her,
To snatch her sucking bairn from her :

And she forgot that he had grown
A hefty lad to be her pride,
A shepherd for skilled piping known
Throughout the hilly Borderside,
Until they took him from her side,
No more to seek his minney's side.

By day or night she cannot rest :
Stravaging over Auchopecairn,
She clutches to her naked breast
An old clout-dolly, like a bairn ;
And moans : "My bairn — my hinny bairn !
Death shall not have my wee bit bairn !"

NOTES AND QUESTIONS ON "KATHERINE VEITCH"

The mother, suddenly hearing that her son, a soldier, "fell at Loos", makes no audible demonstration, but her mind loses its balance under the shock. Ever afterward she thinks of the son as again an infant, no longer the "hefty lad", the shepherd renowned throughout the country-side for his playing on the flute.

Day and night she roams and cannot rest, but clasping a rag doll, she moans, "Death shall not have my wee bit bairn."

Read Lucy Larcom's poem, "Hannah at the Window Binding Shoes", for a similar example of derangement. From what dialect are the words "bairn", "hinny"? Explain "stravaging", "Auchopecairn."

## THE STONE

"And will you cut a stone for him,
To set above his head?
And will you cut a stone for him —
A stone for him?" she said.

Three days before, a splintered rock
Had struck her lover dead —
Had struck him in the quarry dead,
Where, careless of the warning call,
He loitered, while the shot was fired —
A lively stripling, brave and tall,
And sure of all his heart desired. . . .
A flash, a shock,
A rumbling fall . . .
And, broken 'neath the broken rock,
A lifeless heap, with face of clay;
And still as any stone he lay,
With eyes that saw the end of all.

I went to break the news to her;
And I could hear my own heart beat
With dread of what my lips might say.
But some poor fool had sped before;
And flinging wide her father's door,
Had blurted out the news to her,
Had struck her lover dead for her,
Had struck the girl's heart dead in her,
Had struck life, lifeless, at a word,
And dropped it at her feet:

Then hurried on his witless way,
Scarce knowing she had heard.

And when I came, she stood, alone,
A woman, turned to stone:
And, though no word at all she said,
I knew that all was known.

Because her heart was dead,
She did not sigh nor moan,
His mother wept:
She could not weep.
Her lover slept:
She could not sleep.
Three days, three nights,
She did not stir:
Three days, three nights,
Were one to her,
Who never closed her eyes
From sunset to sunrise,
From dawn to evenfall:
Her tearless, staring eyes,
That seeing naught, saw all.

The fourth night when I came from work,
I found her at my door.
"And will you cut a stone for him?"
She said and spoke no more;
But followed me, as I went in,
And sank upon a chair;
And fixed her grey eyes on my face,
With still, unseeing stare.
And, as she waited patiently,
I could not bear to feel

Those still, grey eyes that followed me,
Those eyes that plucked the heart from me,
Those eyes that sucked the breath from me
And curdled the warm blood in me,
Those eyes that cut me to the bone,
And pierced my marrow like cold steel.

And so I rose, and sought a stone ;
And cut it, smooth and square :
And, as I worked, she sat and watched,
Beside me, in her chair.
Night after night, by candle-light,
I cut her lover's name :
Night after night, so still and white,
And like a ghost she came ;
And sat beside me in her chair ;
And watched with eyes aflame.

She eyed each stroke ;
And hardly stirred :
She never spoke
A single word :
And not a sound or murmur broke
The quiet, save the mallet-stroke.
With still eyes ever on my hands,
With eyes that seemed to burn my hands,
My wincing, overwearied hands,
She watched, with bloodless lips apart,
And silent, indrawn breath :
And every stroke my chisel cut,
Death cut still deeper in her heart :
The two of us were chiseling,
Together, I and death.

And when at length the job was done,
And I had laid the mallet by,

As if, at last, her peace were won,
She breathed his name, and with a sigh,
Passed slowly through the open door:
And never crossed my threshold more.

Next night I laboured late, alone,
To cut her name upon the stone.

Reprinted from "Fires", by Wilfred Wilson Gibson. By special arrangement with The Macmillan Company, Publishers.

### NOTES AND QUESTIONS ON "THE STONE"

*Stanza 1.*   The abruptness of the beginning and the repetition of a part of the first line in the last are characteristic of the old ballad form in which the poem is written.

*Stanza 2.*   What made the lad's death so tragic?   The skillful use of contrast brings this out.

*Stanza 3.*   Here we find the first instance of the repetition of the same words at the beginning and end of successive lines, a device used effectively in several stanzas.   To what does "struck life, lifeless", line 9, owe its force?   Why does the poet speak of the woman as "turned to stone"?   Is it possible that the title "The Stone" has two meanings?

*Stanza 5.*   Note the difference in the length of the lines here and in the preceding stanzas: can you discover the poet's purpose?

*Stanza 6.*   What peculiarity, noted before, has this stanza?

*Stanza 7.*   Observe the medial rhyme in lines 5 and 7 and, as you read the stanza aloud, listen for the effect.   What figures of speech add force to the stanza?

*Stanza 8.*   What variation in line-length adds vividness?   Find a word used many times in stanza 6 which is repeated many more times in stanza 7 and here; what impression does Mr. Gibson wish you to get from this?

*Stanza 9.*   Observe how the simplicity of the statements adds to the effectiveness.

*Stanza 10.*   Why is this stanza so short?   Bring out the force of "alone" as you read the stanza aloud.

*In General.*   In reading this poem aloud be sure to give the frequent pauses their full value, for they are an important part of the rhythm. You will also find it interesting to trace the varying rhyme-scheme.

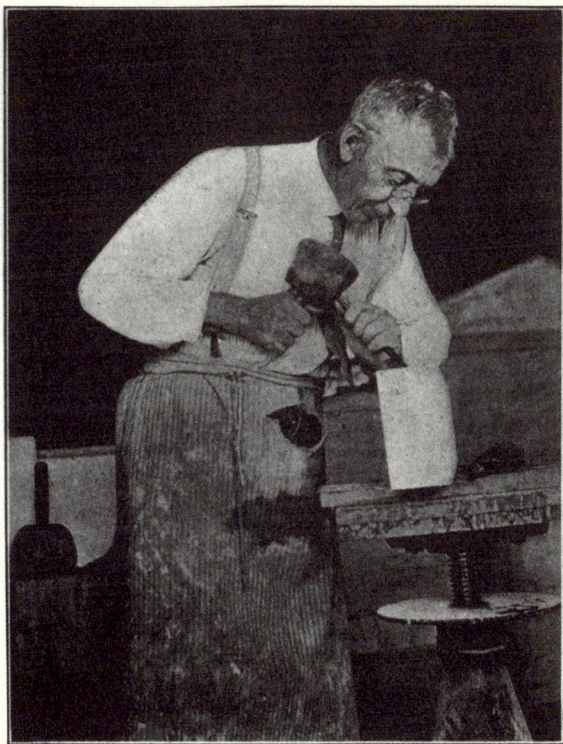

NIGHT AFTER NIGHT, BY CANDLE–LIGHT
I CUT HER LOVER'S NAME

CARL SANDBURG

# CARL SANDBURG

In the "seventies" two worthy persons, the man having had but three months of schooling and the woman two years, left Sweden and came to Galesburg, Illinois. Here the man obtained work as a black-smith in a railroad shop, but there were so many other men by the name of August Johnson in the same shop that the family name was changed to Sandburg. In 1878 a son was born, to whom the name of Carl was given.

All through his boyhood and early manhood Carl Sandburg was forced to work his way almost unaided. Leaving school at the age of thirteen, he first drove a milk wagon, next worked in a barber shop, then shifted scenery in a theatre, drove a truck in a brick yard and molded clay in a pottery shop.

At seventeen Carl started for the West, where he washed dishes in a Denver hotel, threshed wheat in Kansas, and worked on a construction camp. Homesick, he returned to Galesburg, but the Spanish War broke out and he joined the first company to set foot in Porto Rico. At the close of the war he possessed the largest amount of money he had ever had, one hundred dollars, so he entered Lombard College at Galesburg. While he was paying his way through by ringing the college bell and doing janitor work in the gymnasium, his literary ambition was awakened and he began to write for the college paper, of which he soon became editor. This work, and that which he did as college correspondent for a newspaper, paved the way for editorial work, which he did later for several prominent papers. He is now on the editorial staff of the *Chicago Daily News* and has written many poems brimming with the spirit of America, especially the West. His book "The Prairie Years", a biography of Lincoln, is a notable contribution.

Carl Sandburg cares little for the ways of society and is careless in his personal appearance, but he has a voice like a 'cello, so beautiful that people who listen to his reading of his poems are enraptured. His work varies in quality from the merest doggerel to thoughts of surpassing beauty and strength.


## GRASS

Pile them high at Austerlitz and Waterloo.
Shovel them under and let me work —
    I am the grass; I cover all.

And pile them high at Gettysburg
And pile them high at Ypres and Verdun.

234        CONTEMPORARY VERSE

Shovel them under and let me work.
Two years, ten years, and passengers ask the conductor:
    What place is this?
    Where are we now?

    I am the grass.
    Let me work.

NOTES AND QUESTIONS ON "GRASS"

Austerlitz, a small town famous for a great victory by Napoleon;
Waterloo, the place where he met his last, crushing defeat.   What does
Sandburg accomplish by naming the two in the same line?   "Shovel
them under" is literally true; do you like its stark brutality of statement?   Why is line 3 so effective?   What is shown by the questions asked the conductor?   Why is this a good method?   As you
read the poem aloud, notice the quiet whispering of the lines.   Of
what is it expressive?


PRAYERS OF STEEL

Lay me on an anvil, O God.
Beat me and hammer me into a crowbar.
Let me pry loose old walls;
Let me lift and loosen old foundations.

Lay me on an anvil, O God.
Beat me and hammer me into a steel spike.
Drive me into the girders that hold a skyscraper together.
Take red-hot rivets and fasten me into the central girders.
Let me be the great nail holding a skyscraper through blue
    nights into white stars.

NOTES AND QUESTIONS ON "PRAYERS OF STEEL"

Stanza 1.   The first half of the poem voices the prayer of steel to
be made into an instrument to destroy the old in order to make way
for the new; is that what usually happens in a city?

*Stanza 2.* Now the great skyscraper is in the process of construction. Why does the steel wish to be a nail in the *central* girder? Note the beauty of "through blue nights", etc. How is the height of the skyscraper suggested?

Have you ever stood before a great steel building in process of erection and felt a thrill of admiration at its majesty and the wonder of its construction? Is steel then a proper subject for a poem?

## SMOKE AND STEEL

Smoke of the fields in spring is one,
Smoke of the leaves in autumn another.
Smoke of a steel-mill roof or a battleship funnel,
They all go up in a line with a smokestack,
Or they twist . . . in the slow twist . . . of the wind.

If the north wind comes they run to the south.
If the west wind comes they run to the east.
    By this sign
    all smokes
    know each other.
Smoke of the fields in spring and leaves in autumn,
Smoke of the finished steel, chilled and blue,
By the oath of work they swear: "I know you."

Hunted and hissed from the center
Deep down long ago when God made us over,
Deep down are the cinders we came from —
You and I and our heads of smoke.

    \*   \*   \*   \*   \*   \*   \*

Some of the smokes God dropped on the job
Cross on the sky and count our years
And sing in the secrets of our numbers;
Sing their dawns and sing their evenings,

Sing an old log-fire song :
    You may put the damper up,
    You may put the damper down,
    The smoke goes up the chimney just the same.

Smoke of a city sunset skyline,
Smoke of a country dusk horizon —
    They cross on the sky and count our years.

        *   *   *   *   *   *   *

    A bar of steel — it is only
Smoke at the heart of it, smoke and the blood of a man,
A runner of fire ran in it, ran out, ran somewhere else,
And left — smoke and the blood of a man
And the finished steel, chilled and blue.

So fire runs in, runs out, runs somewhere else again,
And the bar of steel is a gun, a wheel, a nail, a shovel,
A rudder under the sea, a steering-gear in the sky ;
And always dark in the heart and through it,
    Smoke and the blood of a man.
Pittsburg, Youngstown, Gary — they make their steel with
    men.

In the blood of men and the ink of chimneys
The smoke nights write their oaths :
Smoke into steel and blood into steel ;
Homestead, Braddock, Birmingham, they make their steel
    with men.
Smoke and blood is the mix of steel.

    The birdmen drone
    in the blue ; it is steel
    a motor sings and zooms.

        *   *   *   *   *   *   *

Steel barb-wire around The Works.
Steel guns in the holsters of the guards at the gates of The
    Works.

Steel ore-boats bring the loads clawed from the earth by
steel, lifted and lugged by arms of steel, sung on its
way by the clanking clam-shells.
The runners now, the handlers now, are steel; they dig
and clutch and haul; they hoist their automatic
knuckles from job to job; they are steel making steel.
Fire and dust and air fight in the furnaces; the pour is
timed, the billets wriggle; the clinkers are dumped:
Liners on the sea, skyscrapers on the land; diving steel
in the sea, climbing steel in the sky.

       \*   \*   \*   \*   \*   \*   \*

Luck moons come and go:
Five men swim in a pot of red steel.
Their bones are kneaded into the bread of steel:
Their bones are knocked into coils and anvils
And the sucking plungers of sea-fighting turbines.
Look for them in the woven frame of the wireless station.
So ghosts hide in steel like heavy-armed men in mirrors.
Peepers, skulkers — they shadow-dance in laughing tombs.
They are always there and they never answer.

   They laugh at the cost.
   They lift the birdmen into the blue.
   It is steel a motor sings and zooms.

In the subway plugs and drums,
In the slow hydraulic drills, in gumbo or gravel,
Under dynamo shafts in the webs of armature spiders,
They shadow-dance and laugh at the cost.

       \*   \*   \*   \*   \*   \*   \*

Pearl cobwebs in the windy rain,
in only a flicker of wind,
are caught and lost and never known again.

A pool of moonshine comes and waits,
but never waits long: the wind picks up
loose gold like this and is gone.

A bar of steel sleeps and looks slant-eyed
on the pearl cobwebs, the pools of moonshine;
sleeps slant-eyed a million years,
sleeps with a coat of rust, a vest of moths,
a shirt of gathering sod and loam.

The wind never bothers . . . a bar of steel.
The wind picks only . . . pearl cobwebs . . . pools of
moonshine.

From "Smoke and Steel", by Carl Sandburg. Copyright, 1920, by Harcourt, Brace & Co., Inc.

### NOTES AND QUESTIONS ON "SMOKE AND STEEL"

In the first two stanzas Sandburg connects the smokes of different industries by a common oath; what is that oath? In the next stanza man is connected with the smokes by his head of smoke, in other words, by his desire to spend himself in creative work as signified by smoke.

In the next section you find the old log-fire song in the last three lines of the first stanza.

*Section three* again emphasizes the relation of man to industry. How does the poet show the sacrifice of human life in the national industry of steel making? Have you any idea how many lives are lost each year in this and other industries of America? What fine use of onomatopœia do you find here?

*Section four* gives a good summary of the progress made in the use of steel in the last few years.

*Section five.* Note with how few strokes this horrible picture of the death of the five men is given; what words make it so vivid? Does Sandburg believe the results justify the sacrifice?

The last section contains a very strong contrast. Why was the cobweb used in this contrast? Why is it called "loose gold"?

In general note the slow graceful cadences of the poem in exact imitation of the motion of a column of smoke. Have you ever noticed the beauty of the curves of smoke? How do you know Sandburg has?

VACHEL LINDSAY

# VACHEL LINDSAY

Cymbalist, prophet, priest, wandering minstrel, maker of "fool pictures", prohibitionist, "movie" enthusiast, all these rôles combined to make Nicholas Vachel Lindsay one of the most interesting men in literature of his day. Nicholas has been omitted in his pen-name and Vachel rhymes with Rachel. If this remarkable young American could have chosen his birth-place it would, doubtless, have been the very spot which fate chose for him, namely, Springfield, Illinois, hallowed by the crowding memories of Abraham Lincoln.

Three years at Hiram College, Ohio, and five in art schools in Chi-

cago and New York, fitted him for his life work. To prove that a
wandering minstrel could earn his bed and board even in prosaic
and commercial America of the Twentieth Century, he tramped over
a greater part of the United States with no money in his pockets, only
his poems printed in pamphlet form, which he exchanged for food
and lodging. Read his "A Handy Guide for Beggars" for a humorous
account of these tramps. Everywhere he preached his gospel of
beauty, the text of which is, "Bad public taste is mob law; good
public taste is democracy."

Ever after he was a boy Vachel Lindsay made pictures, pictures
which were as interesting and as unlike any others as were his poems,
and his time was divided between drawing and the writing of poetry
which is perhaps more distinctly American in its viewpoint and spirit
than that of any other American now writing.

"Why is he called a cymbalist?" you may ask. Because his poems
resound with the loud but musical sounds made by the cymbals, and
yet some are as sweet and tender as the song of a bird. No man
understood better than Vachel Lindsay how to use rhythm, rhyme,
and the Aids to Musical Sounds in Poetry (See Introduction). The
orchestral effect of his poems is unsurpassed. He died suddenly December 5, 1931.

## THE BRONCHO THAT WOULD NOT BE BROKEN

A little colt — broncho, loaned to the farm
To be broken in time without fury or harm,
Yet black crows flew past you, shouting alarm,
Calling "Beware", with lugubrious singing . . .
The butterflies there in the bush were romancing,
The smell of the grass caught your soul in a trance,
So why be a-fearing the spurs and the traces,
O broncho that would not be broken of dancing?

You were born with the pride of the lords great and olden
Who danced, through the ages, in corridors golden.
In all the wide farm-place the person most human.
You spoke out so plainly with squealing and capering,

With whinnying, snorting, contorting and prancing,
As you dodged your pursuers, looking askance,
With Greek-footed figures, and Parthenon paces,
O broncho that would not be broken of dancing.

The grasshoppers cheered. " Keep whirling," they said.
The insolent sparrows called from the shed
"If men will not laugh, make them wish they were dead."
But arch were your thoughts, all malice displacing,
Though the horse-killers came, with snake-whips advancing.
You bantered and cantered away your last chance.
And they scourged you; with Hell in their speech and
    their faces,
O broncho that would not be broken of dancing.

"Nobody cares for you," rattled the crows.
As you dragged the whole reaper next day down the rows.
The three mules held back, yet you danced on your toes.
You pulled like a racer, and kept the mules chasing.
You tangled the harness with bright eyes side-glancing,
While the drunk driver bled you — a pole for a lance —
And the giant mules bit at you — keeping their places.
O broncho that would not be broken of dancing.

In that last afternoon your boyish heart broke.
The hot wind came down like a sledge-hammer stroke.
The blood-sucking flies to a rare feast awoke.
And they searched out your wounds, your death-warrant
    tracing.
And the merciful men, their religion enhancing,
Stopped the red reaper to give you a chance.
Then you died on the prairie, and scorned all disgraces,
O broncho that would not be broken of dancing.

## NOTES AND QUESTIONS ON "THE BRONCHO THAT WOULD NOT BE BROKEN"

This short narrative poem is full of the spirit of youth, which hates discipline, and you will sympathize with the gay little broncho. It is truly American, for it deals with the life on a western ranch, and is based on an incident witnessed by Lindsay in July, 1912.

*Stanza 1.* How is the note of coming disaster sounded in this stanza?

*Stanza 2.* Why is the broncho spoken of as "the person most human"? Find, if you can, a picture of the Parthenon frieze and see what is meant by "With Greek-footed figures and Parthenon paces."

*Stanza 3.* Are sparrows usually "insolent"? What shows that the little broncho was not malicious? Select the fine descriptive words in lines 5, 6, and 7.

*Stanza 4.* Why did they harness him with the mules?

*Stanza 5.* Why "boyish heart"? What good figure of speech in line 2? Note the sarcasm in line 5 and the alliteration in line 6.

*In General.* Rhyme-scheme. Lines 1, 2, and 3 rhyme; the fourth lines in stanzas 3, 4, and 5 rhyme with each other; every fifth line ends in a rhyme of "dancing"; every sixth line ends in a half rhyme of "dancing"; all seventh lines rhyme with each other; and the eighth line is the same throughout. This rhyme-scheme, coupled with the frequent use of short, merry vowel sounds, is admirably adapted to enhance the dancing idea of the poem.

# THE SANTA–FÉ TRAIL

## (A HUMORESQUE)

I asked the old Negro, "What is that bird that sings so well?" He answered: "That is the Rachel-Jane." "Hasn't it another name, — lark, or thrush, or the like?" "No. Jus' Rachel-Jane."

## I

### In which a Racing Auto comes from the East

This is the order of the music of the morning : —

First, from the far East comes but a crooning.

*To be sung delicately, to an improvised tune.*

The crooning turns to a sunrise singing.
Hark to the *calm*-horn, *balm*-horn, *psalm*-
horn
Hark to the *faint*-horn, *quaint*-horn, *saint*-
horn . . .

Hark to the *peace*-horn, *chase*-horn, *race*- *To be sung or*
horn. *read with great*
And the holy veil of the dawn has gone. *speed.*
Swiftly the brazen car comes on.
It burns in the East as the sunrise burns.
I see great flashes where the far trail turns.
Its eyes are lamps like the eyes of dragons.
It drinks gasoline from big red flagons.
Butting through the delicate mists of the
morning,
It comes like lightning, goes past roaring.
It will hail all the wind-mills, taunting,
ringing,
Dodge the cyclones,
Count the milestones,
On through the ranges the prairie-dog
tills —
Scooting past the cattle on the thousand
hills. . . .
Ho for the tear-horn, scare-horn, dare- *To be read or*
horn, *sung in a roll-*
Ho for the *gay*-horn, *bark*-horn, *bay*-horn. *ing bass, with*
*Ho for Kansas, land that restores us* *some delibera-*
*When houses choke us, and great books bore* *tion.*
*us!*
*Sunrise Kansas, harvester's Kansas,*
*A million men have found you before us.*

## II

### In which Many Autos pass Westward

I want live things in their pride to remain. *In an even, de-*
I will not kill one grasshopper vain *liberate, narra-*
Though he eats a hole in my shirt like a *tive manner.*
    door.
I let him out, give him one chance more.
Perhaps while he gnaws my hat in his
    whim,
Grasshopper lyrics occur to him.

I am a tramp by the long trail's border,
Given to squalor, rags and disorder.
I nap and amble and yawn and look,
Write fool-thoughts in my grubby book,
Recite to the children, explore at my ease,
Work when I work, beg when I please,
Give crank-drawings, that make folks
    stare,
To the half-grown boys in the sunset glare,
And get me a place to sleep in the hay
At the end of a live-and-let-live day.

I find in the stubble of the new-cut weeds
A whisper and a feasting, all one needs:
The whisper of the strawberries, white and
    red
Here where the new-cut weeds lie dead.

But I would not walk all alone till I die
Without some life-drunk horns going by.
Up round this apple-earth they come
Blasting the whispers of the morning
    dumb: —

Cars in a plain realistic row.
And fair dreams fade
When the raw horns blow.

On each snapping pennant
A big black name : —
The careering city
Whence each car came.
They tour from Memphis, Atlanta, Savan-
nah,
Tallahassee and Texarkana.                    *Like a train-caller*
They tour from St. Louis, Columbus,          *in a Union*
Manistee,                                     *Depot.*
They tour from Peoria, Davenport, Kan-
kakee.
Cars from Concord, Niagara, Boston,
Cars from Topeka, Emporia, and Austin.
Cars from Chicago, Hannibal, Cairo.
Cars from Alton, Oswego, Toledo.
Cars from Buffalo, Kokomo, Delphi,
Cars from Lodi, Carmi, Laomi.
Ho for Kansas, land that restores us
When houses choke us, and great books
bore us!
While I watch the highroad
And look at the sky,
While I watch the clouds in amazing gran-
deur
Roll their legions without rain
Over the blistering Kansas plain —
While I sit by the milestone
And watch the sky,
The United States
Goes by.

Listen to the iron-horns, ripping, racking. *To be given very*
Listen to the quack-horns, slack and *harshly with a*
    clacking. *snapping ex-*
Way down the road, trilling like a toad, *plosiveness.*
Here comes the *dice*-horn, here comes the
    *vice*-horn,
Here comes the *snarl*-horn, *brawl*-horn,
    *lewd*-horn,
Followed by the *prude*-horn, bleak and
    squeaking : —
(Some of them from Kansas, some of them
    from Kansas.)
Here comes the *hod*-horn, *plod*-horn, *sod*-
    horn,
Nevermore - to - *roam* - horn, *loam* - horn,
    *home*-horn.
(Some of them from Kansas, some of them
    from Kansas.)
    Far away the Rachel-Jane *To be read or*
    Not defeated by the horns *sung, well-nigh*
    Sings amid a hedge of thorns : — *in a whisper.*
    "Love and life,
    Eternal youth —
    Sweet, sweet, sweet, sweet,
    Dew and glory,
    Love and truth,
    Sweet, sweet, sweet, sweet."
While smoke-black freights on the double- *Louder and*
    tracked railroad, *louder, faster*
Driven as though by the foul-fiend's ox- *and faster.*
    goad,
Screaming to the west ocean, screaming
    to the east,
Carry off a harvest, bring back a feast,

Harvesting machinery and harness for the
    beast.
The hand-cars whiz, and rattle on the rails,
The sunlight flashes on the tin dinner-
    pails.
And then, in an instant,         *In a rolling bass,*
Ye modern men,              *with increasing*
Behold the procession once again,   *deliberation.*
Listen to the iron-horns ripping, racking,  *With a snappy*
Listen to the *wise*-horn, *desperate-to-*   *explosiveness.*
    *advise*-horn,
Listen to the *fast*-horn, *kill*-horn, *blast*-
    horn. . . .
    Far away the Rachel-Jane     *To be read or*
    Not defeated by the horns     *sung well-nigh*
    Sings amid a hedge of thorns : —  *in a whisper.*
    " Love and life,
    Eternal youth,
    Sweet, sweet, sweet, sweet,
    Dew and glory,
    Love and truth.
    Sweet, sweet, sweet, sweet."
The mufflers open on a score of cars   *To be brawled in*
With wonderful thunder,         *the beginning*
Crack, crack, crack,           *with a snap-*
Crack-crack, crack-crack,       *ping explosive-*
Crack-crack-crack. . . .        *ness, ending in*
Listen to the gold-horn        *a languorous*
Old-horn . . .               *chant.*
Cold-horn . . .
And all of the tunes, till the night comes
    down
On hay-stack, and ant-hill, and wind-
    bitten town.

Then far in the west, as in the beginning,
Dim in the distance, sweet in retreating,
Hark to the faint-horn, quaint-horn, saint-horn,
Hark to the calm-horn, balm-horn, psalm-horn . . .

*To be sung to exactly the same whispered tune as the first five lines.*

They are hunting the goals that they understand : —
San Francisco and the brown sea-sand.
My goal is the mystery the beggars win.
I am caught in the web the night-winds spin.

*This section beginning sonorously, ending in a languorous whisper.*

The edge of the wheat-ridge speaks to me.
I talk with the leaves of the mulberry tree.
And now I hear, as I sit all alone
In the dusk, by another Santa-Fé stone,
The souls of the tall corn gathering round
And the gay little souls of the grass in the ground.
Listen to the tale the cotton-wood tells.
Listen to the wind-mills, singing o'er the wells.
Listen to the whistling flutes without price
Of myriad prophets out of paradise.
Harken to the wonder
That the night-air carries. . . .
Listen . . . to . . . the . . . whisper . . .
Of . . . the . . . prairie . . . fairies

*To the same whispered tune as the Rachel-Jane song — but very slowly.*

    Singing o'er the fairy plain : —
    "Sweet, sweet, sweet, sweet.
    Love and glory
    Stars and rain,
    Sweet, sweet, sweet, sweet. . . ."

From "The Congo and Other Poems", by Vachel Lindsay. By special permission of The Macmillan Company.

NOTES AND QUESTIONS ON "THE SANTA-FÉ TRAIL"

A humoresque, as defined in the dictionary, "is a musical composition of a humorous or capricious nature", and capricious means changing suddenly without reason. As you study the poem you will see that the word was well chosen.

There are three tunes in this unusual poem; the first the racing automobiles, the second the poet's reverie, and the third the song of the Rachel-Jane. One holiday morning at sunrise, while on a tramp through the Southwest, Lindsay was seated on a milestone of the Santa-Fé Trail, which runs parallel with the double tracks of the Santa-Fé Railroad, watching the thousands of holiday autoists speed past on their way to San Francisco and the beaches. He heard in the distance the song of the little bird, the Rachel-Jane. Mr. Lindsay chants or sings his poems, and the manner in which the different lines are to be rendered is indicated in the notes at the right of the lines.

*Section I* pictures the progress of the first automobile on the Trail from the time it is heard but not seen until it passes the watcher and disappears. What finely chosen words describe the sounds in the distance? Why are the words here combined with "horn" just the right ones? Study the words used to describe the horns throughout the poem to get the force of each one. What vowel and consonant sounds make "And the holy veil of the dawn was gone" so quiet a line? Contrast it with the preceding and the following lines. How do you like the description of the automobile? How is the idea of speed secured here? The prairie dog is a small, barking animal, in no other way like a dog, which burrows in the earth of the western prairies. Kansas, with its great open spaces and miles of wheat fields, "the harvester's Kansas", is just the place to appeal to those who are weary of the limitations of houses and books.

*Section II.* Here begins the second tune, the poet's reverie as he sits and muses beside the Trail. How does this show his love of nature? May there be "grasshopper lyrics"? "I am a tramp", etc., gives an accurate account of how Lindsay spent his time while playing the part of an American minstrel. Note the lively imagination in "the whisper of the strawberries." "But I would not walk all alone", etc., indicates that he is again conscious of the speeding automobiles. Why is "life-drunk horns" a fine expression? What figure of speech in "apple-earth"? Note the contrast in "fair dreams" and "raw horns."

Again the automobiles are racing past. What uses of alliteration help to emphasize the thoughts? Locate as many as possible of the cities named to see from what parts of the nation the cars come.  Note the contrast between the poet watching the "clouds in amazing grandeur" and "The United States" going by.  Who is having the better time?  Explain "trilling like a toad."

With "Far away the Rachel-Jane" begins the third tune.  The short lines with the strong simple language are very fine and the lyrical quality of the rhythm is suited to the theme.

Another sharp contrast, as the "smoke-black freights" of the Santa-Fé Railroad add their screams to the other noises.  What is particularly good in this description?  What lines imitate the sounds described?

Again the automobiles tear past with still more furious, deadly speed.  What is the appropriateness of the term "Ye modern men"?

"Far away", etc., the little bird sings on, unabashed by the turmoil.

"Crack, crack", etc., marks the climax of the tune of the automobiles, which continues but with diminishing force until night comes on and we get the repetition of the song at the beginning but with the words in reversed order;  why?

"They are hunting", etc.;  the motorists are doing what appeals to them, just as the poet is.  "My goal is", etc., begins again the poet's reverie after he has tramped all day and is now seated on another milestone.  What evidence do you find that Lindsay is very close to nature?  Do you believe that the tall corn and the grass have souls?  There are people who do.  Here is another poet who believes in fairies.  Why do they sing the same song as the Rachel-Jane?

Could any one but an American have written this poem ?  As you read it aloud again and again, listen to hear how the lines crash and whiz, "skip and turn somersaults", purr like a motor, and sing like a bird.  The three tunes, one speedy and noisy, the second slow and quiet, and the third lyrical, or singing, in quality, are all fundamentally alike.  What is the prevailing rhyme-scheme and where do you find blank verse?  Notice the effect of making the words combined with "horn" rhyme.  Put into good English your reasons for liking or disliking the poem.

ANGELA MORGAN

# ANGELA MORGAN

Poet, social worker, and prophet of optimism, Angela Morgan was
born at Washington, D. C., received her education in both private
and public schools, and later did special work at Columbia University.
When scarcely more than a girl she began to write for the *Chicago
American* and *Chicago Journal,* and later she contributed to Boston

and New York papers, which work gave her a broad knowledge of
social conditions, for she not only reported the doings of the rich but
visited the police courts, the jails, and the slums. She is always
ready to respond to a social need, and that she is recognized as a
brilliant leader is shown by the fact that she was chosen as one of the
delegates to the First International Congress of Women at the Hague
in the first year of the War. She was elected honor poet of National
Poetry Week, 1930, and awarded the gold emblem.

## WORK

### A Song of Triumph

Work!
Thank God for the might of it,
The ardor, the urge, the delight of it —
Work that springs from the heart's desire,
Setting the brain and the soul on fire —
Oh, what is so good as the heat of it,
And what is so glad as the beat of it,
And what is so kind as the stern command,
Challenging brain and heart and hand?

Work!
Thank God for the pride of it,
For the beautiful, conquering tide of it,
Sweeping the life in its furious flood,
Thrilling the arteries, cleansing the blood,
Mastering stupor and dull despair,
Moving the dreamer to do and dare.
Oh, what is so good as the urge of it,
And what is so glad as the surge of it,
And what is so strong as the summons deep,
Rousing the torpid soul from sleep?

Work!
Thank God for the pace of it,
For the terrible, keen, swift race of it;
Fiery steeds in full control,
Nostrils a-quiver to greet the goal.
Work, the Power that drives behind,
Guiding the purposes, taming the mind,
Holding the runaway wishes back,
Reining the will to one steady track,
Speeding the energies faster, faster,
Triumphing over disaster.
Oh, what is so good as the pain of it,
And what is so great as the gain of it?
And what is so kind as the cruel goad,
Forcing us on through the rugged road?

Work!
Thank God for the swing of it,
For the clamoring, hammering ring of it,
Passion of labor daily hurled
On the mighty anvils of the world.
Oh, what is so fierce as the flame of it?
And what is so huge as the aim of it?
Thundering on through dearth and doubt,
Calling the plan of the Maker out.
Work, the Titan; Work, the friend,
Shaping the earth to a glorious end,
Draining the swamps and blasting the hills,
Doing whatever the Spirit wills —
Rending a continent apart,
To answer the dream of the Master's heart.
Thank God for a world where none may shirk —
Thank God for the splendor of work!

NOTES AND QUESTIONS ON "WORK"

Miss Morgan has a way of her own of combining words and using similar constructions and repetition which gives her poems an individuality easily recognized. As you read see if you enjoy this peculiarity of style.

*Stanza 1.* Lines 4 and 9 tell you the kind of work of which the poet is singing. Does modern industry provide the majority of workers with this kind of work? What lines in this stanza are absolutely alike in structure?

*Stanza 2.* Explain why line 3 is a metaphor. Is line 5 to be interpreted literally? To what device does line 7 owe much of its effectiveness?

*Stanza 3.* To what is work compared in lines 3 to 5? To what in the rest of the stanza? What contradictory words in next to the last line add force?

*Stanza 4.* In what does the metaphor in lines 4 and 5 consist? What lines contain the climax of ideas in regard to work?

*In General.* What similarity of structure do you find in all the stanzas? How much longer than the preceding stanza is each one after the first? This is to heighten the effect of the climax. What peculiarities of rhyme do you find? What repetitions?


# IN SPITE OF WAR

In spite of war, in spite of death,
In spite of all man's sufferings,
Something within me laughs and sings
And I must praise with all my breath.
In spite of war, in spite of hate
Lilacs are blooming at my gate,
Tulips are tripping down the path
In spite of war, in spite of wrath.
"Courage!" the morning-glory saith;
"Rejoice!" the daisy murmureth,
And just to live is so divine
When pansies lift their eyes to mine.

The clouds are romping with the sea,
And flashing waves call back to me
That naught is real but what is fair,
That everywhere and everywhere
A glory liveth through despair.
Though guns may roar and cannon boom,
Roses are born and gardens bloom;
My spirit still may light its flame
At that same torch whence poppies came.
Where morning's altar whitely burns
Lilies may lift their silver urns
In spite of war, in spite of shame.

And in my ear a whispering breath,
"Wake from the nightmare! Look and see
That life is naught but ecstasy
In spite of war, in spite of death!"

NOTES AND QUESTIONS ON "IN SPITE OF WAR"

*Stanza 1.* Why is the repetition of "in spite of war" effective?
From what sort of things does the poet derive courage, as told in this
stanza? How can the tulip be spoken of as "tripping"?
*Stanza 2.* What particularly well-chosen words here? Line 8
shows that the poet's faith is based on something higher than nature.
What is the figure of speech employed here, and what does it add?
What makes the last line so effective?
*Stanza 3.* The very brevity of this stanza gives force to the idea.
How does this method differ from that of "Work"?

# WHEN NATURE WANTS A MAN

When Nature wants to drill a man
And thrill a man,
And skill a man,

When Nature wants to mould a man
To play the noblest part;
When she yearns with all her heart
To create so great and bold a man
That all the world shall praise —
Watch her methods, watch her ways!
How she ruthlessly perfects
Whom she royally elects;
How she hammers him and hurts him
And with mighty blows converts him
Into trial shapes of clay which only Nature understands —
While his tortured heart is crying and he lifts beseeching hands! —
How she bends, but never breaks,
When his good she undertakes. . . .
How she uses whom she chooses
And with every purpose fuses him,
By every art induces him
To try his splendour out —
Nature knows what she's about.

When Nature wants to take a man
And shake a man
And wake a man;
When Nature wants to make a man
To do the Future's will;
When she tries with all her skill
And she yearns with all her soul
To create him large and whole . . .
With what cunning she prepares him!
How she goads and never spares him
How she whets him and she frets him
And in poverty begets him. . . .

How she often disappoints
Whom she sacredly anoints,
With what wisdom she will hide him,
Never minding what betide him
Though his genius sob with slighting and his pride may
    not forget!
Bids him struggle harder yet,
Makes him lonely
So that only
God's high messages shall reach him,
So that she may surely teach him
What the Hierarchy planned.
Though he may not understand
Gives him passions to command —
How remorselessly she spurs him,
With terrific ardour stirs him
When she poignantly prefers him!

When Nature wants to name a man
And fame a man
And tame a man;
When Nature wants to shame a man
To do his heavenly best . . .
When she tries the highest test
That her reckoning may bring —
When she wants a god or king! —
How she reins him and restrains him
So his body scarce contains him
While she fires him
And inspires him!
Keeps him yearning, ever burning for a tantalizing goal —
Lures and lacerates his soul.
Sets a challenge for his spirit,
Draws it higher when he's near it —

Makes a jungle, that he clear it;
Makes a desert, that he fear it
And subdue it if he can —
So doth Nature make a man.
Then, to test his spirit's wrath
Hurls a mountain in his path —
Puts the bitter choice before him
And relentlessly stands o'er him.
"Climb, or perish!" so she says . . .
Watch her purpose, watch her ways!

Nature's plan is wondrous kind
Could we understand her mind . . .
Fools are they who call her blind.
When his feet are torn and bleeding
Yet his spirit mounts unheeding,
All his higher powers speeding
Blazing newer paths and fine;
When the force that is divine
Leaps to challenge every failure and his ardour still is
    sweet
And love and hope are burning in the presence of defeat . . .
Lo, the crisis! Lo, the shout
That must call the leader out.
When the people need salvation
Doth he come to lead the nation . . .
Then doth Nature show her plan
When the world has found — a man!

NOTES AND QUESTIONS ON "WHEN NATURE WANTS A MAN"

It will help you to grasp the idea of this poem if you think of some great man who has been ready to answer the call of the nation for leadership in some crisis.

*Stanza 1.* What about the beginning of the poem immediately attracts your attention? What method does Nature use to accomplish the end set forth by the verbs in the first four lines?

*Stanza 2.* Note the verbs in the first lines of this stanza and compare them with those in stanza 1. What method does Nature now pursue? How can making the man lonely cause God's message to reach him? Since "hierarchy" means the supreme power in spiritual affairs, why is it a fine word for the idea? Note the alliteration in the last line.

*Stanza 3.* What does Nature know is absolutely necessary in order to make a god or king? What then is her method described in this stanza? Why is the direct command in the next to the last line so forceful?

*Stanza 4.* Why is the rhyme-scheme of this stanza so different from that of the others? What was the crisis which called out the heroic man whom you have chosen to keep in mind? The last four lines form the conclusion of the thought; why are they so fine for that purpose?

*In General.* Compare the number of two- and three-syllable words in this poem with those of most poems in this book. Is there anything in the theme of the poem which accounts for this difference? What peculiarities of Miss Morgan's style do you find here?

## SONG OF THE NEW WORLD

I sing the song of a new Dawn waking,
A new wind shaking
　　The children of men.
I say that the hearts that are nigh to breaking
　　Shall leap with gladness and live again.
Over the world of woe appalling,
　　Wild and sweet as a bugle cry,
Sudden I hear a new voice calling —
　　"Beauty is nigh!"
Beauty is nigh! Let the world believe it.
　　Love has covered the fields of dead.
Healing is here! Let the earth receive it,
　　Greeting the Dawn with lifted head.

I sing the song of the sin forgiven,
  The deed forgotten, the wrong undone.
Lo, in the East, where the dark is riven,
  Shines the rim of the rising sun.
Healing is here!  O brother, sing it!
  Laugh, O heart, that has grieved so long.
Love will gather your woe and fling it
  Over the world in waves of song.
Hearken, mothers, and hear them coming —
  Heralds crying the day at hand.
Faint and far as the sound of drumming,
  Hear their summons across the land.
Look, O fathers!  Your eyes are holden —
  Armies throng where the dead have lain.
Fiery steeds and chariots golden —
  Gone is the dream of soldiers slain.
Sing, O sing of a new world waking,
  Sing of creation just begun.
Glad is the earth when morn is breaking —
  Man is facing the rising sun!

#### NOTES AND QUESTIONS ON "SONG OF THE NEW WORLD"

Miss Morgan is always optimistic; she is sure that the great ideal for which the World War was fought is soon to be a reality. Why did she begin "Dawn" with a capital? "The hearts that are nigh to breaking" are those who lost dear ones in that war. Explain what you think "Beauty" means, as used here. What is meant by "the sin", "the deed", etc.? What does the metaphor of the rising sun add? Put in your own words the thought of the last line. The increasing sense of world responsibility on the part of large numbers of individuals in all civilized nations is evidence that the poet is right. What other poems that you have read express the same idea?

*Courtesy Frederick A. Stokes Company.*

ALFRED NOYES

# ALFRED NOYES

Alfred Noyes, one of the most melodious poets living, was born in Staffordshire, England, in 1880, and is an Oxford man, having taken his degree at Exeter College, where he was distinguished chiefly for his interest in rowing. He was a member of the college eight for three years and is said still to keep up his practice on the river.  His study contains, besides many books, a couple of oars on one wall, photographs of college teams, and other athletic trophies.

His first poem was published while he was still at college and he then determined to earn his living by writing poetry, so that it is not surprising to find that his first book, "The Loom of the Years", was published when he was but twenty-two years old.

He married an American girl, Miss Garnett Daniels, daughter of a Civil War veteran, who was subsequently sent to England as American consul at one of the important coastwise ports.  Their home is at Rottingdean, a tiny town near the English Channel, inhabited chiefly by fishermen and shepherds, though both Sir Edward Burne-Jones, the great painter, and Rudyard Kipling, his nephew, once lived there. Mr. Noyes was at one time a professor at Princeton University and has made several tours of the United States, lecturing on literary subjects and reading his own poems.  Though devoted to peace, he felt the justice of England's stand during the war and served for a time in the British Foreign Office.

## THE  HIGHWAYMAN

### Part One

The wind was a torrent of darkness among the gusty trees,
The moon was a ghostly galleon tossed upon cloudy seas,
The road was a ribbon of moonlight over the purple moor,
And the highwayman came riding —
          Riding — riding —
The highwayman came riding, up to the old inn-door.

He'd a French cocked-hat on his forehead, a bunch of lace
          at his chin,
A coat of the claret velvet, and breeches of brown doe-skin;
They fitted with never a wrinkle:  his boots were up to the
          thigh!
And he rode with a jewelled twinkle,
          His pistol butts a-twinkle,
His rapier hilt a-twinkle, under the jewelled sky.

Over the cobbles he clattered and clashed in the dark inn-
    yard,
And he tapped with his whip on the shutters, but all was
    locked and barred;
He whistled a tune to the window, and who should be waiting
    there
But the landlord's black-eyed daughter,
      Bess, the landlord's daughter,
Plaiting a dark red love-knot into her long black hair.

And dark in the dark old inn-yard a stable-wicket creaked
Where Tim the ostler listened; his face was white and
    peaked;

His eyes were hollows of madness, his hair like mouldy hay,
But he loved the landlord's daughter,
      The landlord's red-lipped daughter,
Dumb as a dog he listened, and he heard the robber say —

'One kiss, my bonny sweetheart, I'm after a prize to-night,
But I shall be back with the yellow gold before the morning
    light;
Yet, if they press me sharply, and harry me through the day,
Then look for me by moonlight,
      Watch for me by moonlight,
I'll come to thee by moonlight, though hell should bar the
    way.'

He rose upright in the stirrups; he scarce could reach her
    hand,
But she loosened her hair i' the casement! His face burnt
    like a brand
As the black cascade of perfume came tumbling over his
    breast;

And he kissed its waves in the moonlight,
       (Oh, sweet black waves in the moonlight!)
Then he tugged at his rein in the moonlight, and galloped
    away to the West.

## PART TWO

He did not come in the dawning; he did not come at noon;
And out o' the tawny sunset, before the rise o' the moon,
When the road was a gipsy's ribbon, looping the purple
    moor,
A red-coat troop came marching —
       Marching — marching —
King George's men came marching, up to the old inn-door.

They said no word to the landlord, they drank his ale
    instead,
But they gagged his daughter and bound her to the foot of
    her narrow bed;
Two of them knelt at her casement, with muskets at their
    side!
There was death at every window;
       And hell at one dark window;
For Bess could see, through her casement, the road that *he*
    would ride.

They had tied her up to attention, with many a sniggering
    jest;
They had bound a musket beside her, with the barrel
    beneath her breast!
'Now keep good watch!' and they kissed her.  She heard
    the dead man say —
*Look for me by moonlight;*
  *Watch for me by moonlight;*
*I'll come to thee by moonlight, though hell should bar the way!*

She twisted her hands behind her; but all the knots held
    good!
She writhed her hands till her fingers were wet with sweat
    or blood!
They stretched and strained in the darkness, and the hours
    crawled by like years,
Till, now, on the stroke of midnight,
        Cold, on the stroke of midnight,
The tip of one finger touched it! The trigger at least was
    hers!

The tip of one finger touched it; she strove no more for
    the rest!
Up, she stood up to attention, with the barrel beneath her
    breast,
She would not risk their hearing: she would not strive
    again;
For the road lay bare in the moonlight;
        Blank and bare in the moonlight;
And the blood in her veins in the moonlight throbbed to
    her love's refrain.

*Tlot-tlot; tlot-tlot!* Had they heard it? The horse-hoofs
    ringing clear;
*Tlot-tlot, tlot-tlot,* in the distance? Were they deaf that
    they did not hear?
Down the ribbon of moonlight, over the brow of the hill,
The highwayman came riding,
        Riding, riding!
The red-coats looked to their priming! She stood up,
    straight and still!

*Tlot-tlot,* in the frosty silence! *Tlot-tlot,* in the echoing
    night!
Nearer he came and nearer! Her face was like a light!

Her eyes grew wide for a moment; she drew one last deep
    breath,
Then her finger moved in the moonlight,
      Her musket shattered the moonlight,
Shattered her breast in the moonlight and warned him —
    with her death.

He turned; he spurred to the Westward; he did not know
    who stood
Bowed, with her head o'er the musket, drenched with her
    own red blood!
Not till the dawn he heard it, and slowly blanched to hear
How Bess, the landlord's daughter,
      The landlord's black-eyed daughter,
Had watched for her love in the moonlight, and died in the
    darkness there.

Back — he spurred like a madman, shrieking a curse to the
    sky,
With the white road smoking behind him, and his rapier
    brandished high!
Blood-red were his spurs i' the golden noon; wine-red was
    his velvet coat;
When they shot him down on the highway,
      Down like a dog on the highway,
And he lay in his blood on the highway, with the bunch
    of lace at his throat.
       *     *     *     *     *     *     *

*And still of a winter's night, they say, when the wind is in the*
    *trees,*
*When the moon is a ghostly galleon tossed upon cloudy seas,*
*When the road is a ribbon of moonlight over the purple moor,*
*A highwayman comes riding —*
    *Riding — riding —*
*A highwayman comes riding — up to the old inn-door.*

*Over the cobbles he clatters and clangs in the dark inn-yard;*
*And he taps with his whip on the shutters, but all is locked and*
*    barred;*
*He whistles a tune to the window, and who should be waiting*
*    there*
*But the landlord's black-eyed daughter,*
*        Bess, the landlord's daughter,*
*Plaiting a dark red love-knot into her long black hair.*

### NOTES AND QUESTIONS ON "THE HIGHWAYMAN"

### Part One

*Stanza 1.*   Observe that the first three lines are made up of three metaphors containing words of exactly the same length.   Note, also, the repetition in the next two lines.   What impression of the kind of story to follow do you get from this stanza?

*Stanza 2.*   Try to visualize the picture of the highwayman as Noyes describes him.   Note again the repetition.

*Stanza 3.*   What kind of words are used in the first line, and why? Notice how the double adjectives in "dark red love-knot" and "long black hair" make that line prominent.

*Stanza 4.*   What do you think was Noyes's reason for introducing Tim the ostler here and beginning the stanza as he does?   What do the figures of speech in the third and the fifth lines add?

*Stanza 5.*   Is there any special word in this stanza that Noyes wishes you to remember?

### Part Two

*Stanza 1.*   Compare this stanza with the first of Part One.   What color do you think a "gipsy's ribbon" would be?   What other colors are used in this stanza?

*Stanza 2.*   How does this stanza heighten the sense of impending disaster?

*Stanza 3.*   What mistake did the red-coats make?

*Stanza 4.*   In the old Scotch ballads the word "blood" is often pronounced to rhyme with "good", as it is here.

*Stanza 5.*   "Again", here pronounced to rhyme with "refrain" in line 5.   How is the road described in this stanza?

*Stanza 6.* "Tlot-tlot", a word made for the occasion, is an excellent example of onomatopœia. What skillful use of the interrogative form do you find here? Of repetition?

*Stanza 7.* What do the words used in the first line imitate? Why the repetition of "moonlight" and "shattered"?

*Stanza 8.* Why the short clauses in the first line?

*Stanza 9.* Notice the contrast between the appearance of the road, the velvet coat and the rapier, now and when we first saw them. Find skillful use of repetition in this stanza. The reference to the "bunch of lace at his throat" is dramatic. Why?

\*     \*     \*     \*     \*     \*     \*     \*     \*

Why are almost the exact words of stanzas 1 and 3 repeated here? What do you think Tim the ostler had to do with the fate of the highwayman? Would this make a good "movie"? Does it fulfill the requirements of a ballad as defined in this book?

# FORTY SINGING SEAMEN

"In our lands be Beeres and Lyons of dyvers colours as ye redd, grene, black, and white. And in our land be also unicornes and these Unicornes slee many Lyons. . . . Also there dare no man make a lye in our lande, for if he dyde he sholde incontynent be sleyn." — *Mediæval Epistle of Pope Prester John.*

Across the seas of Wonderland to Mogadore we plodded,
  Forty singing seamen in an old black barque,
And we landed in the twilight where a Polyphemus nodded
  With his battered moon-eye winking red and yellow
      through the dark!
    For his eye was growing mellow,
    Rich and ripe and red and yellow,
  As was time, since old Ulysses made him bellow in the
      dark!
*Cho.* — Since Ulysses bunged his eye up with a pine-torch
    in the dark!

*Were* they mountains in the gloaming or the giant's ugly
    shoulders
  Just beneath the rolling eyeball, with its bleared and
    vinous glow,
Red and yellow o'er the purple of the pines among the
    boulders
  And the shaggy horror brooding on the sullen slopes
    below,
    *Were* they pines among the boulders
    Or the hair upon his shoulders?
  We were simple singing seamen, so of course we didn't
    know,
*Cho.* — We were simple singing seamen, so of course we
    couldn't know.

But we crossed a plain of poppies, and we came upon a
    fountain
  Not of water, but of jewels, like a spray of leaping fire;
And behind it, in an emerald glade, beneath a golden moun-
    tain
  There stood a crystal palace, for a sailor to admire;
    For a troop of ghosts came round us,
    Which with leaves of bay they crowned us,
  Then with grog they well nigh drowned us, to the depth
    of our desire!
*Cho.* — And 'twas very friendly of them, as a sailor can
    admire!

There was music all about us, we were growing quite for-
    getful
  We were only singing seamen from the dirt of London-
    town,
Though the nectar that we swallowed seemed to vanish
    half regretful

As if we wasn't good enough to take such vittles down,
   When we saw a sudden figure,
     Tall and black as any nigger,
  Like the devil — only bigger — drawing near us with a
    frown!
*Cho.* — Like the devil — but much bigger — and he wore a
    golden crown!


And "What's all this?" he growls at us! With dignity
   we chaunted,
  "Forty singing seamen, sir, as won't be put upon!"
"What? Englishmen?" he cries, "Well, if ye don't mind
   being haunted,
   Faith you're welcome to my palace; I'm the famous
    Prester John!
    Will ye walk into my palace?
    I don't bear 'ee any malice!
   One and all ye shall be welcome in the halls of Prester
    John!"
*Cho.* — So we walked into the palace and the halls of
    Prester John!


Now the door was one great diamond and the hall a hollow
   ruby —
  Big as Beachy Head, my lads, nay bigger by a half!
And I see the mate wi' mouth agape, a-staring like a booby,
  And the skipper close behind him, with his tongue out
   like a calf!
   Now the way to take it rightly
   Was to walk along politely
Just as if you didn't notice — so I couldn't help but laugh!
*Cho.* — For they both forgot their manners and the crew
   was bound to laugh!

But he took us through his palace and, my lads, as I'm a
    sinner,
  We walked into an opal like a sunset-coloured cloud —
"My dining-room," he says, and quick as light we saw a
    dinner
    Spread before us by the fingers of a hidden fairy crowd;
      And the skipper, swaying gently
      After dinner, murmurs faintly,
    "I looks to-wards you, Prester John, you've done us very
      proud!"
*Cho.* — And we drank his health with honours, for he *done*
    us *very* proud!

Then he walks us to his garden where we sees a feathered
    demon
  Very splendid and important on a sort of spicy tree!
"That's the Phoenix," whispers Prester, "which all eddi-
    cated seamen
    Knows the only one existent, and *he's* waiting for to flee!
      When his hundred years expire
      Then he'll set hisself afire
    And another from his ashes rise most beautiful to see!"
*Cho.* — With wings of rose and emerald most beautiful to
    see!

Then he says, "In yonder forest there's a little silver river,
  And whosoever drinks of it, his youth shall never die!
The centuries go by, but Prester John endures forever
    With his music in the mountains and his magic on the sky!
      While *your* hearts are growing colder,
      While your world is growing older,
    There's a magic in the distance, where the sea-line
    meets the sky."
*Cho.* — It shall call to singing seamen till the fount o' song
    is dry!

So we thought we'd up and seek it, but the forest fair de-
fied us, —
First a crimson leopard laughs at us most horrible to
see,
Then a sea-green lion came and sniffed and licked his chops
and eyed us,
While a red and yellow unicorn was dancing round a
tree!
*We* was trying to look thinner
Which was hard, because our dinner
Must ha' made us very tempting to a cat o' high degree!
*Cho.* — Must ha' made us very tempting to the whole
menarjeree!

So we scuttled from that forest and across the poppy
meadows
Where the awful shaggy horror brooded o'er us in the
dark!
And we pushes out from shore again a-jumping at our
shadows
And pulls away most joyful to the old black barque!
And home again we plodded
While the Polyphemus nodded
With his battered moon-eye winking red and yellow
through the dark!
*Cho.* — Oh, the moon above the mountains, red and yellow
through the dark!

Across the seas of Wonderland to London-town we blun-
dered,
Forty singing seamen as was puzzled for to know
If the vision that we saw was caused by — here again we
pondered —
A tipple in a vision forty thousand years ago.

Could the grog we *dreamt* we swallowed
Make us *dream* of all that followed?
We were only simple seamen, so of course we didn't know!
*Cho.* — We were simple singing seamen, so of course we
couldn't know!

### NOTES AND QUESTIONS ON "FORTY SINGING SEAMEN"

Prester John was a fabulous Christian monarch believed to have
lived in the twelfth century.  Sir John Mandeville says: An emperor
of India who was a Christian went into a church in Egypt on the
Saturday of Whitsun week where a bishop was ordaining priests.
"And he beheld and listened the service fulle tentyfly."  He then
said that he would no longer be called emperor but priest of the Church
and that he would have the name of the first priest of the church who
was John, and so he has ever since been called Prester (priest) John.
— *Century Dictionary.*

*Stanza 1.*  The first line strikes the keynote of weirdness and fancy
which are to prevail throughout the whole poem.  Mogadore, a seaport
in Morocco which is important commercially.  Why is "plodded"
an excellent word to use here?  Polyphemus, the Cyclops, had only
one eye, which was situated in the middle of his forehead.  It was the
gentle custom of Polyphemus to devour the unfortunate seamen who
were shipwrecked on his island, but Ulysses succeeded in drugging
him and then bored out his eye with a red-hot pine torch.  The
alliteration in "rich and ripe and red" is noteworthy.

*Stanza 2.*  Note the repetition of "red and yellow" and the alliteration in line 4 and in the chorus.

*Stanza 3.*  What does the simile in line 2 add?  "Admire" here
means "wonder at"; does it mean the same in the chorus?

*Stanza 4.*  Note how the expression "sailors from the dirt of London-town" brings out the contrast between the sailors and the brilliant scene.  How must "figure" be pronounced to preserve the
rhyme?

*Stanza 5.*  Note the humor of the conversation in this stanza.

*Stanza 6.*  "Beachy Head" is a chalk headland on the coast of
Sussex, projecting into the English Channel, and is 575 feet high.

*Stanza 7.* Select the words and expressions that make this a beautiful stanza in spite of its humor.

*Stanza 8.* "Demon", spirit. The Phoenix in ancient Oriental mythology was a wonderful bird of great beauty, which after living five or six hundred years in the Arabian wilderness, the only one of its kind, built for itself a funeral pile of spices and aromatic gums, lighted the pile by the fanning of its wings, and was burned upon it, but from its ashes revived in the freshness of youth. Note the color words in the chorus.

*Stanza 9.* What human longing as old as the world itself is expressed here?

*Stanza 10.* This is the climax of the story; how has Noyes made it dramatic?

*Stanza 11.* Why is "scuttled" a good word to describe their flight? What is the purpose of the similarity between this stanza and the first?

*Stanza 12.* What very expressive word do you find in the first line? "Tipple", an intoxicating drink. Why does Noyes leave the question of the sailors unanswered?

*In General.* This is considered one of the best of modern ballads, having the singing quality which so distinguishes all true ballads. The imagery, also, is admirable, and the story rich and rollicking. The usual ballad stanza is described in the notes on "Father Gilligan"; consult these and see how this poem differs. In stanzas 1, 3, 4, and 5 notice that there is a word within the last line rhyming with the last word of the two preceding lines. The chorus, which is better suited to the Forty Singing Seamen, takes the place of the usual refrain of the old ballads. The long lines with a marked pause halfway are admirably adapted to the spirit of the story.

## THE ELFIN ARTIST

In a glade of an elfin forest
　　When Sussex was Eden-new,
I came on an elvish painter
　　And watched as his picture grew.
A harebell nodded beside him.
　　He dipt his brush in the dew.

And it might be the wild thyme about him
   That shone in that dark strange ring;
But his brushes were bees' antennae,
   His knife was a wasp's blue sting;
And his gorgeous exquisite palette
   Was a butterfly's fan-shaped wing.

And he mingled its powdery colours
   And painted the lights that pass,
On a delicate cobweb canvas
   That gleamed like a magic glass,
And bloomed like a banner of elf-land,
   Between two stalks of grass;

Till it shone like an angel's feather
   With sky-born opal and rose,
And gold from the foot of the rainbow,
   And colours that no man knows;
And I laughed in the sweet May weather,
   Because of the themes he chose.

For he painted the things that matter,
   The tints that we all pass by,
Like the little blue wreaths of incense
   That the wild thyme breathes to the sky;
Or the first white bud of the hawthorn,
   And the light in a blackbird's eye;

And the shadows on soft white cloud-peaks
   That carolling skylarks throw,
Dark dots on the slumbering splendours
   That under the wild wings flow,
Wee shadows like violets trembling
   On the unseen breasts of snow;

With petals too lovely for colour
That shake to the rapturous wings,
And grow as the bird draws near them,
And die as he mounts and sings; —
Ah! only those exquisite brushes
Could paint these marvellous things.

From "Elfin Artist", by Alfred Noyes. Copyright, Frederick A. Stokes Company.

### NOTES AND QUESTIONS ON "THE ELFIN ARTIST"

This poem shows that Alfred Noyes, like Walter de la Mare and Richard Le Gallienne, has kept the vivid imagination of a child, and has combined with it the poet's keen observation of nature. What is the rhyme-scheme? Note how the alternating rhymed and unrhymed lines bring out the idea and add to the music of the poem. Why are the simple words used best suited to the ideas?

*Stanza 1.* Why does the poet use "elfin" in line 1 and "elvish" in line 3? Is there any difference in meaning? "Sussex", a county in the south of England. "Eden-new", perfect in its fresh beauty as the Garden of Eden was before sin entered.

*Stanza 2.* Is the bee's sting blue? Why would the butterfly's wing make a good palette?

*Stanza 3.* Have you ever seen colors reflected in a cobweb in the morning? What makes the last three lines of this stanza and the first three of the next particularly good?

*Stanza 4.* Have you ever tried to find the pot of gold at the foot of the rainbow? To whom does "he" in the last line refer?

*Stanza 5.* This enumerates the themes of the elfin artist; study each one separately and see how many of these you have ever thought of. Have you ever seen "the light in a blackbird's eye"?

*Stanzas 6 and 7* continue the list of themes. "Slumbering splendours" describes the white cloud peaks. Note the alliteration and the liquid "l"s in lines 3 and 4.

*Stanza 7.* The first four lines describe the violets of stanza 6. What is the purpose of the last two lines? What other poems that relate to the skylark do you know?

# JOYCE KILMER

Joyce Kilmer, who was killed while bravely doing his duty in the World War, was one of the most promising of our American poets as well as a most charming gentleman. Full of life and enthusiasm, he was greatly loved and admired by all who knew him. He was born in New Brunswick, New Jersey, in 1886, attended Rutgers College two years, and then went to Columbia University, receiving his degree in 1908. The same year he married Aline Murray and became Latin Master in the Morristown High School. In 1909, though but twenty-three years old, he was made assistant editor of the Standard Dictionary and later became a member of the staff of the *New York Times Book Review*, which position he held when he enlisted in the army. By the time he was thirty he had attained unusual prominence in the literary world for so young a man; he was recognized as a poet of no mean ability; he was a lecturer, a critic, an editor, and so had an opportunity to meet many prominent men and women who came to New York.

*Courtesy G. H. Doran Co.*

JOYCE KILMER

Roused to deep indignation by the sinking of the *Lusitania*, Kilmer joined the Officers' Reserve Training Corps, but soon resigned. He

# 278      CONTEMPORARY VERSE

enlisted as a private in the army three weeks after Congress declared war, and soon became a sergeant in the Seventh Regiment, National Guard, New York. He was acting unofficially as adjutant to Major Donovan of the old Rainbow Division during the Marne advance where it was his duty to precede the battalion to discover the location of the enemy's guns and position. He was found lying with a bullet in his brain on the ground as if looking over the edge of a natural trench. He had crawled ahead to get a view of the enemy and had raised his head to look over the trench. It is the rule not to bury enlisted men with officers, but Joyce Kilmer had won so much respect and admiration that the commander of the regiment ordered his grave to be dug next to that of heroic Lieutenant Oliver Ames, who had just lost his life.

It is said that a copy of "Rouge Bouquet", written in memory of some of their number killed by a shell in March, was to be found in the tattered blouse of almost every soldier in the regiment. This poem was read at the funeral of its brave young author as described in the extract from a letter written home by Alexander Woolcott, formerly dramatic editor of the *New York Times*.

"You will see that there is a refrain which calls for bugle notes and I am told that at the funeral service where the lines were first read, the desperately sad notes of 'Taps' sounded faintly from a distant grove when the refrain invoked them. The lines were read by Joyce's own beloved Father Duffy and those who were there told me the tears streamed down the face of every boy in the regiment. They just blubbered."

His widow, herself a poet of no mean ability, bravely tries to carry on in the same noble fashion as did her husband.

## THE WHITE SHIPS AND THE RED

With drooping sail and pennant
   That never a wind may reach,
They float in sunless waters
   Beside a sunless beach.
Their mighty masts and funnels
   Are white as driven snow,
And with a pallid radiance
   Their ghostly bulwarks glow.

Here is a Spanish galleon
  That once with gold was gay,
Here is a Roman trireme
  Whose hues outshone the day.
But Tyrian dyes have faded
  And prows that once were bright
With rainbow stains wear only
  Death's livid, dreadful white.

White as the ice that clove her
  That unforgotten day,
Among her pallid sisters
  The grim *Titanic* lay.
And through the leagues above her
  She looked aghast and said:
"What is this living ship that comes
  Where every ship is dead?"

The ghostly vessels trembled
  From ruined stern to prow:
What was this thing of terror
  That broke their vigil now?
Down through the startled ocean
  A mighty vessel came,
Not white, as all dead ships must be,
  But red, like living flame!

The pale green waves about her
  Were swiftly, strangely dyed
By the great scarlet stream that flowed
  From out her wounded side.
And all her decks were scarlet
  And all her shattered crew.
She sank among the white ghost ships
  And stained them through and through.

The grim *Titanic* greeted her
  "And who art thou?" she said :
"Why dost thou join our ghostly fleet
  Arrayed in living red?
We are the ships of sorrow
  Who spend the weary night
Until the dawn of Judgment Day,
  Obscure and still and white."

"Nay," said the scarlet visitor,
  "Tho I sink through the sea
A ruined thing that was a ship
  I sink not as did ye.
For ye met with your destiny
  By storm or rock or fight,
So through the lagging centuries
  Ye wear your robes of white.

"But never crashing iceberg,
  Nor honest shot of foe,
Nor hidden reef has sent me
  The way that I must go.
My wound that stains the waters,
  My blood that is like flame,
Bear witness to a loathly deed,
  A deed without a name.

"I went not forth to battle,
  I carried friendly men,
And children played about my decks,
  The women sang — and then —
And then — the sun blushed scarlet
  And Heaven hid her face,
The world that God created
  Became a shameful place.

"My wrong cries out for vengeance,
  The blow that sent me here
Was aimed in Hell.  My dying scream
  Has reached Jehovah's ear.
Not all the seven oceans
  Shall wash away the stain:
Upon a brow that wears a crown
  I am the brand of Cain."

When God's great voice assembles
  The fleet on Judgment Day,
The ghosts of ruined ships will rise
  In sea and strait and bay.
Tho they have lain for ages
  Beneath the changeless flood,
They shall be white like silver,
  But one — shall be like blood.

NOTES AND QUESTIONS ON "THE WHITE SHIPS AND THE RED"

The Red Ship is the *Lusitania*, which was sunk by a German submarine in violation of all international law.

*Stanza 1.* This stanza gives a vivid picture of sunken ships; select the words that give the impression of death.

*Stanza 2.* "Spanish galleon", an ancient stately ship of four decks, often very beautifully ornamented. "Trireme", a ship with three banks of oars, hence its name; a typical Roman ship with a Greek name. The dyes of Tyre were famous for their brilliancy and lasting quality.

*Stanza 3.* "That unforgotten day", the *Titanic* was sunk by striking an iceberg in mid-ocean as she was making her maiden trip from Liverpool to Boston in 1912. Why did Kilmer speak of the *Lusitania* as "a living ship"? What is gained by personifying the ships?

*Stanzas 4–10.* Trace this personification to the end of stanza 10.

*Stanza 10.* Cain was branded with the word signifying "Murderer." For the reason see Gen. IV: 3–15.

*Stanza 11.* See if you can tell what makes this stanza so impressive.

## GATES AND DOORS

### A Ballad of Christmas Eve

There was a gentle hostler
  (And blessed be his name!)
He opened up the stable
  The night Our Lady came.
Our Lady and Saint Joseph,
  And gave them food and bed,
And Jesus Christ has given him
  A glory round his head.

*So let the gate swing open*
  *However poor the yard,*
*Lest weary people visit you*
  *And find their passage barred;*
*Unlatch the door at midnight*
  *And let your lantern's glow*
*Shine out to guide the traveller's feet*
  *To you across the snow.*

There was a courteous hostler
  (He is in Heaven to-night)
He held Our Lady's bridle
  And helped her to alight;
He spread clean straw before her
  Whereon she might lie down,
And Jesus Christ has given him
  An everlasting crown.

*Unlock the door this evening*
  *And let your gate swing wide,*
**Let** *all who ask for shelter*
  *Come speedily inside.*

*What if your yard be narrow?*
  *What if your house be small?*
*There is a Guest is coming*
  *Will glorify it all.*

There was a joyous hostler
  Who knelt on Christmas morn
Beside the radiant manger
  Wherein his Lord was born.
His heart was full of laughter,
  His soul was full of bliss
When Jesus, on His mother's lap,
  Gave him His hand to kiss.

*Unbar your heart this evening*
  *And keep no stranger out,*
*Take from your soul's great portal*
  *The barrier of doubt.*
*To humble folk and weary*
  *Give hearty welcoming,*
*Your breast shall be to-morrow*
  *The cradle of a King.*

### NOTES AND QUESTIONS ON "GATES AND DOORS"

To what event do stanzas 1, 3, and 5 refer? Compare them to see how they resemble each other in structure and grouping of words. How do the last two lines in each differ from the other six?

To whom are stanzas 2, 4, and 6 addressed? Notice that in stanza 2 we are admonished to open the gate, in stanza 4 to unlock the door, but in stanza 6 to unbar the heart; why is this order of ideas given? What name do you give that arrangement?

*In General.* Simple words and directness are the outstanding characteristics of this appealing poem; why are these qualities best suited to the theme?

## TREES

I think that I shall never see
A poem lovely as a tree.

A tree whose hungry mouth is prest
Against the earth's sweet flowing breast;

A tree that looks at God all day,
And lifts her leafy arms to pray;

A tree that may in summer wear
A nest of robins in her hair;

Upon whose bosom snow has lain;
Who intimately lives with rain.

Poems are made by fools like me,
But only God can make a tree.

### NOTES AND QUESTIONS ON "TREES"

The best known of Joyce Kilmer's poems is "Trees", which is dear
to every lover of nature.   Notice its structure; only the first and last
stanzas contain complete statements;  the other four are simply
clauses, each giving a different description of a tree.   Which one do
you like best?   What figure of speech prevails in these descriptive
clauses and what is its effect?   Observe the similarity of the rhyme in
the first and last stanzas;  do you suppose that was done purposely?
How would you describe the language used?   Count the words of two
or more syllables and see how many they average to a stanza.   Can
you account for the popularity of the poem?

## ROUGE BOUQUET

In a wood they call the Rouge Bouquet
There is a new-made grave to-day,
Built by never a spade nor pick
Yet covered with earth ten meters thick.

I THINK THAT I SHALL NEVER SEE
A POEM LOVELY AS A TREE

There lie many fighting men,
    Dead in their youthful prime,
Never to love nor laugh again
    Nor taste the Summertime.
For Death came flying through the air
And stopped his flight at the dugout stair,
Touched his prey and left them there,
    Clay to clay.
He hid their bodies stealthily
In the soil of the land they sought to free
    And fled away.
Now over the grave abrupt and clear
    Three volleys ring;
And perhaps their brave young spirits hear
    The bugle sing:
"Go to sleep!
" Go to sleep!
" Slumber well where the shot screamed and fell.
" Let your rifles rest on the muddy floor,
" You will not need them any more.
" Danger's past;
" Now at last,
" Go to sleep!"

There is on earth no worthier grave
To hold the bodies of the brave
Than this place of pain and pride
Where they nobly fought and nobly died.
Never fear but in the skies
    Saints and angels stand
Smiling with their holy eyes
    On this new-come band.
St. Michael's sword darts through the air
And touches the aureole on his hair

As he sees them stand saluting there,
    His stalwart sons;
And Patrick, Brigid, Columkill
Rejoice that in veins of warriors still
    The Gael's blood runs.
And up to heaven's doorway floats,
    From the wood called Rouge Bouquet,
A delicate cloud of bugle notes
    That softly say:
"Farewell!
"Farewell!
"Comrades true, born anew, peace to you!
"Your souls shall be where the heroes are
"And your memory shine like the morning-star.
"Brave and dear,
"Shield us here.
"Farewell!"

### NOTES AND QUESTIONS ON "ROUGE BOUQUET"

This beautiful lyric in memory of nineteen of our boys in khaki, who were killed and buried by a bomb exploded in a wood in France, March 7, 1918, though so sad that it can scarcely be read without tears, is full of exultation because of their bravery. See the account of Joyce Kilmer's death for interesting facts about the poem.

*Stanza 1.* Note the simplicity of the language used in describing the fate of these fine fellows. Why is Death personified? Why is "He hid their bodies stealthily" so good a way to express it? Do you believe "their brave young spirits" did hear the bugle notes? Which line of the refrain is most touching?

*Stanza 2.* It is particularly appropriate to have St. Michael salute them, for he is the Archangel mentioned in the Bible, regarded as the leader of the whole host of angels and representing the Church triumphant. According to the Roman Catholic Church he was employed to defeat Lucifer and is represented in a coat of armor with a glory around his head, a dart in his hand, and trampling on the fallen Lucifer. "Patrick", St. Patrick, who was born in Scotland and crossed the channel to Ireland in the middle of the fifth century to convert the Irish to Christianity. "Brigid", St. Brigid, a friend of St. Patrick, and one of the most remarkable Irishwomen of the fifth century, Patroness of Ireland. "Columkill", a great missionary saint, a statesman, a scholar, and a poet — beloved of the Scotch as well as of the Irish. "Gael", a Scottish or Irish Celt. The refrain of this stanza is as applicable to Joyce Kilmer himself as to those for whom it was written.

*In General.* Notice the effect of the short lines in contrast to the long ones. The rhythm of the refrain is in perfect imitation of "taps", sounded for the dead; try to bring this out in your reading. The rhyme-scheme also is very interesting and should be carefully worked out, for it is very complicated. Note especially line 22 in each stanza; which contains triple rhymes but rhymes with no other lines. Study the lines which seem most musical to you and, by consulting "Aids to Musical Sound in Poetry ", see if you can discover what combinations of sounds make them so beautiful.

WILLIAM ROSE BENÉT                *Photo. by Pinchot.*

# WILLIAM ROSE BENÉT

The idea that a poet is never a good fighting man is disproved by
the record of William Rose Benét, who rose to the rank of second
lieutenant in the air service of the United States during the World
War; in fact, he was born of an army family, his paternal grandfather having been Brig. Gen. Stephen Benét.   He was born in 1886

at Fort Hamilton, New York Harbor, prepared for college at Albany Academy, and was graduated from the Sheffield Scientific School, Yale University. He has lived in the South and the West as well as in the East, so that he knows his native land thoroughly. Having been at one time on the editorial staff of the *Century Magazine*, he was later Associate Editor of the *Literary Review* of the *New York Post*, and contributing Editor of the *Saturday Review of Literature*.

The special charm of Benét's poems lies in his brilliant imagination and the exceptional choice of words which produce effects alike musical and sonorous. His brother, Stephen Vincent Benét, also established his right to be called a poet of the first rank when he published his great poem "John Brown's Body."

## MERCHANTS FROM CATHAY

How that
They came

Their heels slapped their bumping mules; their fat chaps glowed.
Glory unto Mary, each seemed to wear a crown!
Like sunset their robes were on the wide, white road:
So we saw those mad merchants come dusting into town!

Of their
Beasts

Two paunchy beasts they rode on and two they drove before.
May the Saints all help us, the tiger-stripes they had!
And the panniers upon them swelled full of stuffs and ore!
The square buzzed and jostled at a sight so mad.

And their
Boast

They bawled in their beards, and their turbans they wried.
They stopped by the stalls with curvetting and clatter.

As bronze as the bracken their necks and
faces dyed —
And a stave they sat singing, to tell us of
the matter.

**With its
Burthen**

*"For your silks, to Sugarmago! For your
dyes, to Isfahan!
Weird fruits from the Isle o' Lamaree!
But for magic merchandise,
For treasure-trove and spice,
Here's a catch and a carol to the great, grand
Chan,
The King of all the Kings across the sea!*

**And
Chorus**

*"Here's a catch and a carol to the great, grand
Chan:
For we won through the deserts to his sunset
barbican,
And the mountains of his palace no Titan's
reach may span
Where he wields his seignorie!*

**A first
Stave
Fearsome**

"Red-as-blood skins of Panthers, so bright
against the sun
On the walls of the halls where his pillared
state is set
They daze with a blaze no man may look
upon!
And with conduits of beverage those floors
run wet!

**And a sec-
ond Right
hard To
Stomach**

"His wives stiff with riches, they sit before
him there.
Bird and beast at his feast make song and
clapping cheer.

And jugglers and enchanters, all walking on
    the air,
Make fall eclipse and thunder — make moons
    and suns appear!

And a
third
Which
is a
Laughable
Thing

"Once the Chan, by his enemies sore-prest,
    and sorely spent,
    Lay, so they say, in a thicket 'neath a tree
Where the howl of an owl vexed his foes from
    their intent:
    Then that fowl for a holy bird of reverence
    made he!

Of the
Chan's
Hunting

"And when he will a-hunting go, four ele-
    phants of white
    Draw his wheeling daïs of lignum aloes
    made;
And marquises and admirals and barons of
    delight
    All courier his chariot, in orfrayes arrayed!

We gape
to Hear
them end

"*A catch and a carol to the great, grand Chan!*
    *Pastmasters of disasters, our desert caravan*
    *Won through all peril to his sunset barbican,*
    *Where he wields his seignorie!*
    *And crowns he gave us! We end where we*
    *began.*
    *A catch and a carol to the great, grand Chan,*
    *The King of all the Kings across the sea!*"

And are in
Terrors,

Those mad, antic Merchants! . . . Their
    stripèd beasts did beat
    The market-square suddenly with hooves
    of beaten gold!

The ground yawned gaping and flamed beneath our feet!
They plunged to Pits Abysmal with their
wealth untold!

And dread   And some say the Chan himself in anger dealt
it is           the stroke —
Devil's       For sharing of his secrets with silly, common
Work!          folk:
              But Holy, Blessèd Mary, preserve us as you
              may
              Lest once more those mad Merchants come
              chanting from Cathay!

### NOTES AND QUESTIONS ON "MERCHANTS FROM CATHAY"

This, the title poem of Benét's first published volume of verses,
shows the oriental cast of his imagination and his use of musical
effects by choice of words and much alliteration.

Try to get the picture of the Merchants by studying the words used
in describing them and the effect they produced on the on-lookers.
Where does the direct quotation which begins in stanza 3 end?

Explain "the great, grand Chan", "barbican", "seignorie." Why
did the people so fear the Merchants from Cathay?

## HOW TO CATCH UNICORNS

Its cloven hoofprint on the sand
Will lead you — where?
Into a phantasmagoric land —
Beware!

There all the bright streams run up-hill.
The birds on every tree are still.
But from stocks and stones, clear voices come
That should be dumb.

If you have taken along a net,
A noose, a prod,
You'll be waiting in the forest yet . . .
Nid — nod!

In a virgin's lap the beast slept sound,
They say . . . but I —
I think (Is anyone around?)
That's just a lie!

If you have taken a musketoon
To flinders 'twill flash 'neath the wizard moon.
So I should take browned batter-cake,
Hot-buttered inside, like foam to flake.

And I should take an easy heart
And a whimsical face,
And a tied-up lunch of sandwich and tart,
And spread a cloth in the open chase.
And then I should pretend to snore . . .

And I'd hear a snort and I'd hear a roar,
The wind of a mane and a tail, and four
Wild hoofs prancing the forest-floor.

And I'd open my eyes on a flashing horn —
And see the Unicorn!

Paladins fierce and virgins sweet . . .
But he's never had anything to eat!
Knights have tramped in their iron-mong'ry . . .
But nobody thought — that's all! — he's hungry!

### ADDENDUM

Really hungry!   Good Lord deliver us,
The Unicorn is not carnivorous!

This poem illustrates the author's fanciful and sometimes whimsical style. The unicorn is a fabulous creature, called the *monoceros* by the ancients, described as having one long horn, and as being a native of India. It was unlike any known animal.

Explain why the lunch prepared as a bait to catch the unicorn would fail.

Define musketoon, wizard, carnivorous.

## THE FALCONER OF GOD

I flung my soul to the air like a falcon flying.
I said, "Wait on, wait on, while I ride below!
    I shall start a heron soon
    In the marsh beneath the moon —
A strange white heron rising with silver on its wings,
        Rising and crying
    Wordless, wondrous things;
    The secret of the stars, of the world's heart-strings
        The answer to their woe.
Then stoop thou upon him, and grip and hold him so!"

My wild soul waited on as falcons hover.
I beat the reedy fens as I trampled past.
    I heard the mournful loon
    In the marsh beneath the moon.
And then, with feathery thunder, the bird of my desire
        Broke from the cover
    Flashing silver fire.
    High up among the stars I saw his pinions spire.
        The pale clouds gazed aghast
As my falcon stooped upon him, and gript and held him fast.

My soul dropped through the air — with heavenly
        plunder? —
Gripping the dazzling bird my dreaming knew?

Nay! but a piteous freight,
A dark and heavy weight
Despoiled of silver plumage, its voice forever stilled, —
    All of the wonder
Gone that ever filled
Its guise with glory.   O bird that I have killed,
    How brilliantly you flew
Across my rapturous vision when first I dreamed of you!

Yet I fling my soul on high with new endeavor,
And I ride the world below with a joyful mind.
    *I shall start a heron soon*
    *In the marsh beneath the moon —*
*A wondrous silver heron its inner darkness fledges!*
    I beat forever
The fens and the sedges.
The pledge is still the same — for all disastrous pledges,
    All hopes resigned!
My soul still flies above me for the quarry it shall find!

### NOTES AND QUESTIONS ON "THE FALCONER OF GOD"

This poem contains none of the whimsical effect which appears in much of Benét's poetry as, for instance, in "Merchants from Cathay." It is a splendid example of symbolism, a religious lyric in which the poet's imagination sweeps on in exultant endeavor.   The falcon is the spirit of man, while the heron is some fleeting ideal of loveliness which the soul is trying to capture.

*Stanza 1* represents man sending forth his soul (the falcon) to capture the beautiful thing (the heron) which he will start up.

*Stanza 2* shows the capture of "the bird of my desire."

*Stanza 3* portrays the disappointment of the falconer when the bird of his dream brought to earth proves

> "A dark and heavy weight
> Despoiled of silver plumage."

But in the last stanza the poet shows that man, in spite of repeated disappointments in the quest of beauty, is sure that sometime he will find what his soul longs for.

Note the use of fine, vigorous, musical words; also the long swinging lines in contrast to the shorter ones. The rhyme-scheme is an interesting one. What is the effect of making the last line of each stanza rhyme with the second?

Look up the ancient sport of hawking to understand the imagery of the poem.

Read Coleridge's "Ancient Mariner." Which poem do you enjoy the more? Why?

# WINIFRED M. LETTS

Winifred M. Letts is a native of Ireland, in which country she was born in 1887. She enters with ready sympathy into the life of the poor. Her poem "In Service" shows her appreciation of the working girl. Besides her poems Miss Letts has written several novels and books for children. In the World War she served in the base hospitals as nurse. Her experiences there bore fruit in the poem, "The Spires of Oxford", which has made her name known around the world.

## IN SERVICE

Little Nellie Cassidy has got a place in town,
    She wears a fine white apron,
    She wears a new black gown,
An' the quarest little cap at all with straymers hanging
    down.

I met her one fine evening stravagin' down the street,
    A feathered hat upon her head,
    And boots upon her feet.
"Och, Mick," says she, "may God be praised that you and
    I should meet.

"It's lonesome in the city with such a crowd," says she;
    "I'm lost without the bog-land,
    I'm lost without the sea,
An' the harbor an' the fishing-boats that sail out fine and
    free.

"I'd give a golden guinea to stand upon the shore,
    To see the big waves lepping,
    To hear them splash and roar,
To smell the tar and the drying nets, I'd not be asking more.

"To see the small white houses, their faces to the sea,
    The childher in the doorway,
    Or round my mother's knee;
For I'm strange and lonesome missing them, God keep
    them all," says she.

Little Nellie earns fourteen pounds and more,
    Waiting on the quality,
    And answering the door —
But her heart is some place far away upon the Wexford shore.

NOTES AND QUESTIONS ON "IN SERVICE"

*Stanza 1.* Note the clearness of the picture of Little Nellie and the way her position is made plain.

*Stanza 2.* What is shown about her former dress by Mick's remark concerning her hat and boots? Meaning of "stravaging"?

*Stanza 3.* Have you ever been lonesome in a crowd? From what sort of place had Nellie come?

*Stanzas 4 and 5.* Select the important details which make the picture in Nellie's mind clear to you.

*Stanza 6.* What are her wages in our money? Will money drive away homesickness? Wexford?

*In General.* Who is telling the incident? Is the rhyme-scheme a common one for stanzas of four lines?

## QUANTITY AND QUALITY

The poor have childher and to spare,
But with the quality they're rare,
Where money's scarce the childher's many,
Where money's thick you'll scarce find any,
Some wanted here, too many there —
    It's quare.

Now, if the rich and poor could share,
There'd soon be childher everywhere;

But God have pity on the mother
That gives her child up to another;
An' so you'll find a mansion bare,
A cabin rich in all that's fair —
     It's quare.

NOTES AND QUESTIONS ON "QUANTITY AND QUALITY"

*Stanza 1.* "Childher" is the usual form of the word employed in Ireland. Compare Denis McCarthy's poem by that name in this book. "The quality", a term commonly employed by the poorer classes in England and Ireland when referring to the richer classes.

*Stanza 2.* What causes the sudden change of thought after line 2?

*In General.* What unusual rhyme-scheme do you find in both stanzas? Would you like this if there were many stanzas? Why? There is frequent use of metonymy here, as "the poor" for "poor people"; find others. Why is this better than literal language? What makes the last line of each stanza so effective?

## THE MONKEY'S CAROL

Kind Christian souls who pass me by
  On business intent,
I pray you think on such as I
  Who pine in banishment.
    I wear a little coat of red,
    A little bonnet on my head.
    Kind gentles, throw a coin to me
    And God reward your charity.

My master grinds the music out
  To cheer the sullen street;
The children gather round about
  And dance with joyous feet.
    Have pity on the poor old man

And give him pennies all who can;
Have pity on his monkey too,
And God be pitiful to you.

Once long ago my heart was light
Amongst my brethren in the south,
Fulfilled with joy I slept at night,
The taste of mangoes in my mouth.
But now I go from door to door.
Have pity, gentles, on the poor.
My master is both weak and old,
And I am trembling in the cold.

Your kitchens have a fragrant scent
With pies and puddings on each side,
I wish you all much merriment
And peace and love this Christmastide.
If you have nuts or fruit for me
God will reward your charity;
For if you give the poor their share
God will not leave your platters bare.

NOTES AND QUESTIONS ON "THE MONKEY'S CAROL"

*Stanza 1.* What device has the poet used to make the appeal pathetic? What familiar picture do lines 5 and 6 give?

*Stanza 2.* What contrasts does this contain? Why is "sullen" so fine a word to use here?

*Stanza 3.* Why is the use of monkeys by hand-organ men so cruel? Picture their discomfort in both summer and winter.

*Stanza 4.* Does Miss Letts represent the monkey as bearing any resentment in his heart?

*In General.* The metre is very regular and the foot used is the iambus, a short syllable followed by a long. See how many such feet there are in each line of the stanzas. This is the metre of many of the old English carols.

## ANGELIC SERVICE

No angel is so high
But serveth clowns and kings
And doeth lowly things;
He in this serviceable love can see
The symbol of some heavenly mystery, —
So common things grow wings.

No angel bravely dressed
In larkspur-coloured gown,
But he will bend him down
And sweep with careful art the meanest floor,
Singing the while he sweeps and toiling more
Because he wears a crown.

Set water on to boil,
An angel helps thee straight;
Kneeling beside the grate
With pursèd mouth he bloweth up the flame
Chiding the tardy kettle that for shame
Would make an angel wait.

Make thou conserves, the while
Two little cherubs stand·
Tip-toe at either hand,
And one would help thee stir, and one would skim
The golden juice that foams about the brim,
So serveth thy command.

And that same toil-worn broom
So humble in thine eyes,
Perhaps has donned disguise

WEXFORD VILLAGE
Birthplace of Winifred Letts

And is a seraph on this errand bent,
To show thee service is a sacrament
And Love wears servant's guise.

### NOTES AND QUESTIONS ON "ANGELIC SERVICE"

*Stanza 1.* This stanza sets forth a general truth, while the succeeding ones give specific examples of that truth; state the truth in your own words. What is the purpose of the contrast in line 2? "Serviceable love" means love that is able to serve. What figure of speech in the last line?

*Stanza 2.* "Larkspur-coloured", bright dark blue. Express "toiling more", etc., in your own words. How would a creature less fine than an angel treat so lowly a task?

*Stanza 3.* If you remember that the Celts have very vivid imaginations and that many of them believe in good fairies and that angels personally help human beings, this stanza and the succeeding ones will not seem so strange to you.

*Stanza 4.* "Conserve", a rich preserve that has to be stirred while it is cooking, for it is so thick that it would easily burn; and it must also be skimmed.

*Stanza 5.* This stanza, perhaps, will seem the most fantastic of all to you matter-of-fact young persons of to-day, but let your imagination have free rein, do not question too closely, and get the lesson taught. Why is "toil-worn" a good descriptive phrase to use of the broom? What other poems in this book contain the same idea of supernatural help?

## THE SPIRES OF OXFORD

### (As Seen from the Train)

I saw the spires of Oxford
　　As I was passing by,
The gray spires of Oxford
　　Against a pearl-gray sky.
My heart was with the Oxford men
　　Who went abroad to die.

The years go fast in Oxford,
　　The golden years and gay,
The hoary Colleges look down
　　On careless boys at play.
But when the bugles sounded war
　　They put their games away.

They left the peaceful river,
　　The cricket-field, the quad,
The shaven lawns of Oxford
　　To seek a bloody sod —
They gave their merry youth away
　　For country and for God.

### THE SPIRES OF OXFORD

God rest you, happy gentlemen;
  Who laid your good lives down,
Who took the khaki and the gun
  Instead of cap and gown.
God bring you to a fairer place
  Than even Oxford town.

#### NOTES AND QUESTIONS ON "THE SPIRES OF OXFORD"

In the midst of the Word War the writer, from a railway train, saw in the distance the gray spires of Oxford University. The sharp contrast between its peace and quiet, the pearl-gray sky, the river, the sports, and the terrible scenes of blood-red war to which so many students had gone forth, is well portrayed in this poem which is easily one of the finest and one of the most stirring and popular of the many war poems.

Why are the college years spoken of as "golden"? What is gained by the contrast between the "hoary colleges" and the "careless boys at play"? Explain "cricket-field", "quad." On what is the first line of the last stanza based?

Try writing a poem in the same rhyme and rhythm as this about the boys who went to the war from some school or college that you know about.

MARGARET WIDDEMER

# MARGARET WIDDEMER

Margaret Widdemer, a native of Doylestown, Pennsylvania, is one of the poets who were "born, not made." As a child she relates that she used to go alone into her grandmother's parlor and dance, without music, in delight at the rhythms she could make. She early produced some very creditable poems, and after being graduated from the Drexel Institute Library School in 1909 she became a regular contributor to the magazines. Her first published poem, "Factories", attracted favorable notice and was widely quoted.

Miss Widdemer's poems are in two volumes: "Factories, with Other Poems", 1915; and "The Old Road to Paradise" (1918). The latter divided with Carl Sandburg's "Cornhuskers" the Columbia Poetry Prize in 1918. Her "Collected Poems" appeared in 1928.

She has published two books of short stories, four novels, and several books for girls.

# FACTORIES

I have shut my little sister in from life and light
  (For a rose, for a ribbon, for a wreath across my hair),
I have made her restless feet still until the night,
  Locked from sweets of summer and from wild spring air;
I who ranged the meadowlands, free from sun to sun,
  Free to sing and pull the buds and watch the far wings fly,
I have bound my sister till her playing time was done —
  Oh, my little sister, was it I?   Was it I?

I have robbed my sister of her day of maidenhood
  (For a robe, for a feather, for a trinket's restless spark).
Shut from love till dusk shall fall, how shall she know good,
  How shall she go scatheless through the sun-lit dark?
I who could be innocent, I who could be gay,
  I who could have love and mirth before the light went by,
I have put my sister in her mating-time away —
  Sister, my young sister, was it I?   Was it I?

I have robbed my sister of the lips against her breast
  (For a coin, for the weaving of my children's lace and lawn),
Feet that pace beside the loom, hands that cannot rest —
  How can she know motherhood, whose strength is gone?
I who took no heed of her, starved and labor-worn,
  I, against whose placid heart my sleepy gold-heads lie,

Round my path they cry to me, little souls unborn —
God of Life! Creator! It was I! It was I!

This poem is one of the more conservative of Margaret Widdemer's poems. She takes upon herself, representing happy womanhood, the burden of responsibility for the sufferings and deprivations of the girls who work in factories. Her genuine sympathy gives real pathos to the poem.

Note how the contrast continued through each stanza serves to accentuate the wrong done "little sister" and the cruelty of robbing her of joy.

In what respects are the stanzas identical? In what unlike? What was the purpose in this?

## A BOY OF THE GHETTO

He goes out with his Dreams
   Through the dingy city square,
Purple- and silver-winged
   They go with him everywhere.

The quarreling hags at the windows
   Have voices unkind, unsweet,
But his Dreams have silver voices
   And starrily-slippered feet;

The workmen push on the pavement
   And laugh and curse as they go,
But he is far with his Dreams
   On a road they do not know;

He walks far off with the Dreams
   That whisper and sing beside,
And his face is glad and still
   And his eyes are burning-wide;

He goes out with his Dreams
Through a golden wonder-place
With the light of God in his eyes
And the peace of God in his face.

NOTES AND QUESTIONS ON "THE BOY OF THE GHETTO"

The little Italian boy in the "Land of Make Believe" passes serenely along the way, untroubled and unafraid, for he lives for the time being in a world of his own, the world of imagination.

Is the boy unusual, or do you know any boys who enjoy "dreams" of what the future has for them? Dreams which make them unmindful of discomfort and lack of harmony in the present?

## THE WATCHER

She always leaned to watch for us,
  Anxious if we were late,
In winter by the window,
  In summer by the gate.

And though we mocked her tenderly,
  Who had such foolish care,
The long way home would seem more safe
  Because she waited there.

Her thoughts were all so full of us —
  She never could forget!
And so I think that where she is
  She must be watching yet.

Waiting till we come home to her,
  Anxious if we are late —
Watching from Heaven's window,
  Leaning from Heaven's gate.

The picture of the mother watching for the home-coming of her child is one that almost every heart will recognize in its own experience. Youth, light-hearted and feeling little need of such care, laughs — not unkindly.   Now the mother has passed on, the writer cannot think the loving care has ceased to be, but that she is "watching yet."

Why do we assume that the watcher is the mother?

Can you think of a conspicuous instance where the father watched for the son to return?

What is the difference in the character of the homecoming in each case?

# OTHER POEMS YOU WOULD LIKE

| TITLES | AUTHORS |
|---|---|
| Enchanted Hill, The | Walter de la Mare |
| Exeter Road | Amy Lowell |
| Ex Ore Infantium | Francis Thompson |
| Factory Children | Richard Burton |
| Farmer Remembers Lincoln, A | Witter Bynner |
| Fiddler Jones | Edgar Lee Masters |
| First Sight | Anna Hempstead Branch |
| Four Winds, The | Charles Henry Lüders |
| Frost To-night | Edith Thomas |
| Fulfilled Dreams | Richard Burton |
| General Booth Enters into Heaven | Vachel Lindsay |
| Give Me the Splendid Silent Sun | Walt Whitman |
| Gloucester Moors | William Vaughn Moody |
| Going Down Hill on a Bicycle | Henry Charles Beeding |
| Golden Shoes, The | Josephine Preston Peabody |
| Goodby My Fancy | Walt Whitman |
| Good Hours | Robert Frost |
| Grandfather's Love | Sara Teasdale |
| Hark to the Merry Birds | Robert Bridges |
| Hands | Louis Untermeyer |
| Horse Thief, The | William Rose Benét |
| How He Turned Out | Edwin Arlington Robinson |
| Hymn | Paul Laurence Dunbar |
| If | Rudyard Kipling |
| If Only the Dreams Abide | Clinton Scollard |
| I Have a Rendezvous with Death | Alan Seeger |
| Incentive, The | Sara N. Cleghorn |
| In Flanders Fields | John McCrae |
| In Praise of Johnny Appleseed | Vachel Lindsay |
| In the Cool of the Evening | Alfred Noyes |
| Invictus | William Ernest Henley |
| Jest 'fore Christmas | Eugene Field |
| Joy Vender, The | Abbie Farwell Brown |
| Justice | Aline Kilmer |
| Kind Morn | Sara Teasdale |
| Kinship | Angela Morgan |
| Kharmsin | Clinton Scollard |
| Lad That Is You, A | Robert Louis Stevenson |
| Last Watch, The | Bliss Carman |
| Lavender | Alfred Noyes |

# INDEX OF AUTHORS

# INDEX OF TITLES

# INDEX OF FIRST LINES